IMAGES
of America

WATCH HILL

BY RIVER AND BY SEA

For Brian and Magda Rooney,
my parents.

As mighty waves grow from distant breezes,
So do history books grow from family tales shared and time well spent.

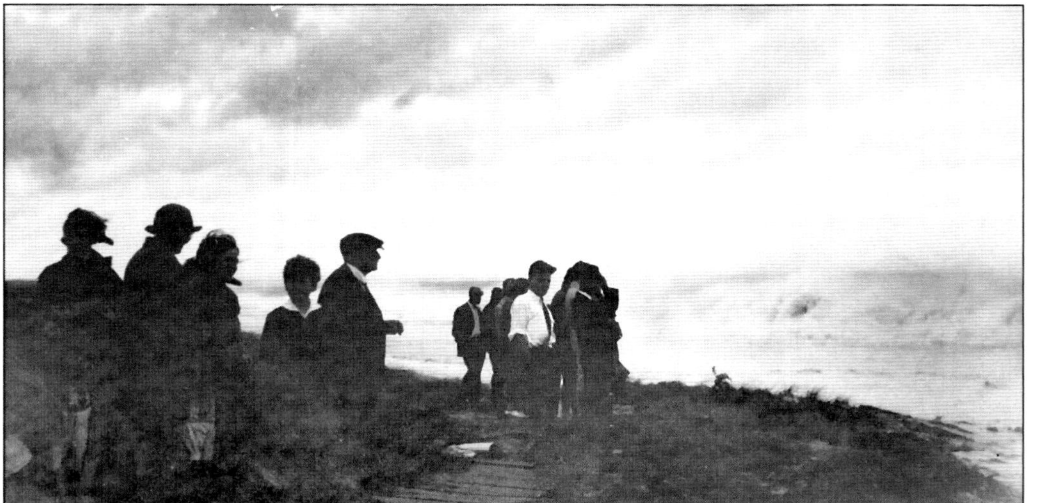

IMAGES
of America

WATCH HILL
BY RIVER AND BY SEA

Brigid Rooney Smith

ARCADIA
PUBLISHING

ISBN 978-0-7385-3552-4

Published by Arcadia Publishing
Charleston, South Carolina

Printed in the United States of America

Library of Congress Catalog Card Number: 99-62494

For all general information contact Arcadia Publishing at:
Telephone 843-853-2070
Fax 843-853-0044
E-Mail sales@arcadiapublishing.com
For customer service and orders:
Toll-Free 1-888-313-2665

Visit us on the Internet at www.arcadiapublishing.com

Cover Photograph: Sitting in the stern of a rowboat rental *c.* 1890, a summer visitor to Watch Hill gazes southeast over long-forgotten salt marshes toward the Plimpton Annex and the Narragansett House. (GHU-Burdick.)

Contents

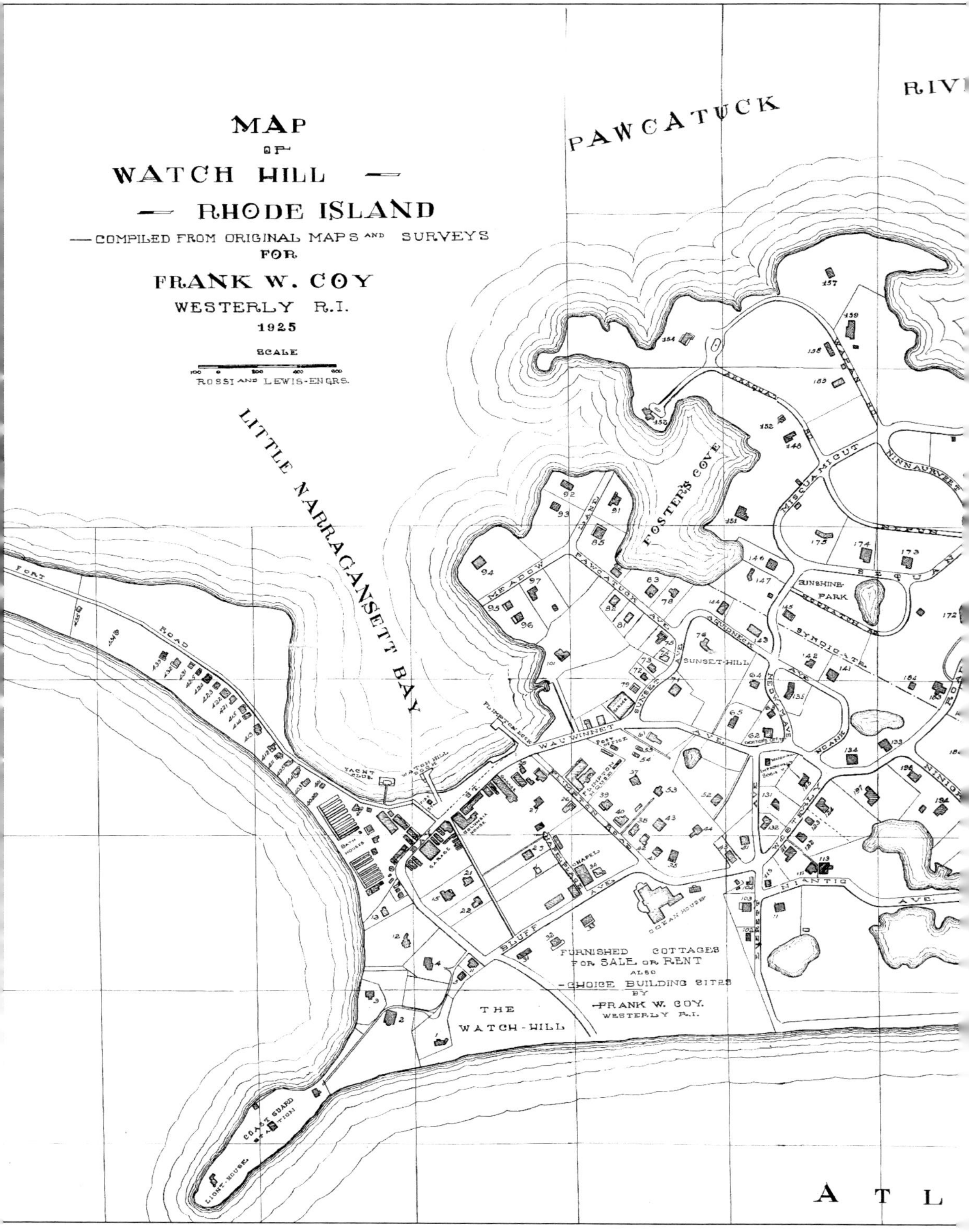
MAP
OF
WATCH HILL
RHODE ISLAND
COMPILED FROM ORIGINAL MAPS AND SURVEYS
FOR
FRANK W. COY
WESTERLY R.I.
1925
SCALE
ROSSI AND LEWIS-ENGRS.
PAWCATUCK
RIV
LITTLE NARRAGANSETT BAY
FOSTER'S COVE
FORT ROAD
MEADOW
PAWCATUCK AVE.
SUNSET-HILL
SUNSHINE PARK
SYNDICATE
WATCH HILL DOCK
YACHT CLUB
BATH HOUSES
BLUFF AVE.
OCEAN HOUSE
CHAPEL
POST OFFICE
NIANTIC AVE.
FURNISHED COTTAGES FOR SALE OR RENT
ALSO
CHOICE BUILDING SITES
BY
FRANK W. COY.
WESTERLY R.I.
THE WATCH-HILL
COAST GUARD STATION
LIGHT-HOUSE
ATL

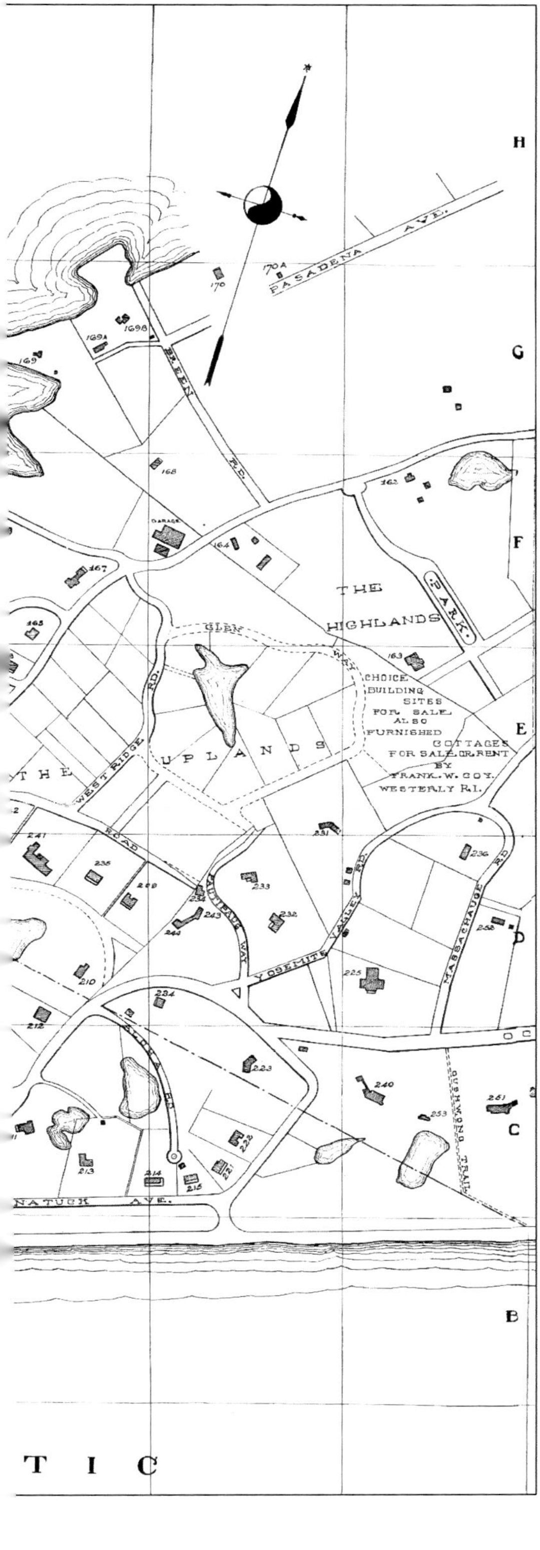

*But look! here come more crowds,
pacing straight for the water, and
seemingly bound for a dive. Strange!
Nothing will content them
but the extremest limit of the land;
loitering under the shady lee of yonder
warehouses will not suffice. No.
They must get just as nigh the water
as they possibly can without falling in.
And there they stand—miles of them—
leagues. Inlanders all,
they come from lanes and alleys,
streets avenues—north, east, south,
and west. Yet here they all unite.*

Herman Melville
Moby Dick; Or, The Whale

(Map courtesy of the Westerly Public Library.)

ACKNOWLEDGMENTS

Before a historic picture can tell a thousand words, it must first be unearthed from the depths of the attic or the cellar into which it has fallen captive. Upon such resurrection, a picture must then be dutifully cared for and, most importantly, provided with as broad a forum as possible to tell its tale.

The precious photographs that are contained in *Watch Hill: By River and By Sea* exist only because there are institutions and private individuals that care enough about things historical to give unsparingly of their time and talents to preserve mementos of our past. As an author, I am grateful beyond words for the generosity displayed by the following altruistic historians:

Dwight Brown Jr. (DB) of Bradford, Rhode Island, has collected and catalogued hundreds of wonderful turn-of-the-century photographs of Westerly and Watch Hill, Rhode Island. The maritime theme of many of these treasured photographs and Mr. Brown's in-depth knowledge of local history are well represented within this book. Thanks also to Anna Brown, his wife, a volunteer at the Westerly Public Library, for her contributions.

George H. Utter (GHU), of *The Westerly Sun* newspaper fame, is a longtime resident of Westerly, Rhode Island, who has amassed an amazing collection of photographs, memorabilia, and antidotes about Watch Hill and its surrounding environs. In particular, he is the keeper of the Burdick Collection of glass-plate negatives that touch upon countless aspects of life along the Pawcatuck River before the turn of the century.

Jane Hoxie Maxson (JM) of Wakefield, Rhode Island, is the daughter, granddaughter, and great-granddaughter of three of Watch Hill's most colorful personalities: Porter Hoxie, George Hoxie, and Wanton Weeks Hoxie, respectively. Her family photographs and family vignettes focus on the village of Watch Hill. Jane also provided invaluable insight and comments on the initial drafts of this book.

John F. Hall Jr. (JH), owner and operator of the Frank Hall Boat Yard in Avondale, Rhode Island, is the fifth generation of the Hall family to live in the same house on the Pawcatuck River. His "local knowledge" and unique photographs bring to life the early 1900s on the river.

Susan Carr (SC) of Westerly, Rhode Island, a descendant of the well-known Nash family of Watch Hill, provided family stories and memories of Fort Road on Napatree that have otherwise been lost to time.

My father, Brian Rooney (BAFR), a longtime visitor and boater at Watch Hill, opened up his precious postcard collection and spent Saturday afternoons "digging" around for tidbits long forgotten.

The citizens of Westerly, Rhode Island, should take great pride in the fact that both the Westerly Public Library (WPL) and the Westerly Historical Society (WHS) contain such vast resources and knowledge. The historical society has a tremendous collection of photographs and the library has not only wonderful photographs, but file upon file of local literature from days long gone by. Civic institutions that serve the populace are powerful institutions indeed.

Thank you one and all.

Introduction

Long ago, beneath the crisp stillness of a harvest moon, Montauk braves once paddled northward from Long Island to pillage the peaceful Niantics who resided at what we now know as Watch Hill. Espied as they were from the Hill itself, the Montauks, or so the old tale goes, were wiped out to a man on East Beach.

In 1614, a Dutch pinnace cautiously rounded the heavily wooded Nap O' Trees in exploratory pursuit of what Adrien Block would ultimately label the East (or *Pawcatuck*) River. Straddling shoals and rock outcroppings, this small vessel dropped "East Hill" off its starboard quarter and tacked cautiously upriver to what we now call Pawcatuck Rock.

During 1637, the Massachusetts Bay Colony reacted to Captain John Mason's victory over the Pequots by laying claim to a great tract of land that lay between the Pequot (or *Thames*) River and the Pawcatuck River as a spoil of war. Eventually, the Colony granted Captain Daniel Gookin of Boston ". . . five hundred acres of land, being bounded on the West wth Poquatucke River, on ye south wth the Sound, on the east wth Thomas Prentice, & on the north wth the wilderness . . ."

Captain Gookin ultimately sold his "five hundred acres" to Symon Lynde in 1671. This tract of land, which included ". . . our farme and housing thereon (being a neck of land) sittuated & being in the Pequitt Cuntery on Pawcutuck River . . .", was referred to for the first time as "Watch Hill" by the Connecticut General Court, which documented this transaction in 1675.

Watch Hill, once a barren knoll, was used by Native Americans and European settlers alike as a high ground, a "watching" place, from which enemies could be detected and local activities observed. In Colonial times, for instance, a watch manned the Hill for the specific purpose of lighting a beacon fire that would warn the locals of any pending danger.

So too does the photographic history of Watch Hill provide us with a towering promontory from which we can observe the rich maritime legacy of the Pawcatuck River and its sister venues, Little Narragansett Bay, Watch Hill Cove, and Fishers Island Sound. Keen-eyed photographers have captured a rich array of "life by the water" from bustling Westerly, Rhode Island, downstream to the snug little village of Watch Hill, Rhode Island.

Where yachts now tug lazily at their tackle behind the lee of Sandy Point, men once farmed seaweed in horse-drawn carts. Where Watch Hill 15s now dance merrily in the quietude of Watch Hill Cove, catboats were once let for hire to any and all who could hand a gaff-rigged mainsail. Where children now dally in the mild surf of Napatree, lives were once lost and capital was sunk amidst the wreckage of the unfortunate sailing vessels that stumbled in from the fury of the Sound.

The Pawcatuck River has been home to whaling captains and shipwrights, farmers and fishermen. It has listened attentively to the clanging tempo of the caulker's mallet and it has winked mischievously at the countless ships that have slid off its weathered stocks en route to far-reaching horizons. Small villages such as Lotteryville, now known as Avondale, built fieldstone docks upon the river's edge to offload cargo and produce. Quaint locales such as Watch Hill and Foster Cove have provided summer sanctuary to affluent transients for over a century.

Napatree and Sandy Point, those peripatetic and fragile sand spits that separate the somnolence of Little Narragansett Bay from the churning tides of Fishers Island Sound, were once joined at right angles at the Nap (or the current terminus of Napatree Point). From 1839 until September 1938, these two neighbors clung tenaciously to their sandy offshore footholds. After the devastating Hurricane of 1938, the bond was broken and Sandy Point has been traveling north by nor'west ever since. Sailors that travel between Stonington and Watch Hill by way of the "inside" route should take note that the Folly, that magnificent granite foundation on the north shore of Sandy Point, once bore a green marker that urged those traveling east to stay to starboard and those traveling west to stay to port.

Lighthouse Point, the southernmost extremity of the Village of Watch Hill, has nurtured two lighthouses and two life saving stations since the early days of the 1800s. Manned by men who lived and worked upon the sea, these maritime institutions witnessed both redemption for those sailors who were pulled from the sea and resolution for those sailors who were not. The granite wall that stands sentinel at the tip of Lighthouse Point was actually quarried from Millstone Point, Connecticut, the current site of an aging nuclear power plant.

Fishers Island Sound was certainly not going to be a weak link in the East Coast seaboard defense. Fort Mansfield was constructed and commissioned in 1901 on Napatree Point to guard the eastern reaches of Fishers Island Sound. Replete with a garrison of soldiers and 8-inch cannons, the military of the day thought nothing of lobbing live shells into Fishers Island Sound at target barges.

Turn-of-the-century Watch Hill was also replete with massive and opulent waterside hotels. Rambling wooden affairs with porticoes, verandas, and several stories of seaside porches, these resplendent inns made Watch Hill a premier Northeast coastal resort. Arriving by steamer and transported by horse-drawn buggies, summer transients would be feted with incomparable ocean bathing, sailing, dancing, dining, and social gamesmanship.

Yet, it may be the flying-horse carousel that paints the finest portrait of Watch Hill and its environs. Abandoned on the sands of Napatree in 1879, this venerable landmark has withstood the ravages of the sand, the sun, the snow, and, ultimately, the fatal Hurricane of 1938 to carry out its annual charge of providing merriment to the scores of youthful visitors that come down to the sea of a blue-skied summer's day.

So join us on this journey, a journey by way of river and sea, to the quiet bights and prominent hotels of times gone by at Watch Hill, Rhode Island.

One

Down the River

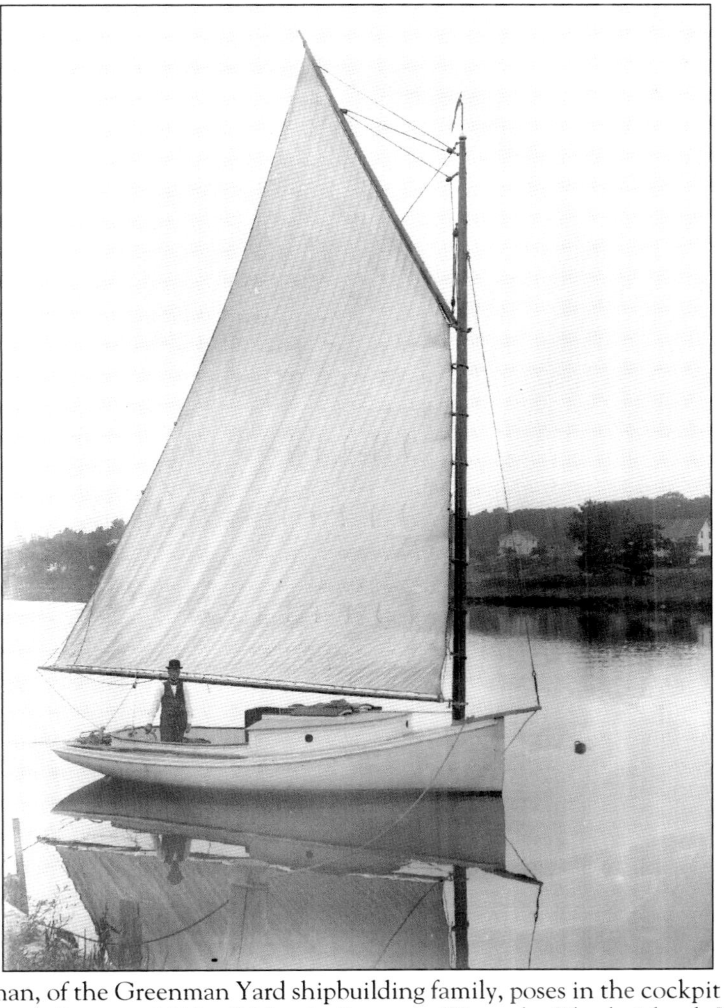

Frank Greenman, of the Greenman Yard shipbuilding family, poses in the cockpit of his catboat on the Pawcatuck River *c.* 1910 off Margin Street in Westerly, Rhode Island. It is not every day that a sailor will tie down such a huge mainsail when his craft is tethered to a dock by both a bow line and a stern line. Watch Hill lies approximately 5 nautical miles downstream from Westerly. (WHS.)

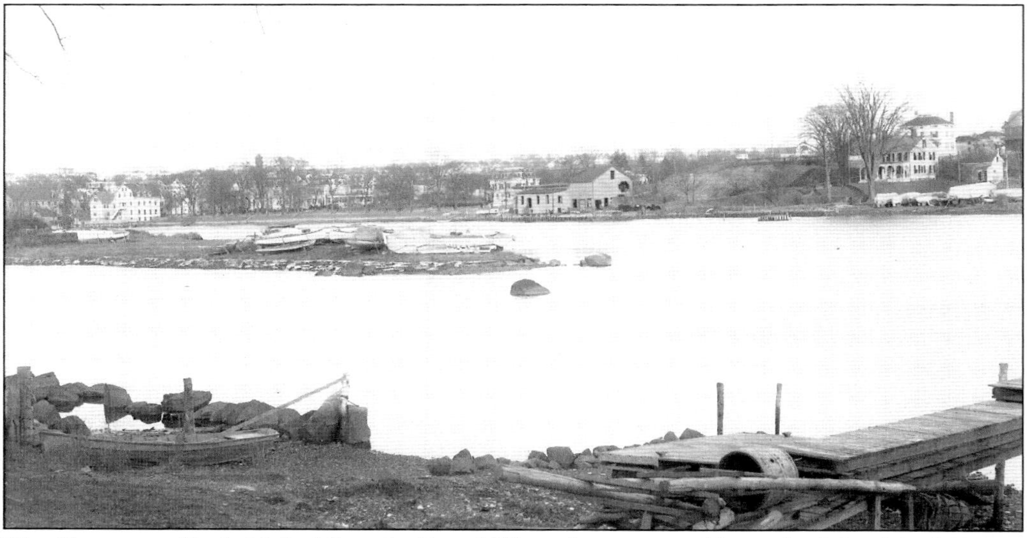

The Greenman Yard shipbuilding facility of Westerly is just visible to the left of the barns in the center of this photo. Long renowned as the most famous shipyard on the Pawcatuck River, the Greenman Yard constructed commercial sailing craft from 1835 until 1874. The spit of land in mid-river, which forms the eastern shore of Jack Cove, has long since receded back into the river itself. (WHS.)

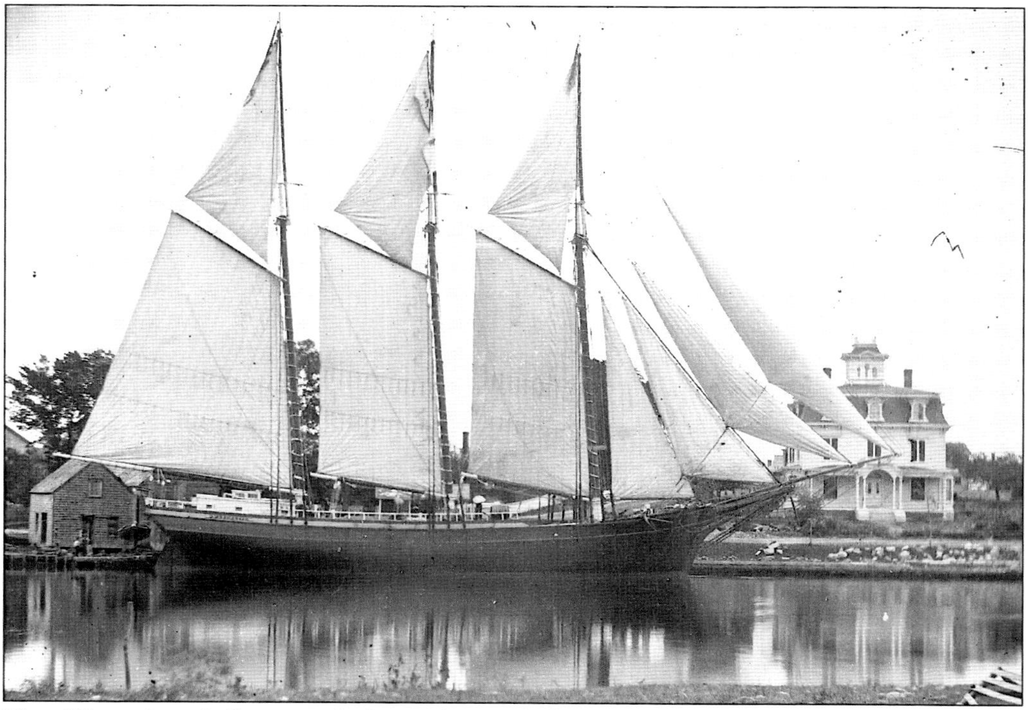

The *Water Line* luffs at a dock in front of the Greenman Yard. Built in 1874, this 400-ton staysail schooner was the last large sailing craft built on the Rhode Island shore of the Pawcatuck River. Note the deck hand, arms akimbo, posing below the boom of the foremast. (JH.)

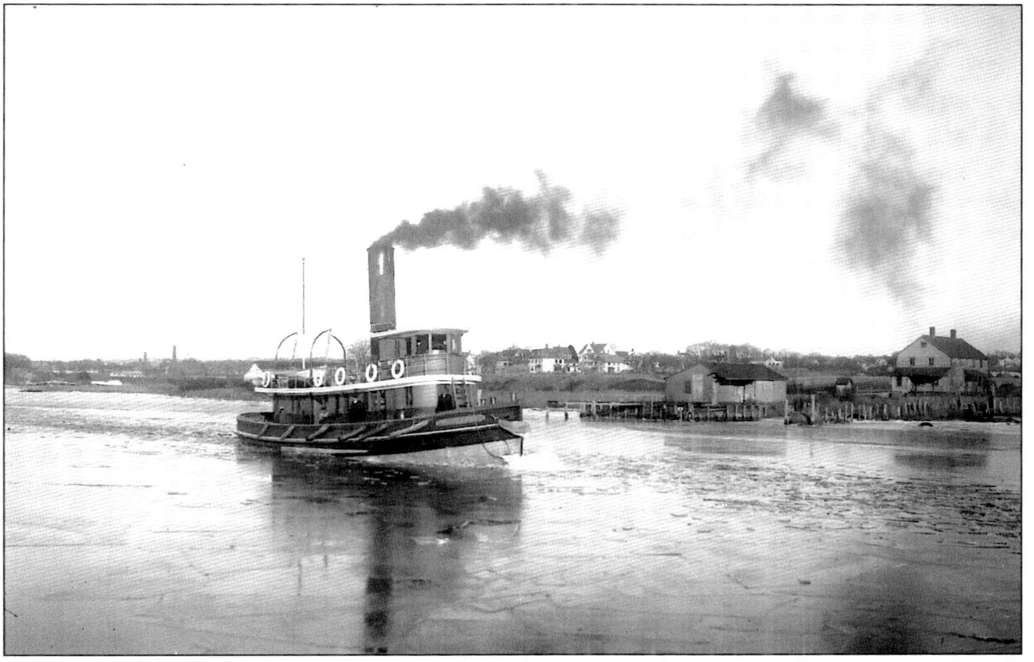

Captain Frank H. Robinson first steamed up the Pawcatuck River in the new tug *Westerly No. 2* on March 21, 1912. Built to tow barges up and down the river, the *Westerly No. 2* also made passenger excursions to the likes of Block Island, Rhode Island, and Greenport, New York. This sturdy tug served until January 24, 1932. In this 1913 winter scene, *Westerly No. 2* is breaking ice on the Pawcatuck. (WHS.)

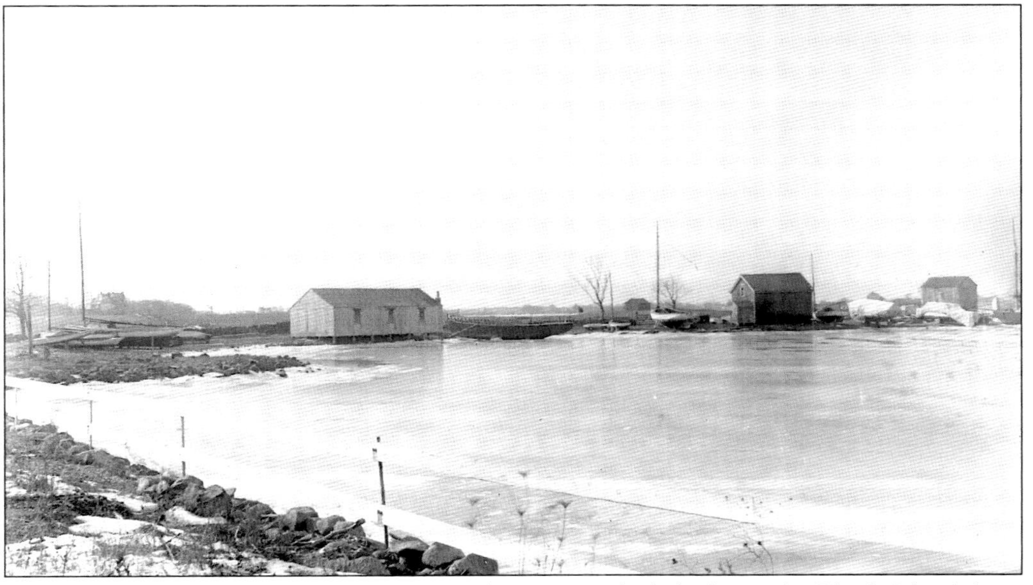

Downriver from Westerly, Thompson Cove forms a neat little bight on the Rhode Island shore of the Pawcatuck River. Looking south from Beach Street during early April 1915, one notes the last vestiges of snow and ice from a severe winter. The southern shore of this cove is currently the site of the Westerly Yacht Club. (WHS.)

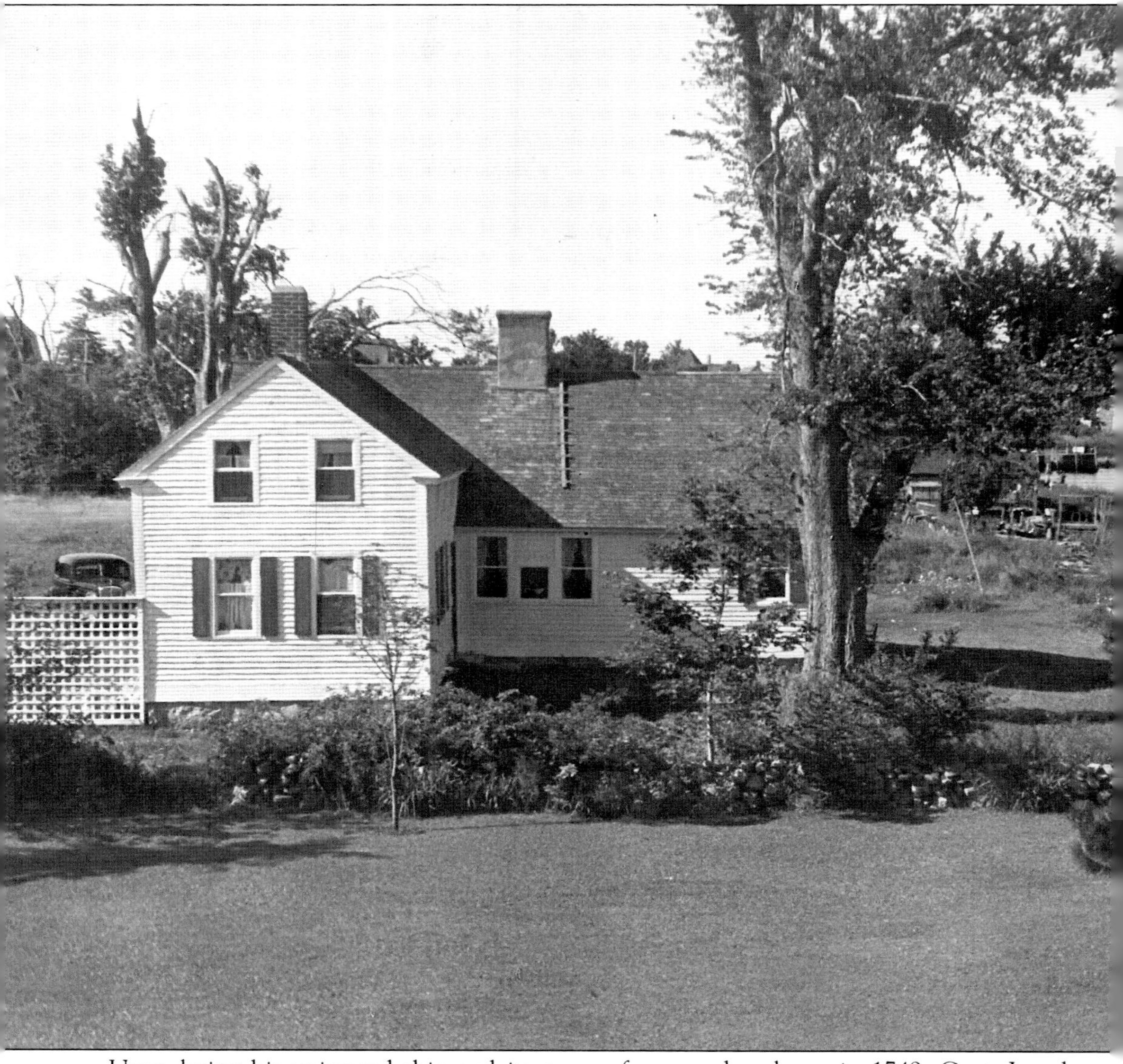

Upon losing his uninsured ship and its cargo of rum and molasses in 1749, Capt. Joseph Pendleton petitioned the RI General Assembly to subdivide his Pawcatuck River farm into 126 lots that could be sold by lottery. This was the origin of the Village of Lotteryville, now known as Avondale, Rhode Island. The Colonial-era dwelling in the left foreground of this 1930s photo was built upon one of these lots. It has housed five generations of the Hall family,

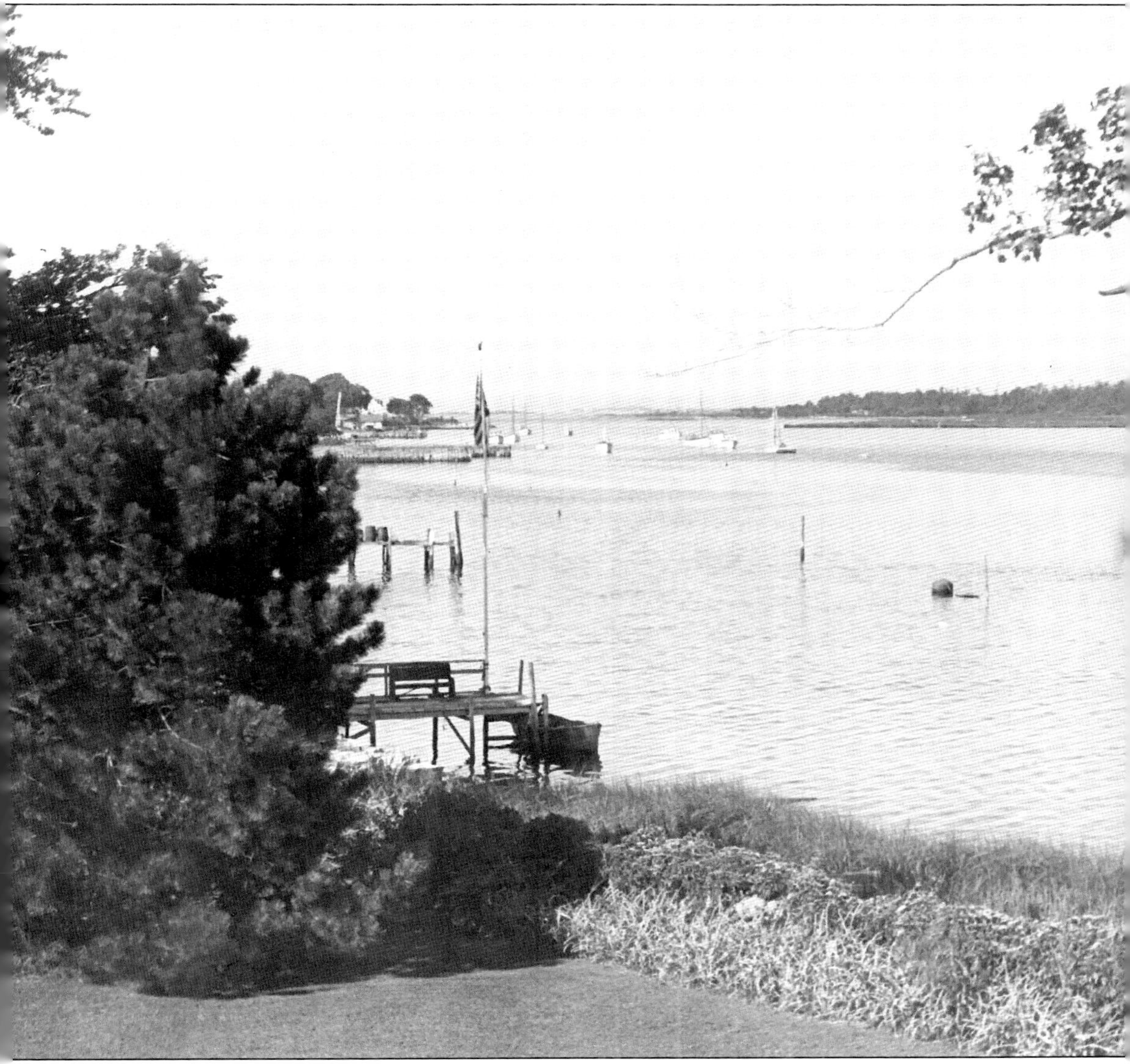

including John P. Hall, whaling master of the *Caledonia* out of Stonington in the 1830s; Daniel C. Hall, organist for Christ Church in Westerly in the early 1900s; and, currently, John F. Hall Jr. and the bustling Frank Hall Boat Yard. Note the shadow of Napatree and Fishers Island in the background at the mouth of the Pawcatuck River. (JH.)

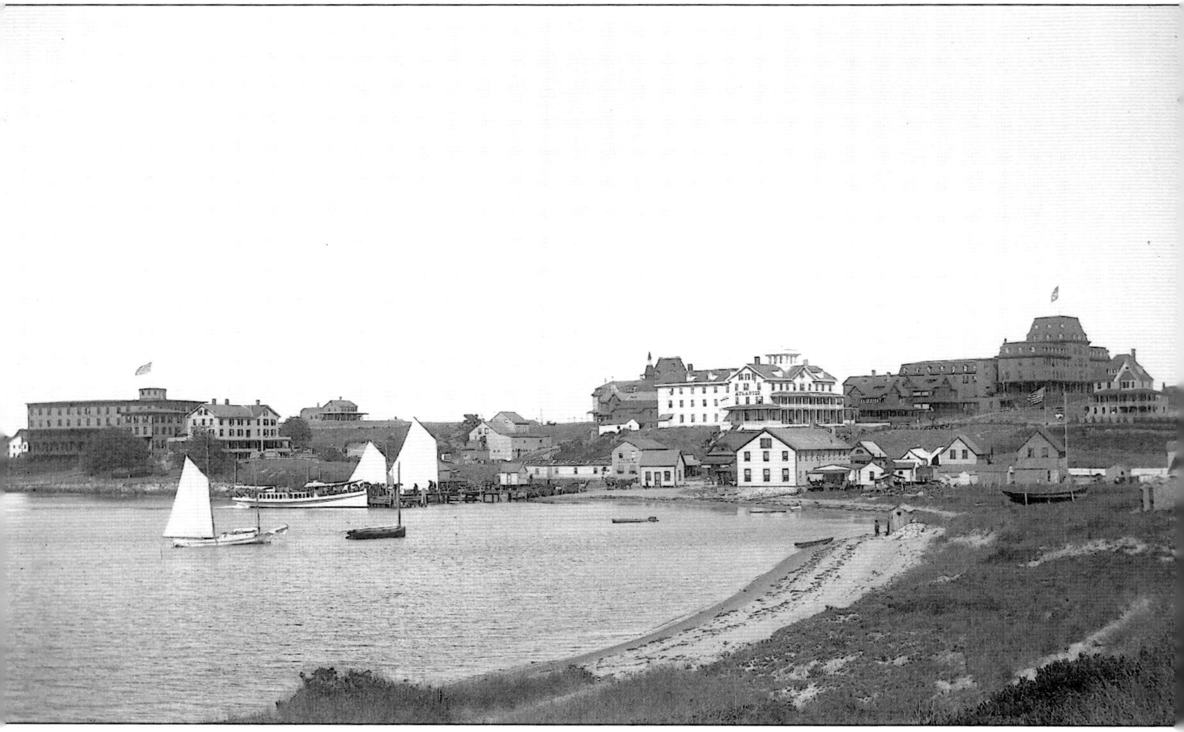

In the 1880s, Watch Hill Cove was guarded by a skyline of rambling wooden structures that included the following, from left to right: the flag-bedecked Plimpton House and Annex; the three-chimneyed Narragansett House; an unidentified cottage; the north wing of the Ocean House; the steepled Watch Hill Chapel; the two-tier porches of the Atlantic House; and the vast Watch Hill House, beneath Old Glory. Prior to the advent of trolley traffic in 1894, Watch Hill was mostly accessible by water. In the earlier days, sailboats such as the *Fanny Golden* and *North Star* sailed between Westerly and Watch Hill with passengers. In later years, the 105-foot sidewheel steamer *Sadie* sailed between Westerly and Watch Hill and the awning-covered *Watch Hill* steamer, depicted in the center foreground of this photo, sailed regularly between Stonington, Connecticut, and Watch Hill. Early deeds refer to Watch Hill Cove as Pawcatuck Bay, Pawcatuck River, and Wilcox Cove. (GHU-Burdick.)

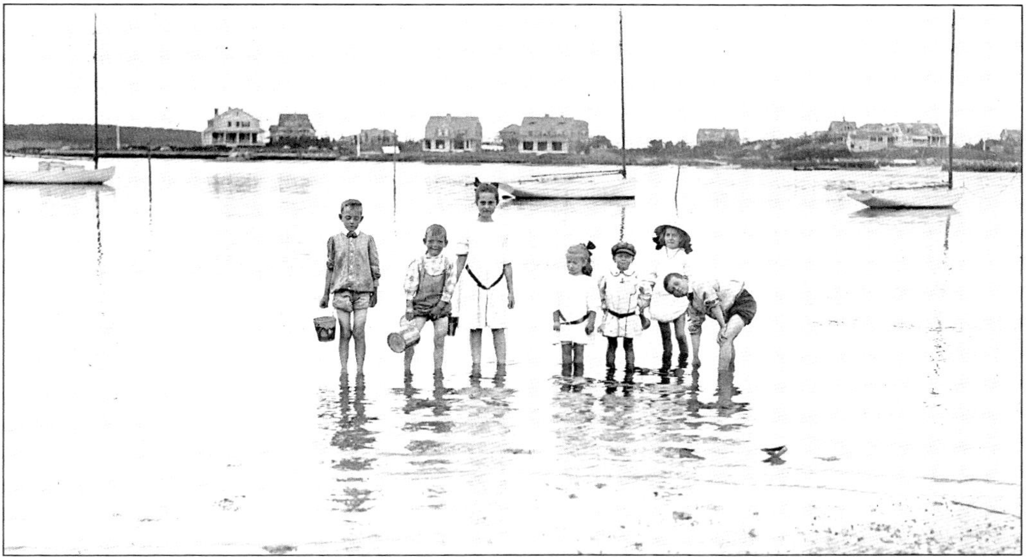

Where a cement retaining wall now encloses the southwest corner of Watch Hill Cove, children once had direct access to its summer wonders during the early 1900s. Porter Hoxie, far right, would go on to become a fire fighter for Watch Hill and a piano player for the silent movies at the Crown Theater on Bay Street. (JM.)

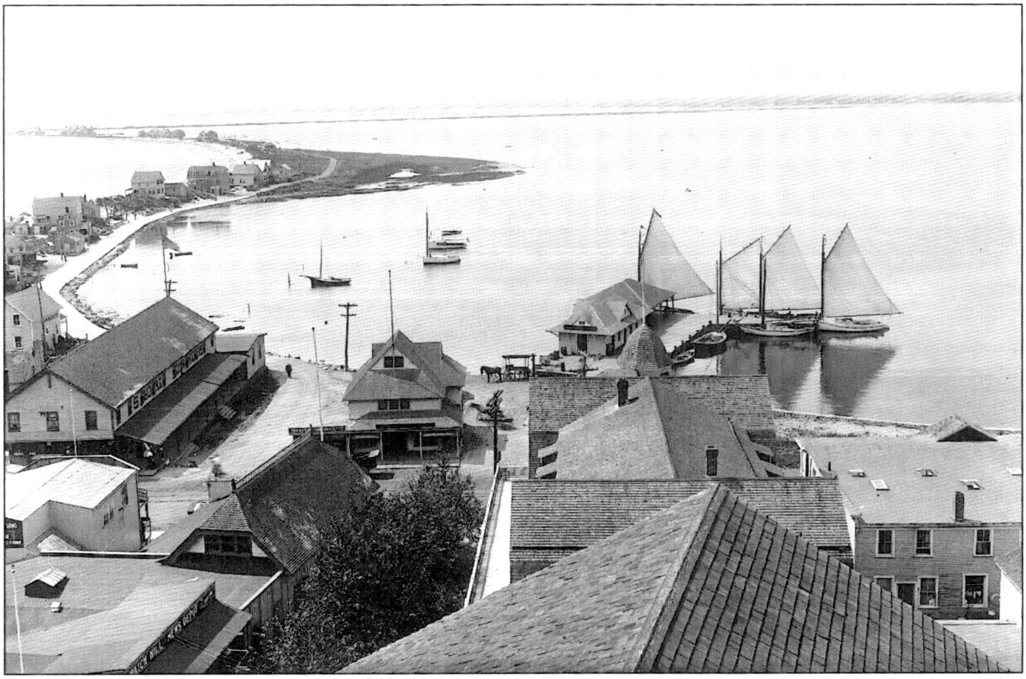

A view from the roof of the Atlantic House in August 1912 reveals that Sandy Point was still connected to Napatree, that numerous cottages lined Fort Road all the way out to Fort Mansfield, and that pre-hurricane Napatree was much wider than it is today. Watch Hill Cove, which was not dredged until 1913, looks barren without its contemporary jetty, numerous moorings, and red and green entrance buoys. (WHS.)

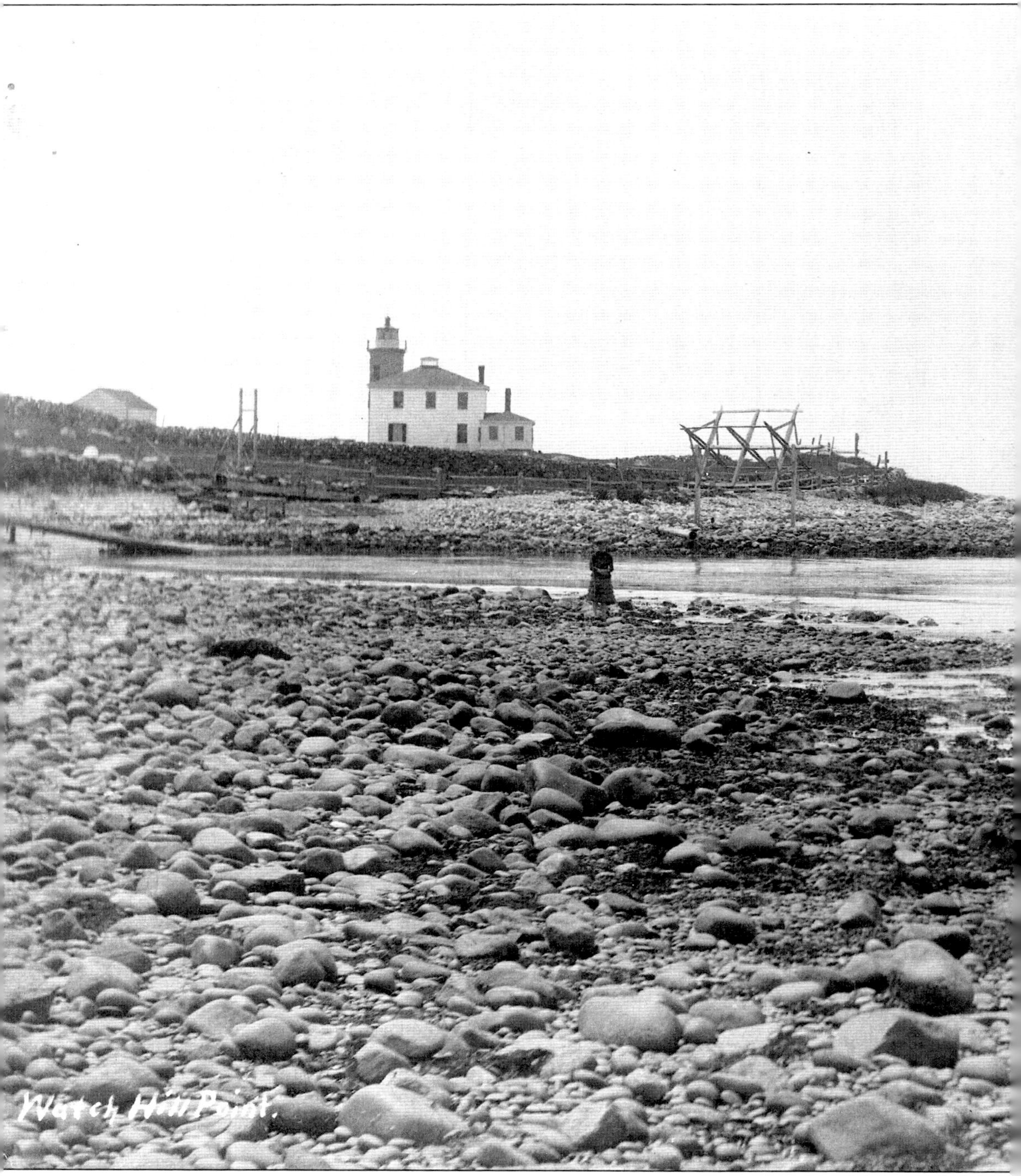

Watch Hill Point, the southernmost extremity of the Village of Watch Hill, houses the Watch Hill Lighthouse that was built in 1855. Jutting out between Fishers Island Sound to the west and Block Island Sound to the east, this small peninsula is the shoulder from which the long sandy arm of Napatree extends between Fishers Island Sound and Little Narragansett Bay. From left to right, this turn-of-the-century scene depicts the ramp from the life saving station sliding

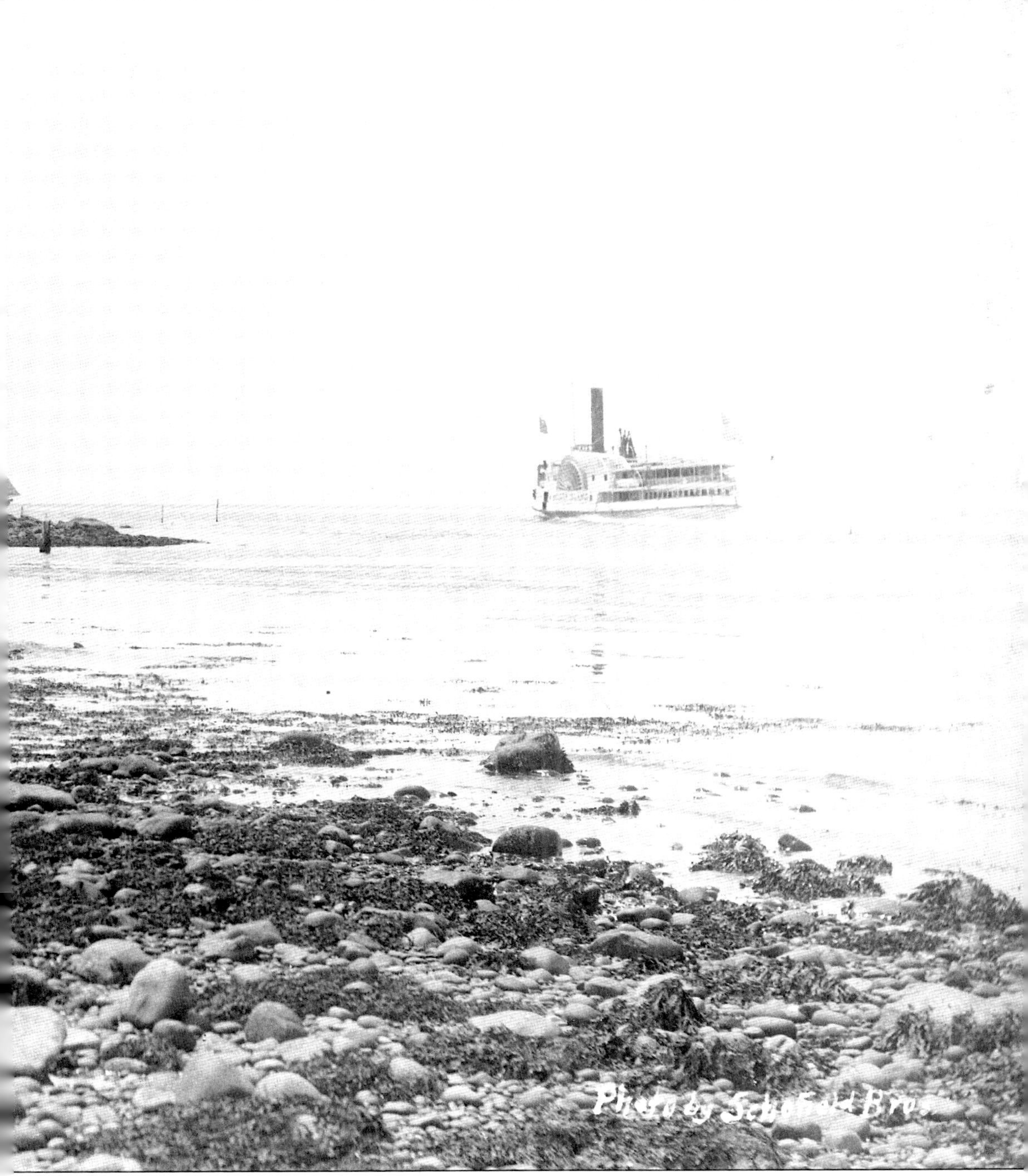

into the Sound; the second lighthouse to stand upon this point (it operates to this very day); a solitary walker; racks for drying fish nets; a two-masted staysail schooner; and the *Block Island* steamer en route to her namesake island. Modern-day visitors would not recognize the many cobblestones that litter what is now the site of several seaside cottages. (WPL.)

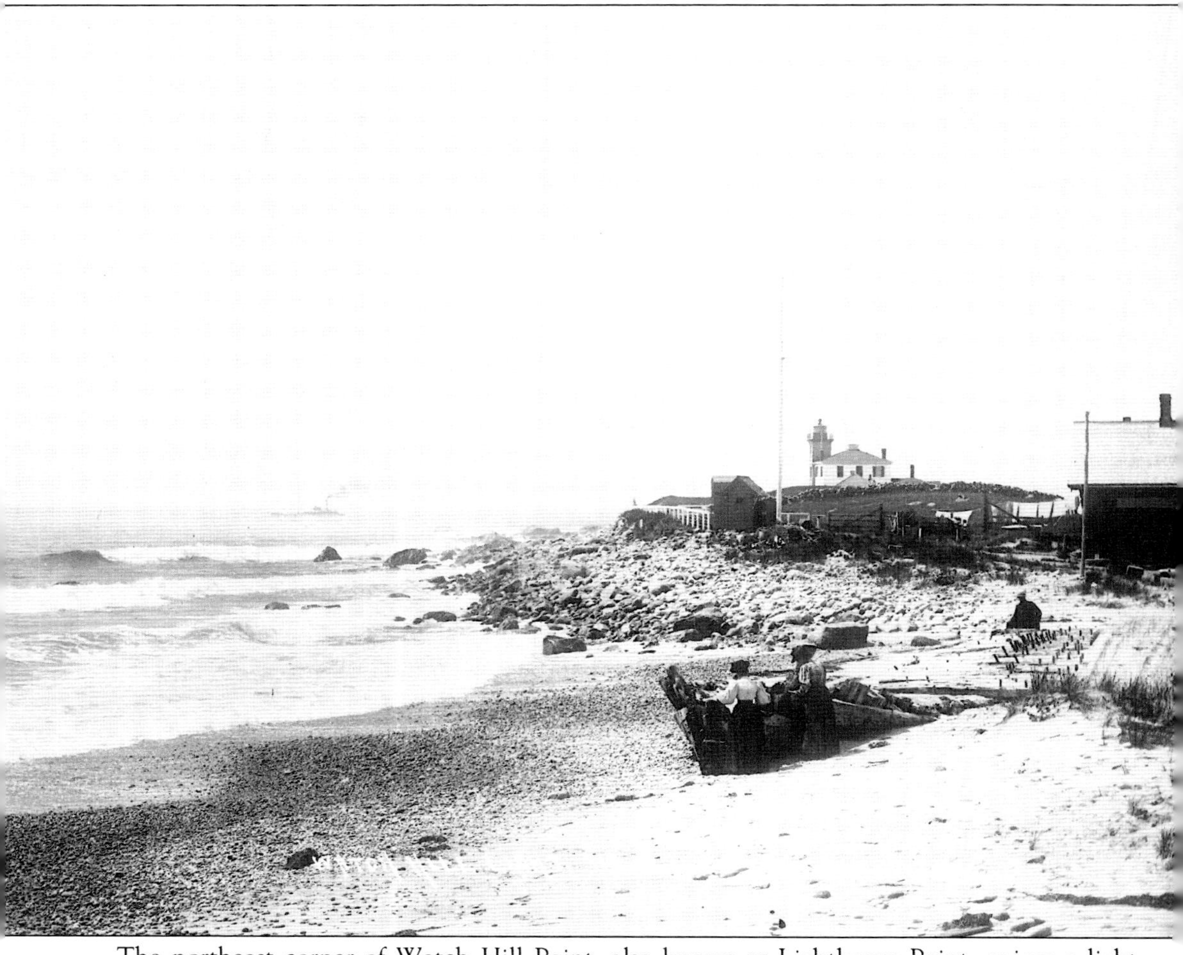

The northeast corner of Watch Hill Point, also known as Lighthouse Point, enjoys a light southeast breeze and gentle surf. Two properly attired ladies and a gentleman examine a rotting hulk that has begun to sink below the hard packed sand of East Beach. Note the clothes drying in the wind before the two-chimneyed life saving station. (GHU-Burdick.)

Two

ON THE COVE

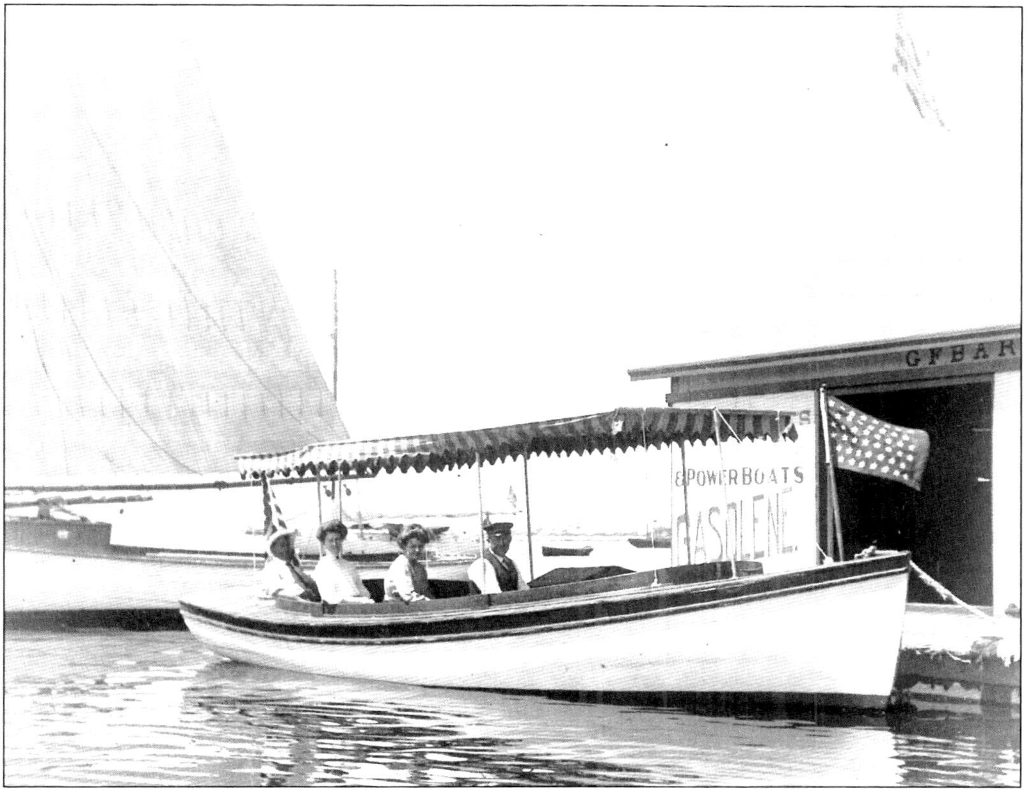

Members of the Barbour family of Avondale have donned their Sunday best for a turn-of-the-century partyboat excursion in a stately wooden launch. Summer residents could readily avail themselves of the numerous partyboats that operated out of Watch Hill Cove throughout the season. A huge gaff sail, replete with three tiers of reefing points, luffs calmly in the summer breeze on the catboat that lies astern of the power launch. The snapping Union Jack on the bow of the Barbour's craft denotes either a Sunday outing or a holiday. (DB.)

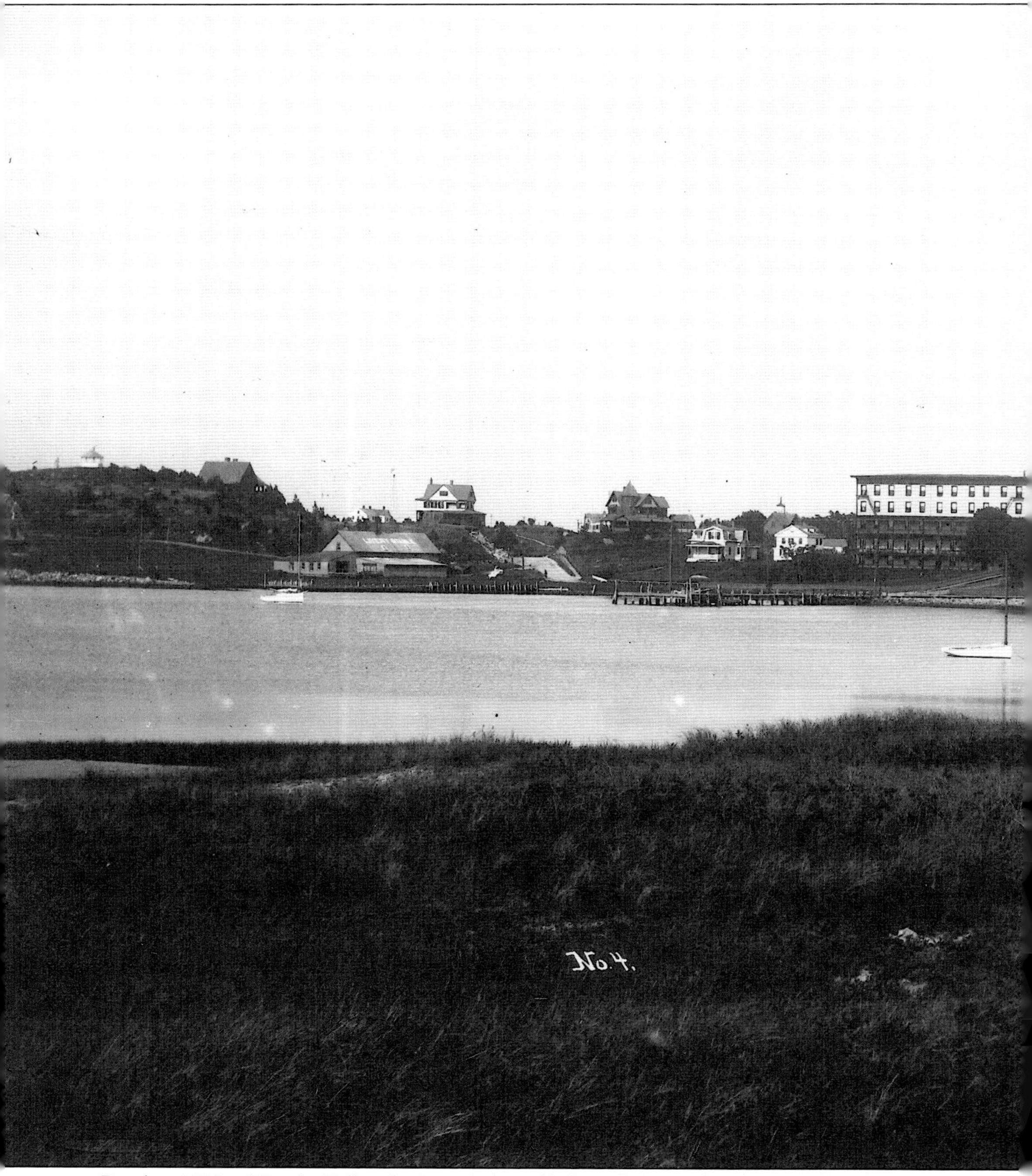

By the 1880s, Watch Hill, which styled itself the "Queen of Atlantic Resorts," had eight significant hotels. Some bore aquatic names such as the Atlantic, the Bay-View, and the Narragansett. Others bore family names such as the Plimpton and the Larkin. For many summer tourists, access to Watch Hill and the hostelries was gained by steamer through Watch Hill Cove. Early developers promoted tourism by noting that "passengers by the Stonington line can

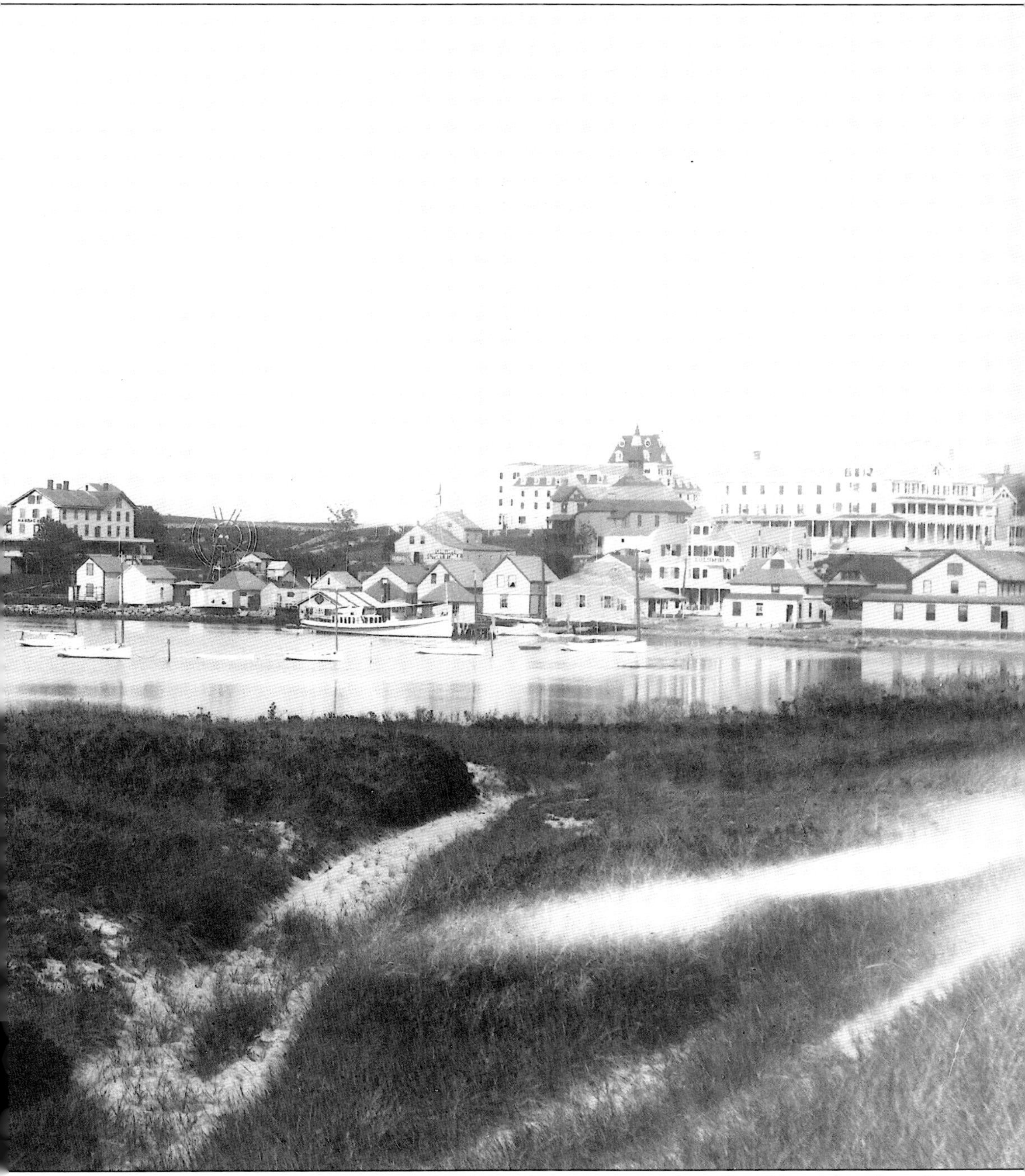

breakfast on board or in Stonington, or take the early boat to Watch Hill and breakfast there." Resorts of every era promote recreation and the cove was a repository for many such activities. Note the livery stable on the far left side of the cove, the Ferris wheel in the center foreground, and the racing yachts that are moored in the cove. (GHU-Burdick.)

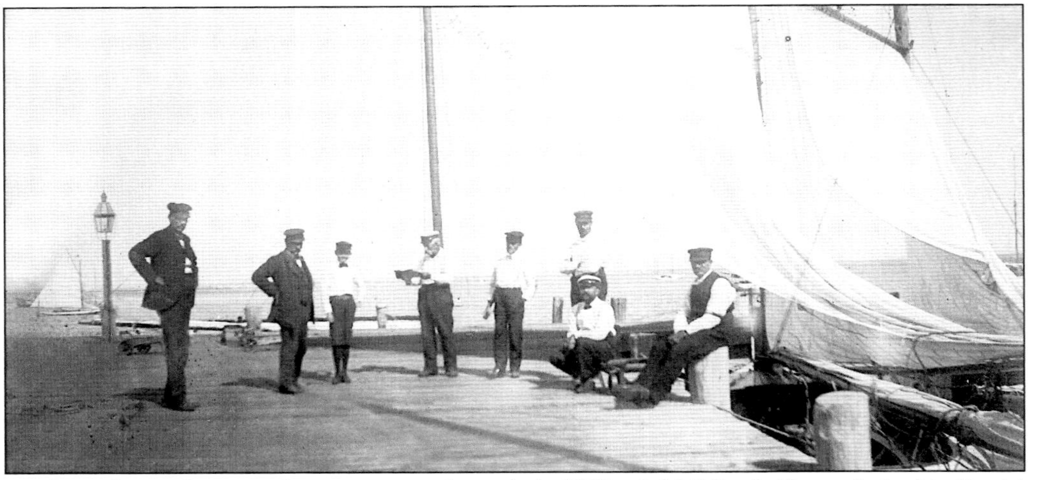

Tradition has it that partyboat captains who sailed off Watch Hill Dock (formerly Larkin Dock) in Watch Hill Cove in the late 1880s invested in a 10-foot plank at the beginning of each summer season that would be propped up on three kegs. Setting upon the plank with jackknives over the course of the summer, they would whittle until the plank "was nearly asunder in several places" (*The Westerly Sun*, July 1914). (JH.)

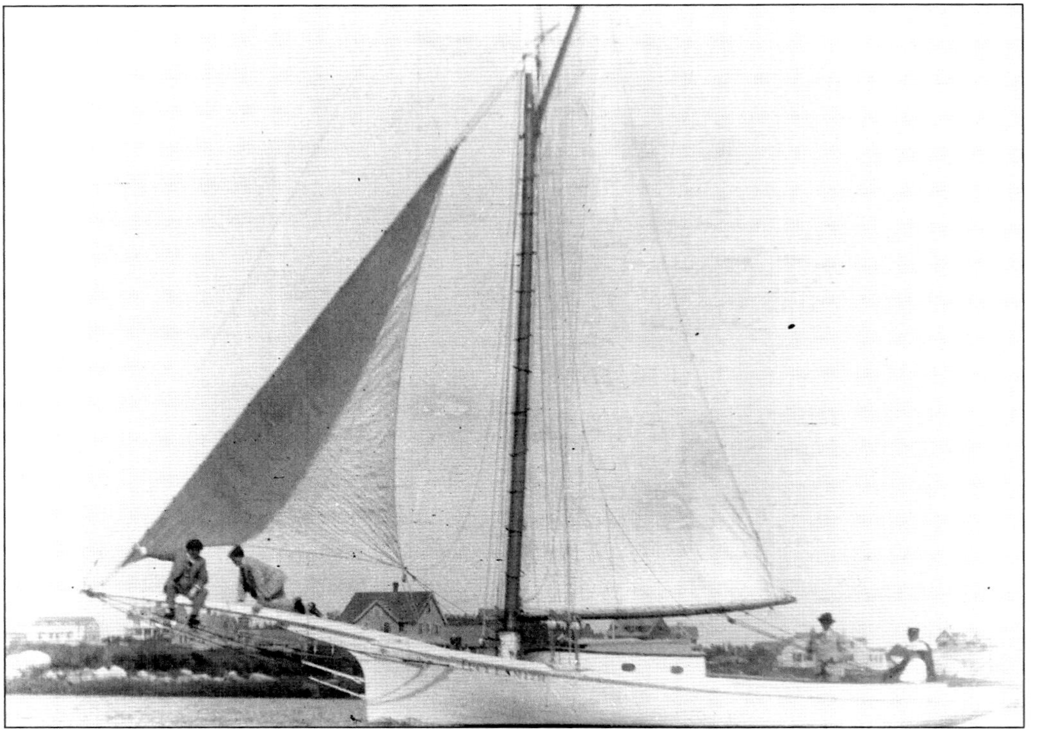

Captain Burdick sailed the *Lucy E. Smith*, a Friendship Sloop from Avondale, as a partyboat during the summer seasons at the turn of the century off Plimpton Dock in Watch Hill Cove. Summer visitors could sail for $5 (half day) and $10 (full day). On moonlit nights, Captain Burdick and his passengers would venture out into Fishers Island Sound and circumnavigate the East Breakwater. (DB.)

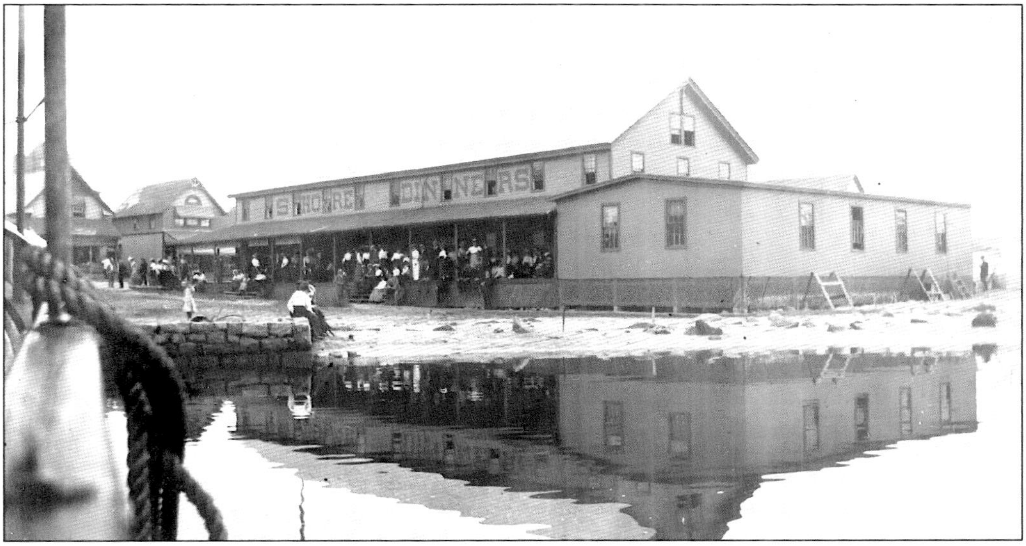

"Whale" Larkin's Shore Dinner, a cove-side restaurant of great repute, would feed up to 800 people at a Sunday afternoon sitting in the late 1880s. Jack Noyes would ring his dinner bell and Policeman Chapman would control the crowd. Waiters served "clam chowder . . . broiled blue fish, mashed potato and turnip, cranberry sauce, clam fritters with wine sauce, green corn on the cob . . . brown bread and butter" (*The Westerly Sun*, July 1914). (DB.)

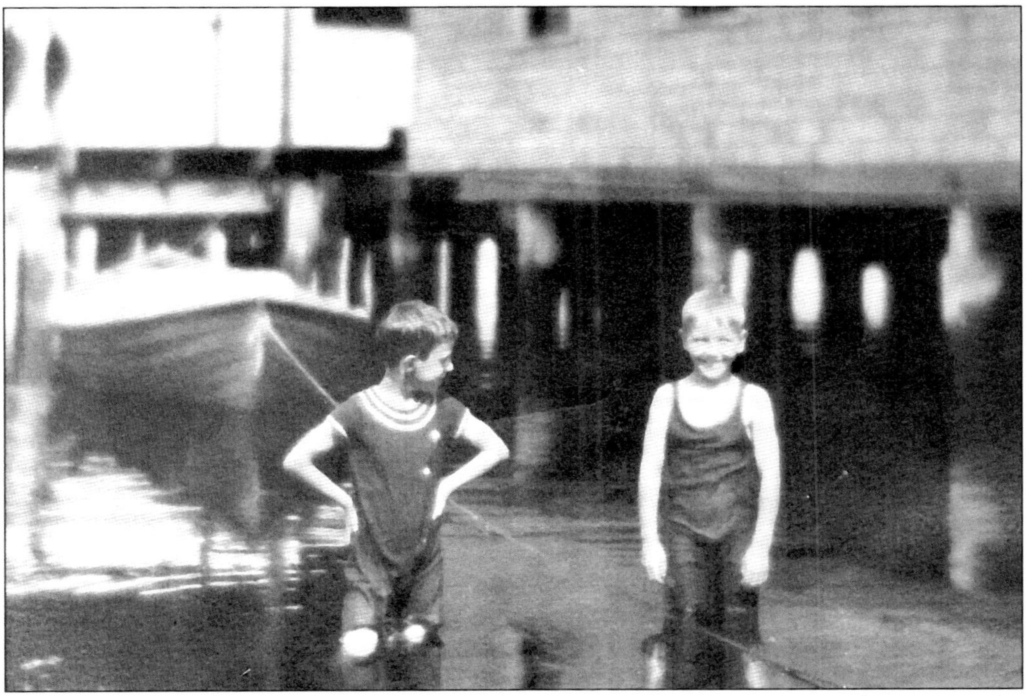

Frank Nash and his cousin, William Watrous, cavort in their one-pieces in the cove to the north of the Watch Hill Dock c. 1905. Frank, whose father, Walter, was once the fire chief of Watch Hill and whose great-great grandfather, Jonathan, was the first keeper of the Watch Hill Lighthouse, lived year-round on Fort Road on Napatree as a child. (SC.)

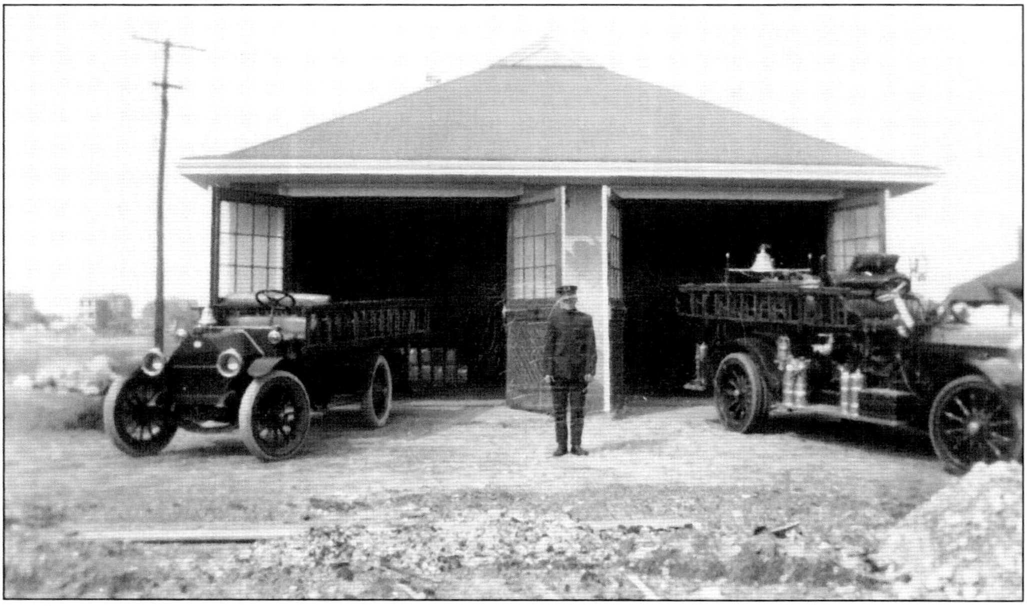

With its stern on the cove by the current location of the Watch Hill Dock and its doors opening on Bay Street, the first firehouse at Watch Hill was well-positioned to provide fire protection to the immediate community at the turn of the century. The Columbia House, a hotel, was located directly across from this site. (JM.)

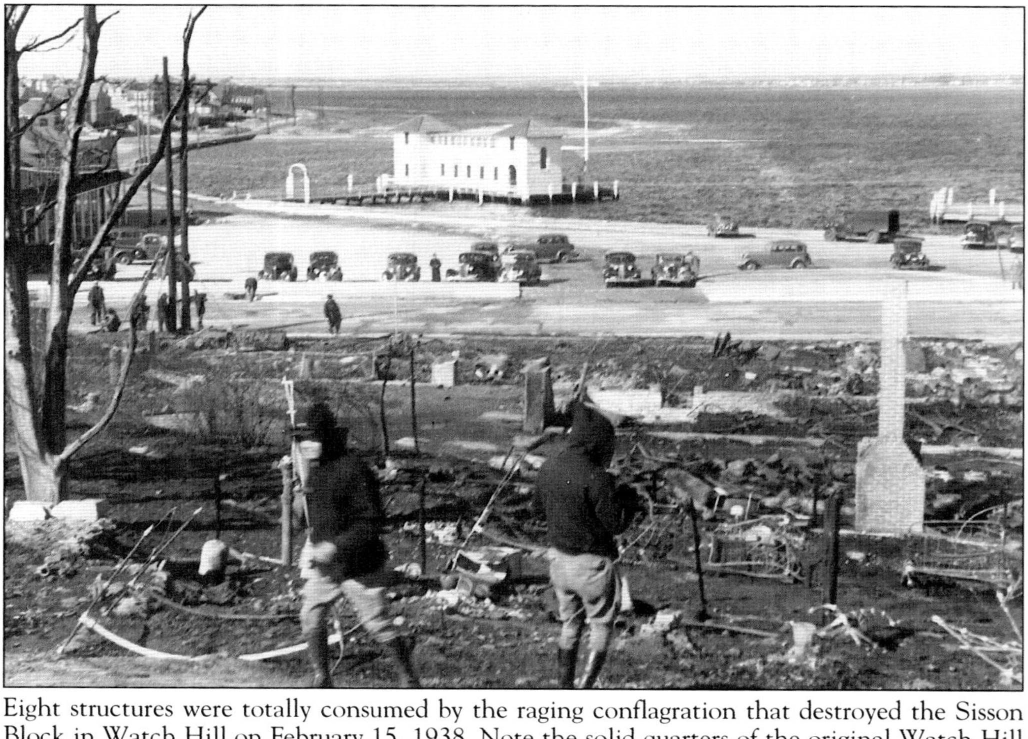

Eight structures were totally consumed by the raging conflagration that destroyed the Sisson Block in Watch Hill on February 15, 1938. Note the solid quarters of the original Watch Hill Yacht Club in the center foreground. (JM.)

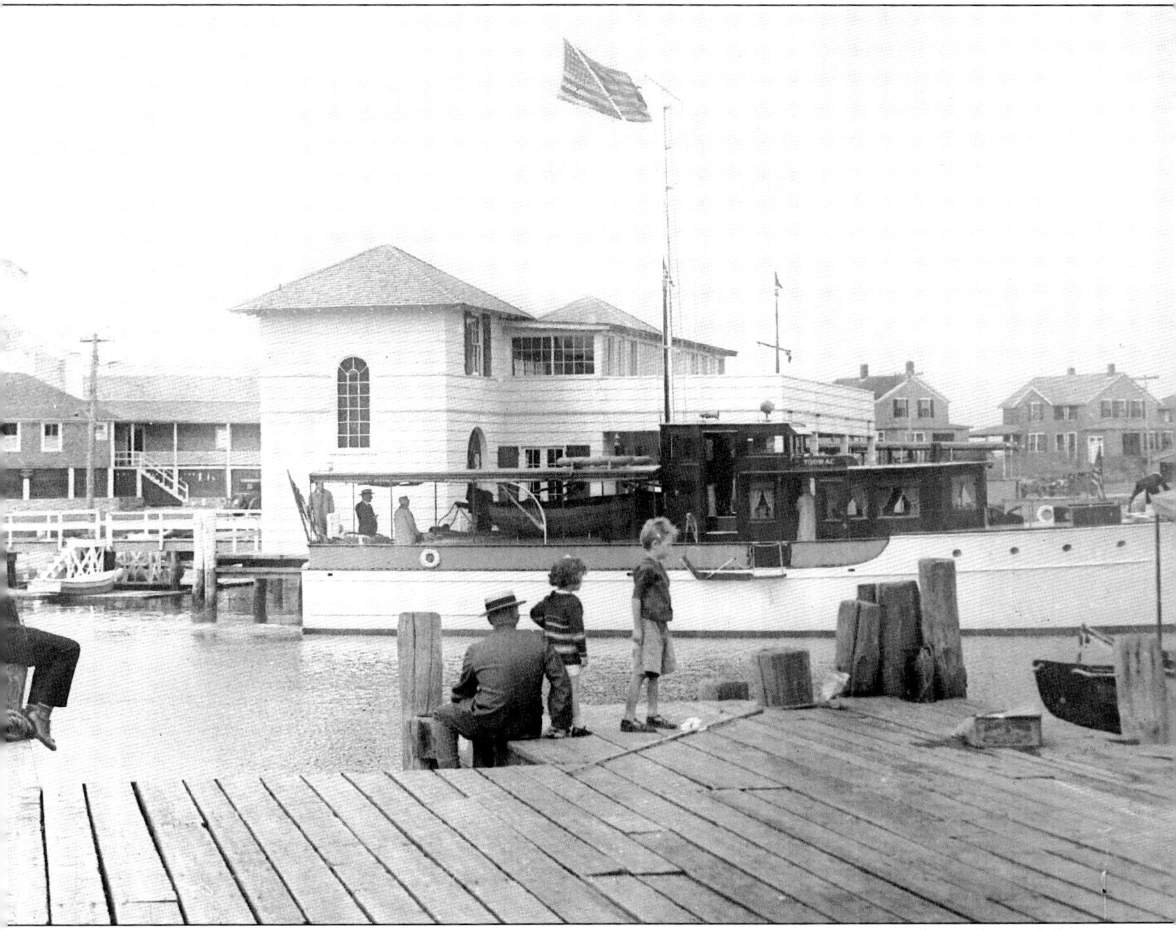

Departing before a northwest breeze, the *Toorac* drops the original Watch Hill Yacht Club astern as it gathers way for the mouth of Watch Hill Cove in the late 1920s or early 1930s. The 65-foot *Toorac* was named by spelling the owner's name, which was C.A. Root, backwards. Frank Hall of Avondale signed on as the chief polisher of the *Toorac* as a 12-year-old boy back in 1925. Polishing 180 pieces of brass every day earned him "a dollar a day and all I could eat . . . we slept in the fo'csle while the guests had cabins . . . but that was OK." The *Toorac*, whose owners summered in Weekapaug, were undaunted mariners who cruised far and wide. Frank Hall recalls a journey that "started at the Westerly Yacht Club, down to New York, up through Lake Champlain to Quebec" (*Tidings*, August 1991). (JH.)

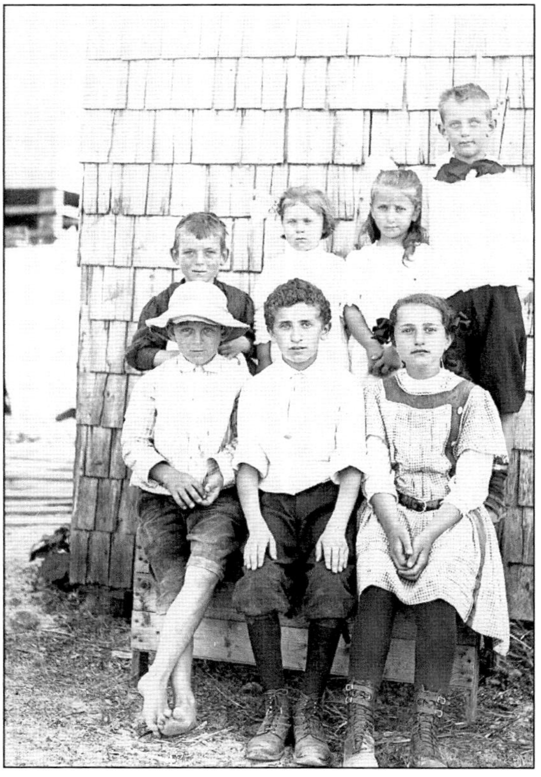

Local children pose for a quick photo against a shingle background on a summer day in Watch Hill. Porter Hoxie, top left, was born in 1899. As an adult, Porter and his father, George, were engaged on special occasions to move a piano from the Misquamicut Golf Club to the Watch Hill Beach Club. Porter was known for playing the piano en route in the back of the truck. (JM.)

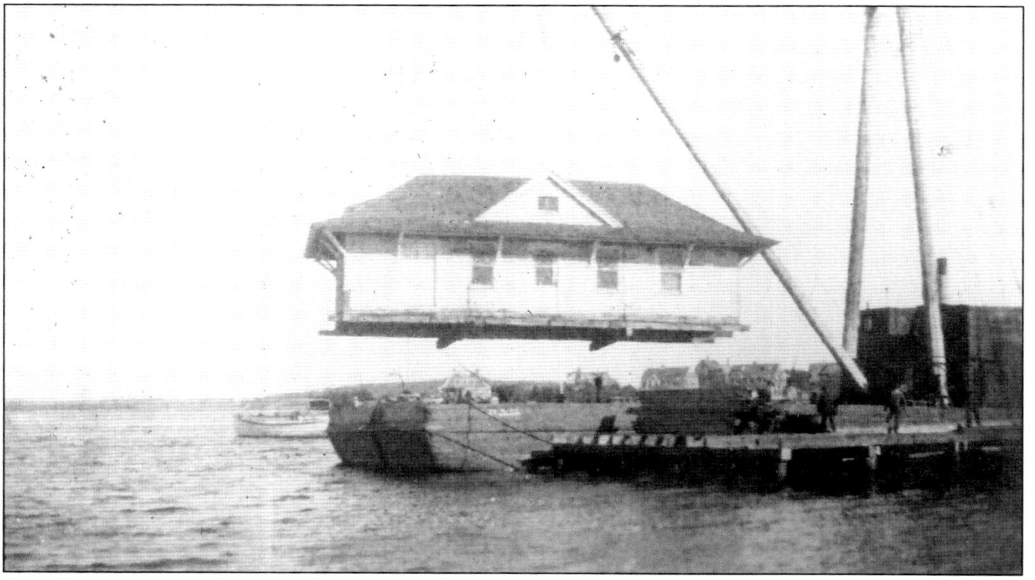

Suspended from a derrick, the pre-hurricane Watch Hill Yacht Club is being readied for its short trip from the Watch Hill Dock to its new home at the present site of the Watch Hill Yacht Club. Commodore John Watts received permission from the Watch Hill Fire District in July 1921 to acquire, move, and utilize a former ticket and express office as the club's quarters. (JM.)

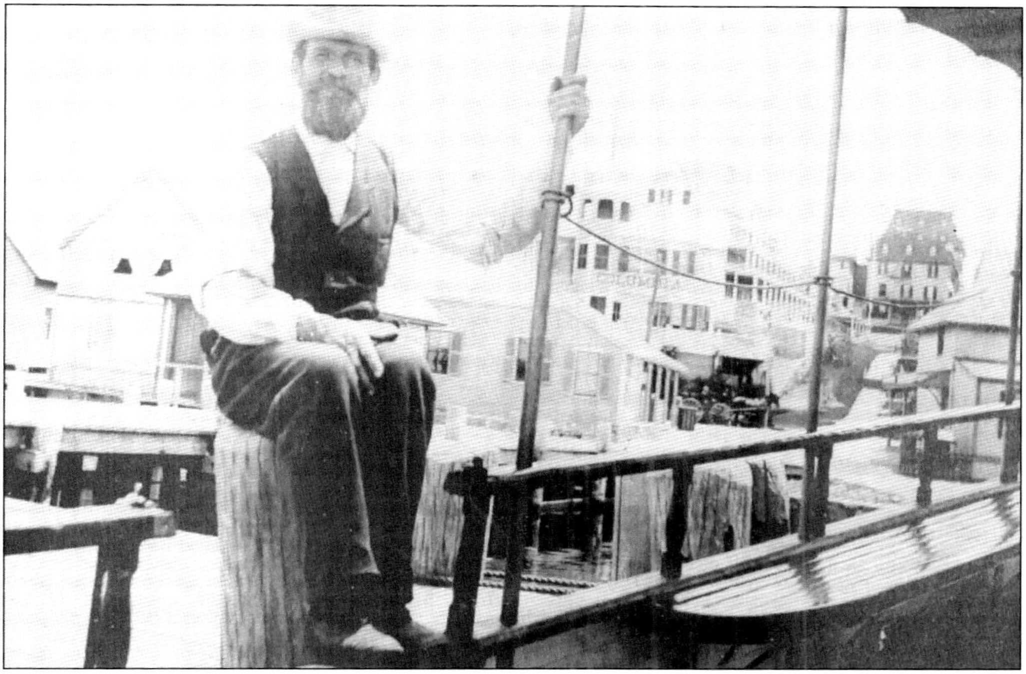

Wanton Weeks Hoxie poses for a photograph while sitting on a pile alongside the *Watch Hill* steamer during the summer of 1901. The Columbia House, which is now the Olympia Tea Room, is visible in the background. Note the horse and carriage on Bay Street. (SC.)

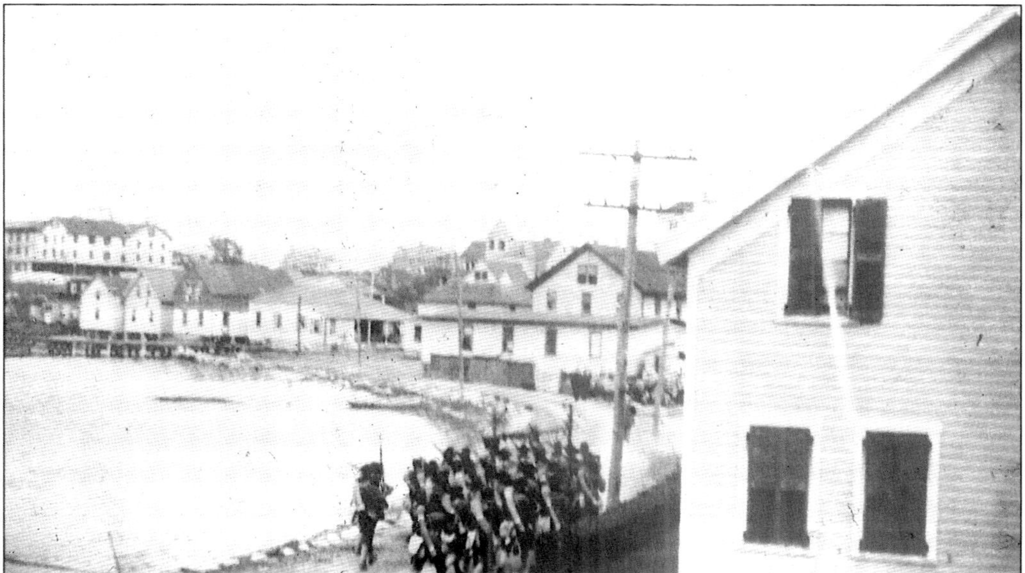

A garrison of soldiers from Fort Mansfield marches down Fort Road toward the cove. Two hundred twenty-eight soldiers once manned Fort Mansfield, which was built upon the "Nap" at Napatree in 1901, with the purpose of defending the western extremity of Fishers Island Sound. It is inconceivable to us today, but "the eight-inch guns were fired in practice, shaking Watch Hill windows well" (*Fort Mansfield*). (JM.)

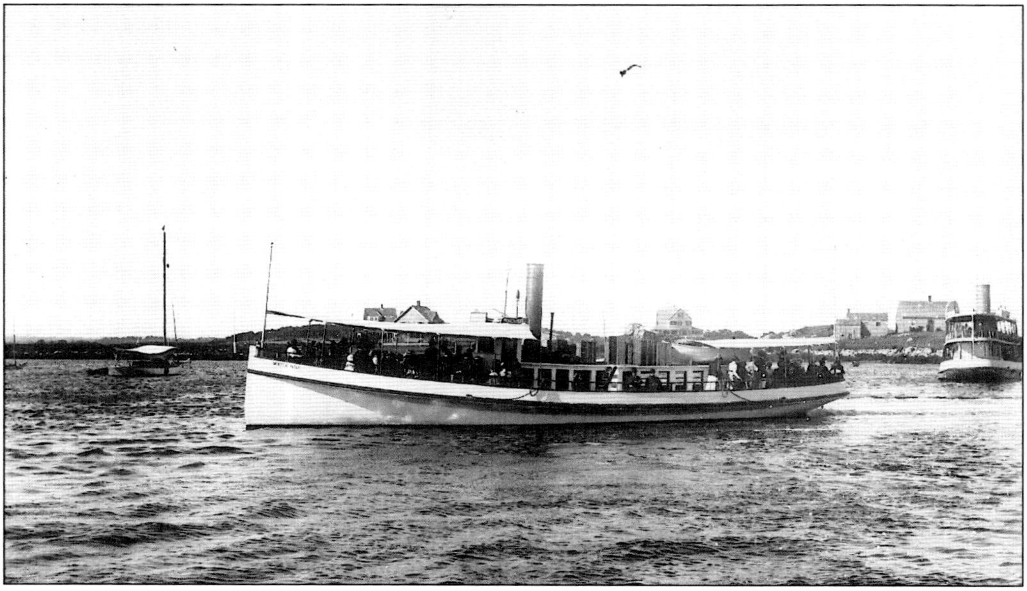

The steamer *Watch Hill* maintained a schedule between Stonington and the cove for two decades after the turn of the century despite several ownership changes. J.I. Maxson acquired and piloted the *Watch Hill* after it had been converted from a steam rig to a gasoline twin-screw rig in 1914. Maxson was also noted for his lovely yawl, the *Wanderer*. (GHU-Burdick.)

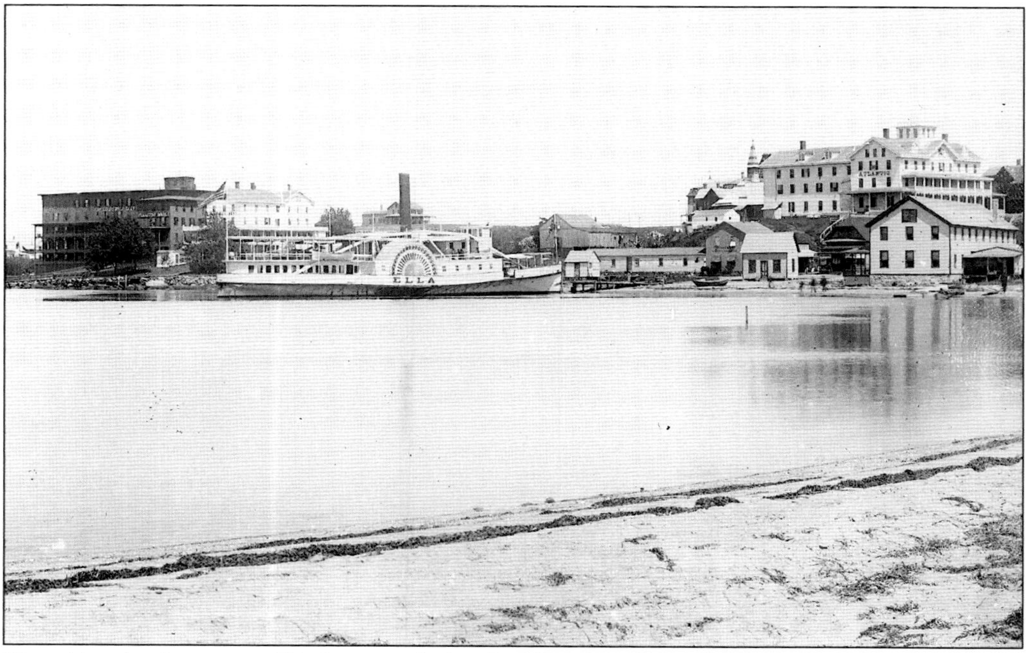

The side-wheel steamer *Ella* lies quietly by the Watch Hill Dock. This 154-foot steamer was "Mystic Built" by the shipbuilding yard of Charles Mallory & Sons in 1864. Intended to run a schedule that called upon Norwich, New London, Mystic, Stonington, and Watch Hill, the *Ella* was chartered by the war department for Civil War service. Returning to duty as a steamer, she was finally abandoned in 1904. (GHU-Burdick.)

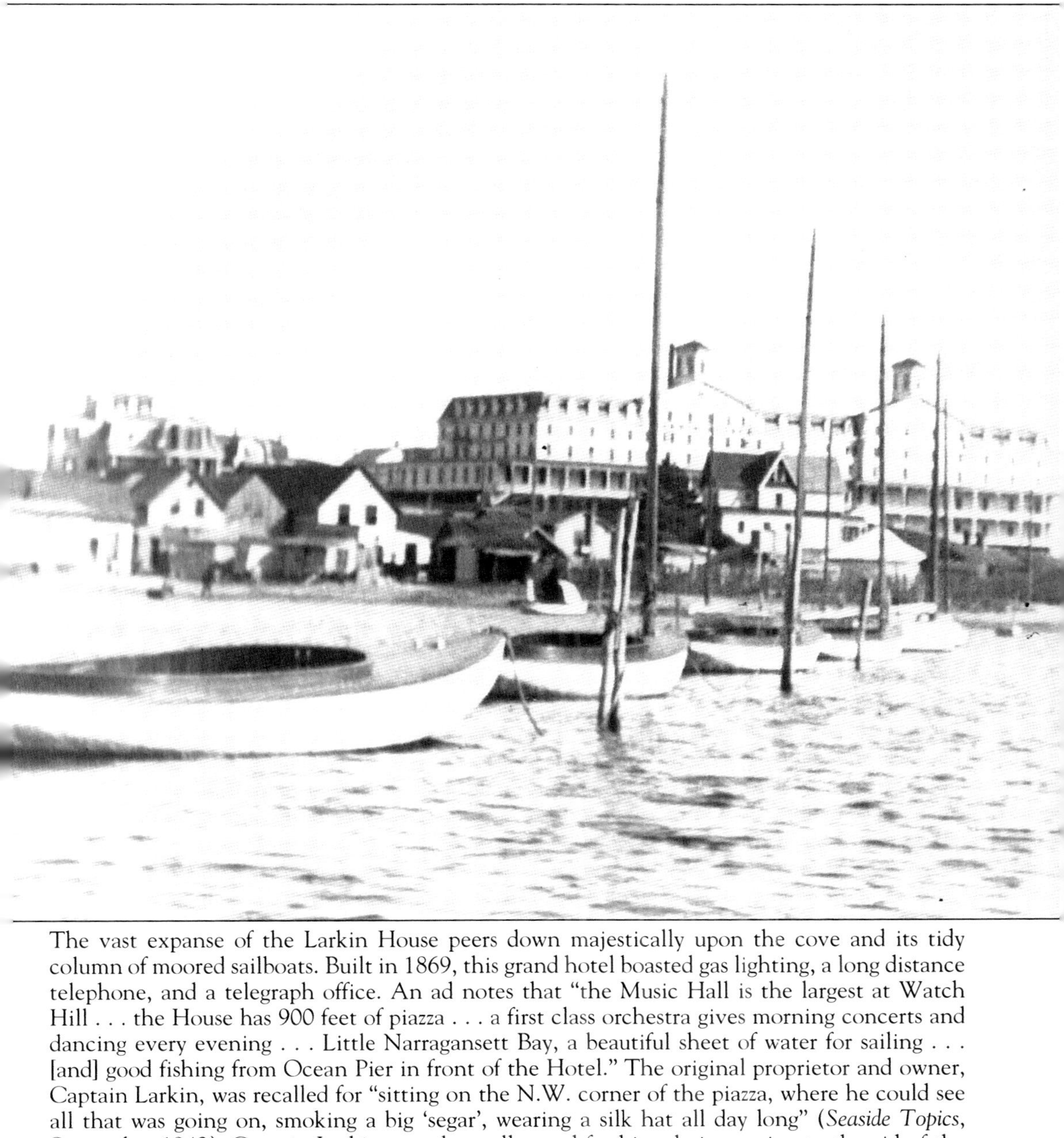

The vast expanse of the Larkin House peers down majestically upon the cove and its tidy column of moored sailboats. Built in 1869, this grand hotel boasted gas lighting, a long distance telephone, and a telegraph office. An ad notes that "the Music Hall is the largest at Watch Hill . . . the House has 900 feet of piazza . . . a first class orchestra gives morning concerts and dancing every evening . . . Little Narragansett Bay, a beautiful sheet of water for sailing . . . [and] good fishing from Ocean Pier in front of the Hotel." The original proprietor and owner, Captain Larkin, was recalled for "sitting on the N.W. corner of the piazza, where he could see all that was going on, smoking a big 'segar', wearing a silk hat all day long" (*Seaside Topics*, September 1942). Captain Larkin was also well noted for his role in coming to the aid of the steamer *Metis* after its fatal wreck off Lighthouse Point during August 1872. He received a congressional medal for his life saving heroics, which he would recount to his guests at least a couple of times a season. (DB.)

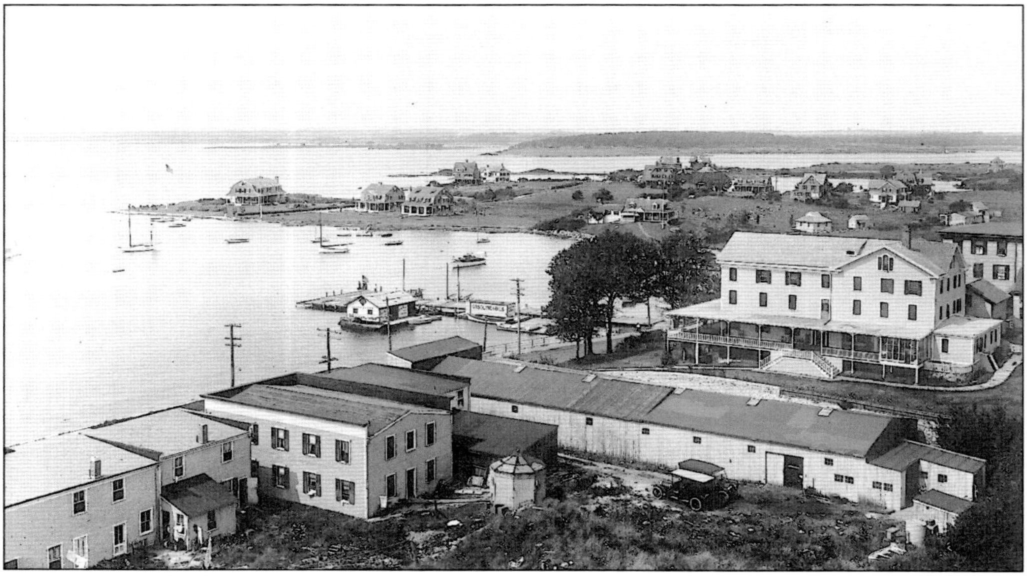

Standing atop the Atlantic House during August 1912, one would notice the vast expanse of placid Little Narragansett Bay at the top left; a ribbon of water that is the Pawcatuck River across the top center; a brief glimpse of Foster Cove hiding just below the Pawcatuck; the rambling porches of the Narragansett House at right center; and Fenelon's garage, the long one-story structure on the bottom right. (WHS.)

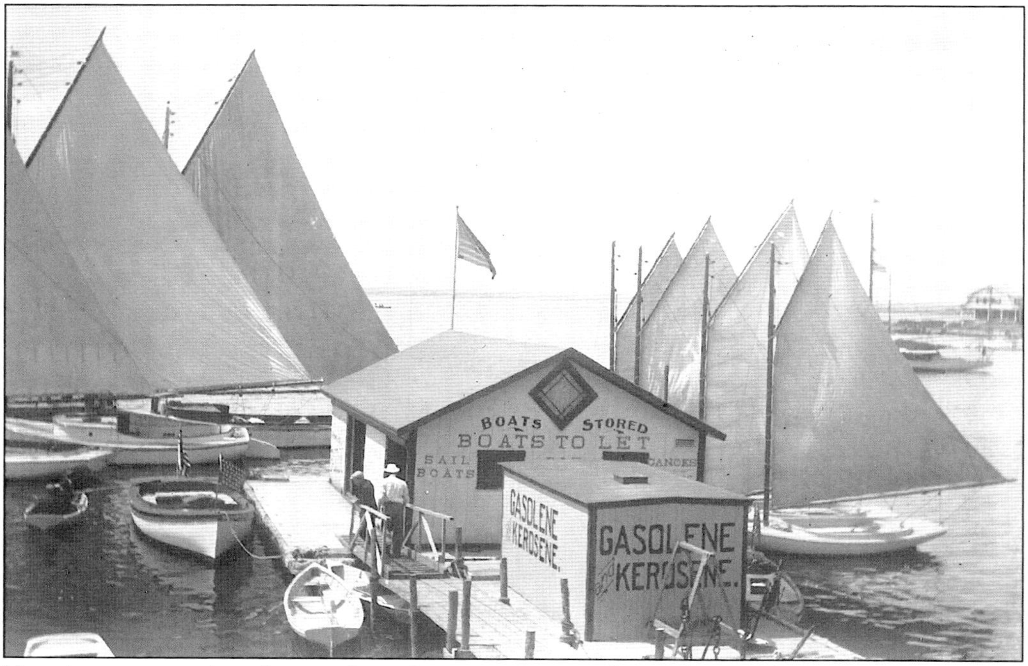

If a picture is worth a thousand words, it sometimes takes a thousand efforts to take care of a picture. George Barbour's "Boats To Let" fleet was rescued from oblivion by the efforts of Dwight Brown Jr., who reclaimed hundreds of curled-up and damaged negatives that had been improperly stored depicting scenes of turn-of-the-century Watch Hill. (DB.)

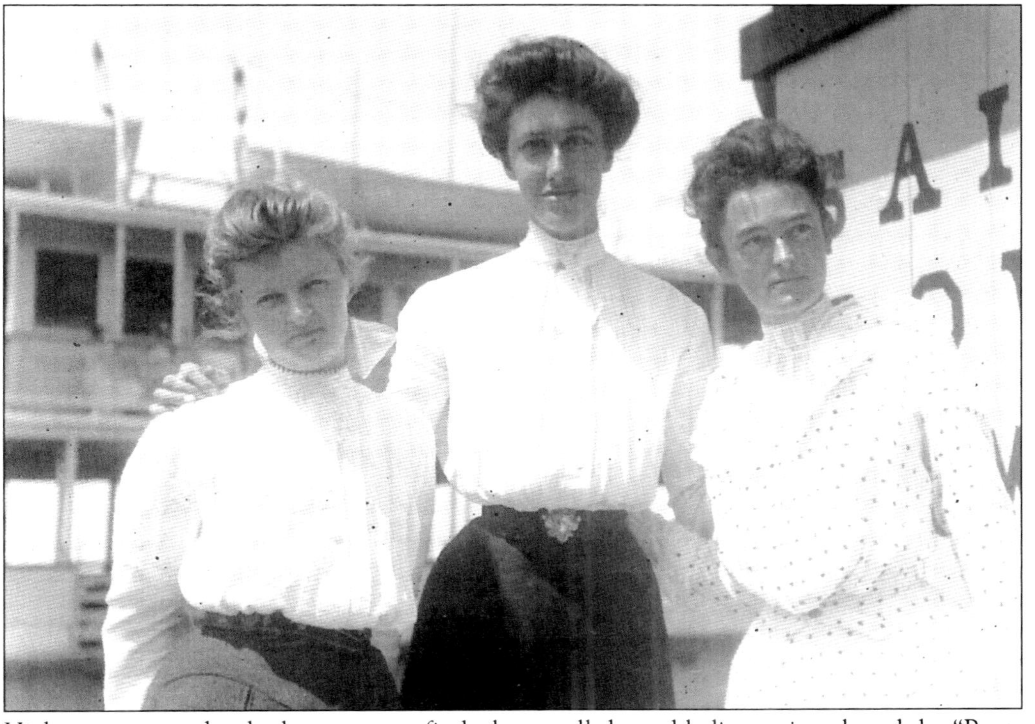

High noon, or so the shadows suggest, finds three well-dressed ladies posing aboard the "Boats To Let" floating dock on a sunny summer's day. Other visitors to the cove were not quite as self-assured in things nautical. Albert Einstein, a summer resident, apparently understood $E=MC^2$ better than red, right, returning. He was notorious for leaving his sailboat high and dry after every outing. (DB.)

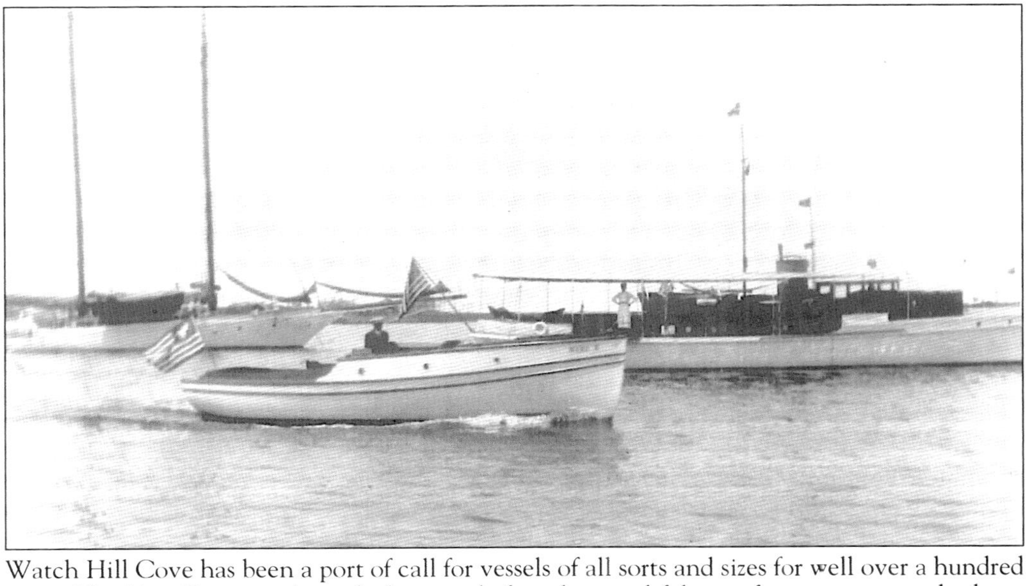

Watch Hill Cove has been a port of call for vessels of all sorts and sizes for well over a hundred years. The *Nina B* steams through the cove before the watchful eye of a passenger on the large canopied yacht in the background. (DB.)

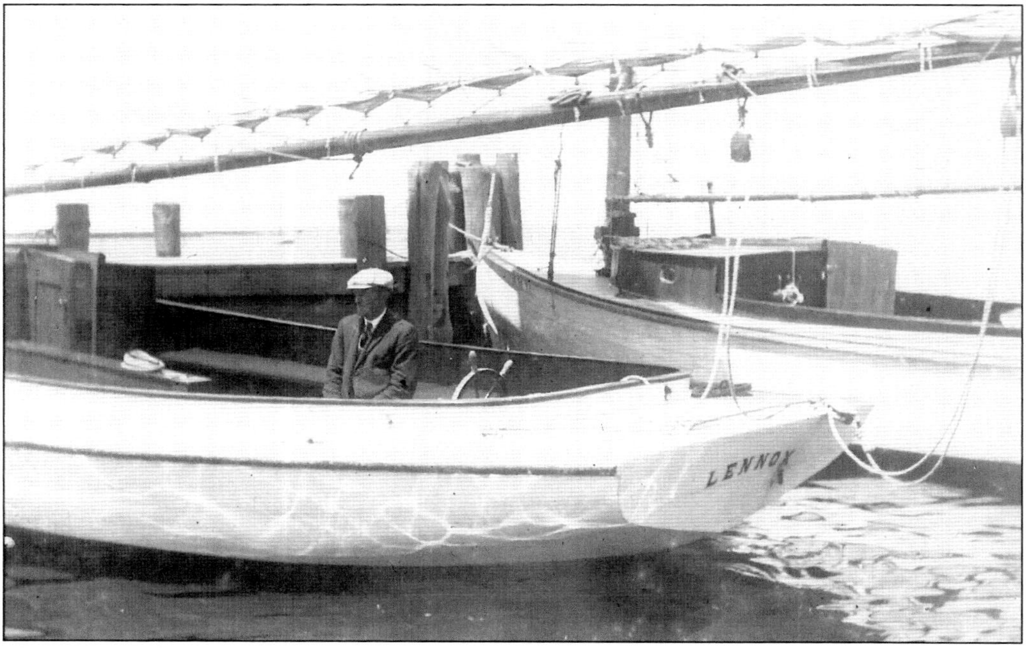

The cat-rigged *Lennox*, which was captained by Roger Dunham, sailed from Watch Hill Dock at the turn of the century. The *Lennox* was one of nearly 30 private party sailboats that were available for hire from both the Plimpton Dock and Watch Hill Dock during the decade prior to 1900. These "partyboats" sailed on both Little Narragansett Bay and Fishers Island Sound for full and half-day excursions. (DB.)

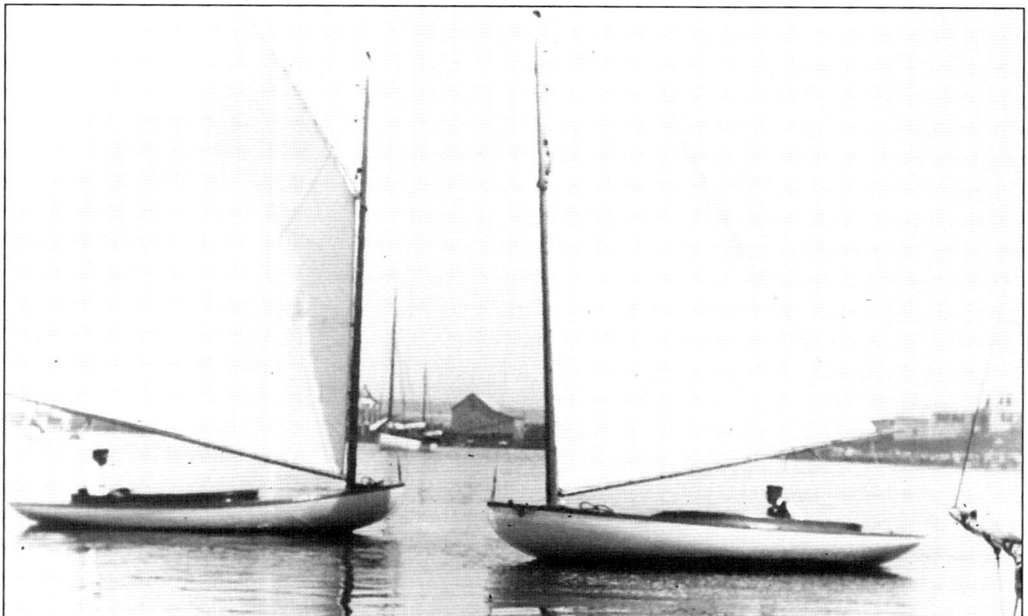

Port tack has right of way—or is it starboard tack? A photograph taken 30 seconds later would tell quite a tale. (DB.)

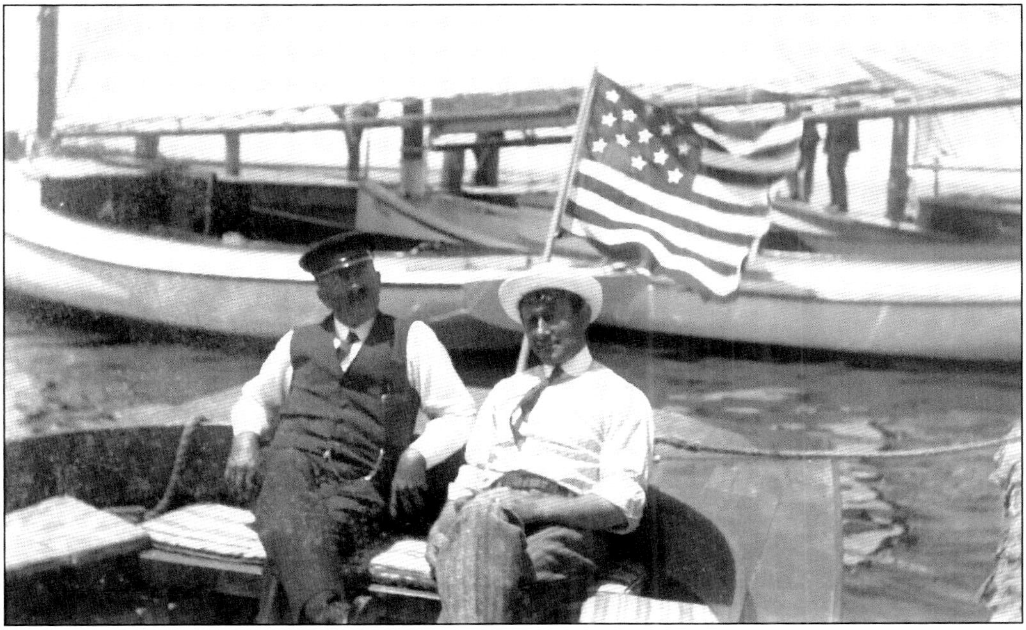

Thirteen stars on a field of blue. (DB.)

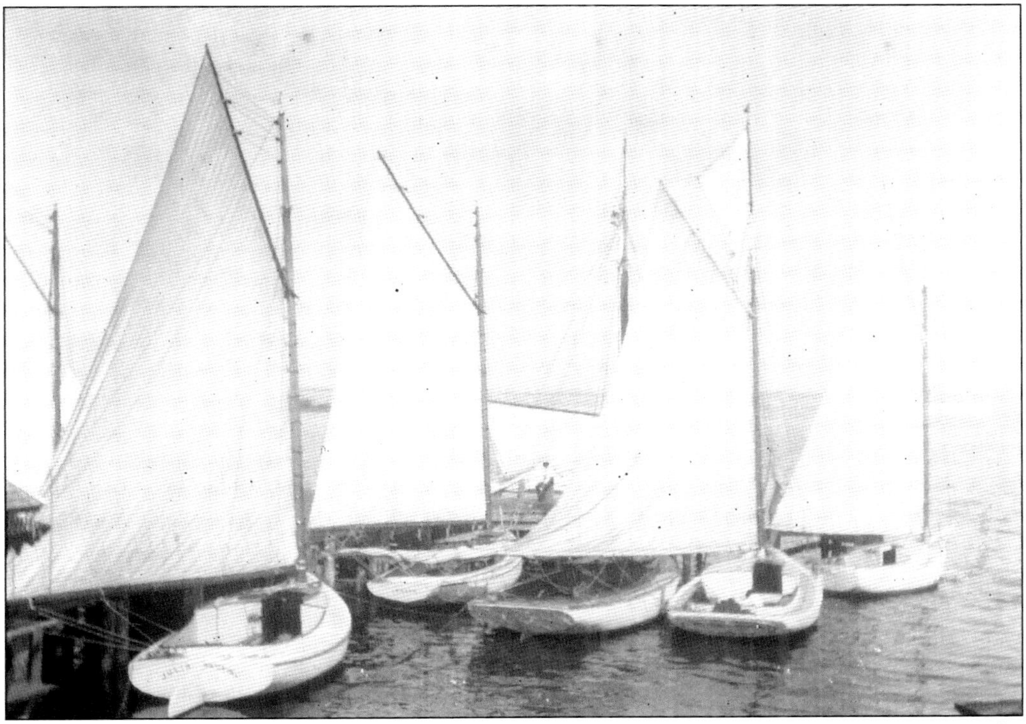

A 1905 advertisement proclaims "Sail Boats For Private Parties . . . boats let with skipper, by the day or hour, at moderate prices. Engage boats ahead by phone to Bannon's Drug Store." Note that the hatchway on three of the catboats enter the right side of the cuddy instead of the center. Also, note that only one of the cats sports the traditional barn-door rudder. (DB.)

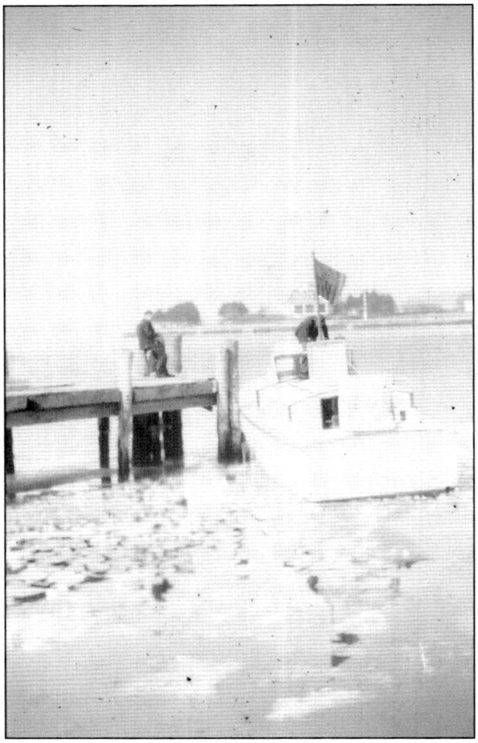

It is the rare contemporary sailor that approaches a dock through ice floes under power or sail; yet, in times gone by, winter ice was a common occurrence. The winter of 1917–18, for instance, laid a solid coat of ice across both the Pawcatuck River and the cove from December until March. (JM.)

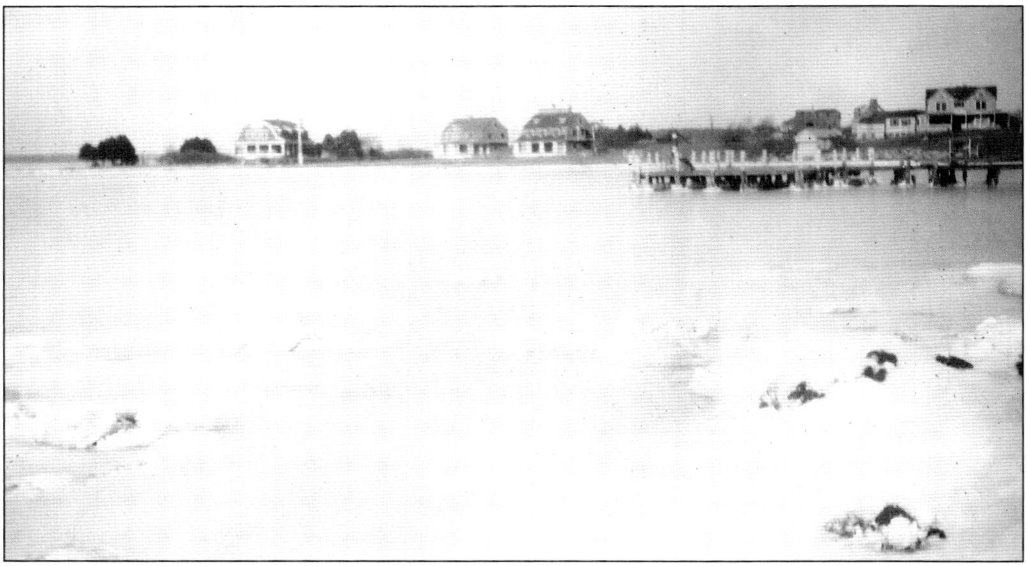

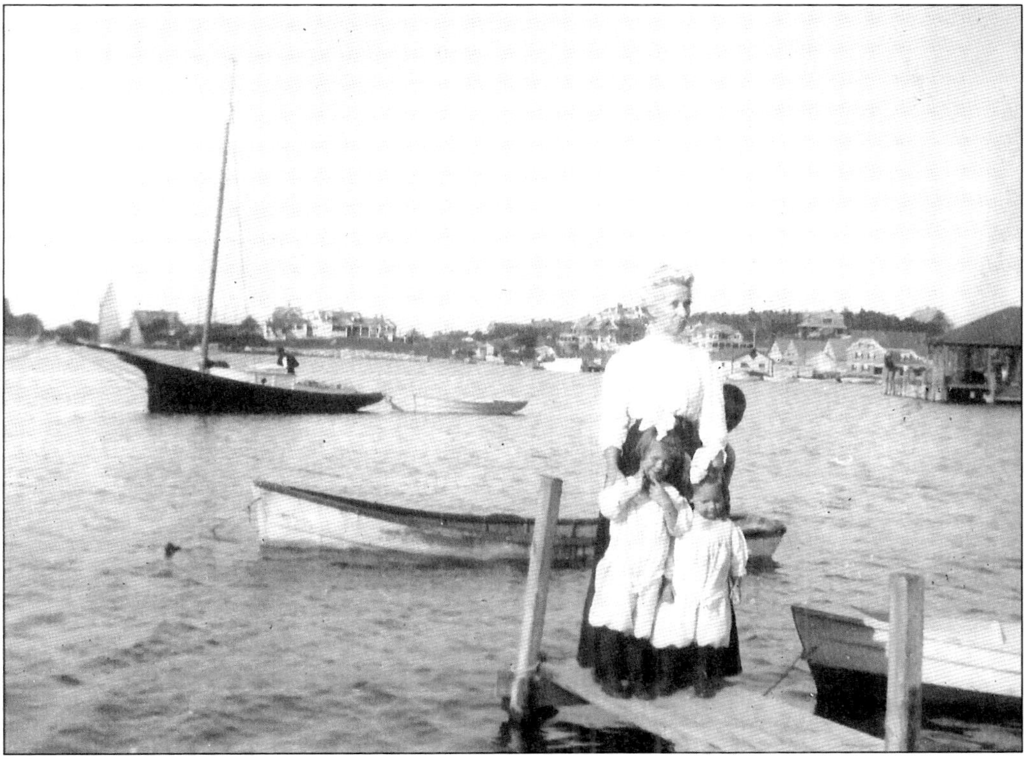

Peek-a-boo! (JM.)

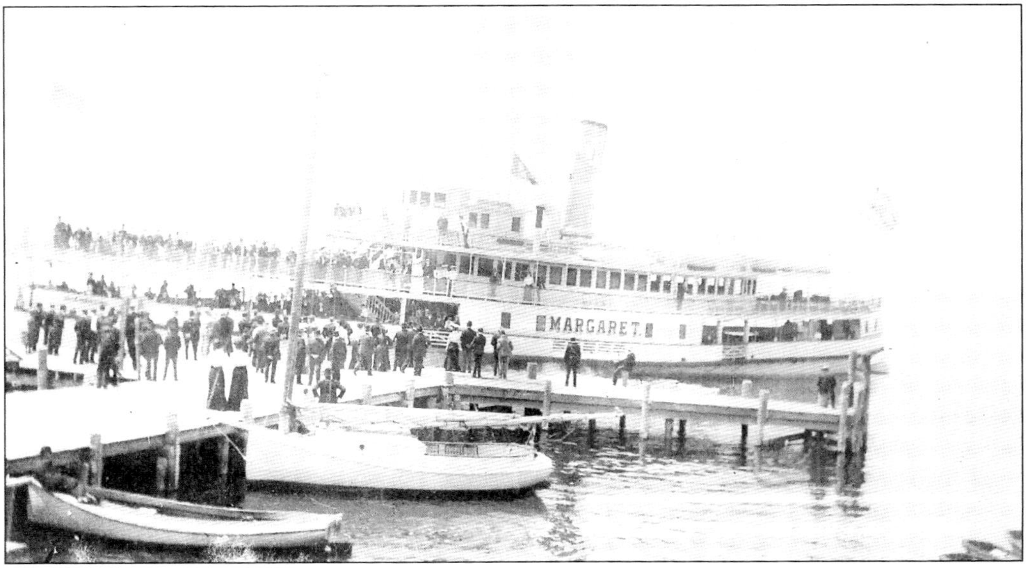

The steamer *Margaret* takes on passengers at Watch Hill Dock in 1904. This was a pivotal year for steamer lines as the "inside route," running from Norwich to New London to Watch Hill Cove, was forever supplanted a year later by the larger and faster steamer *Block Island* and the outside route, running from New London to Block Island with stops at the new steamer dock by Lighthouse Point. (JH.)

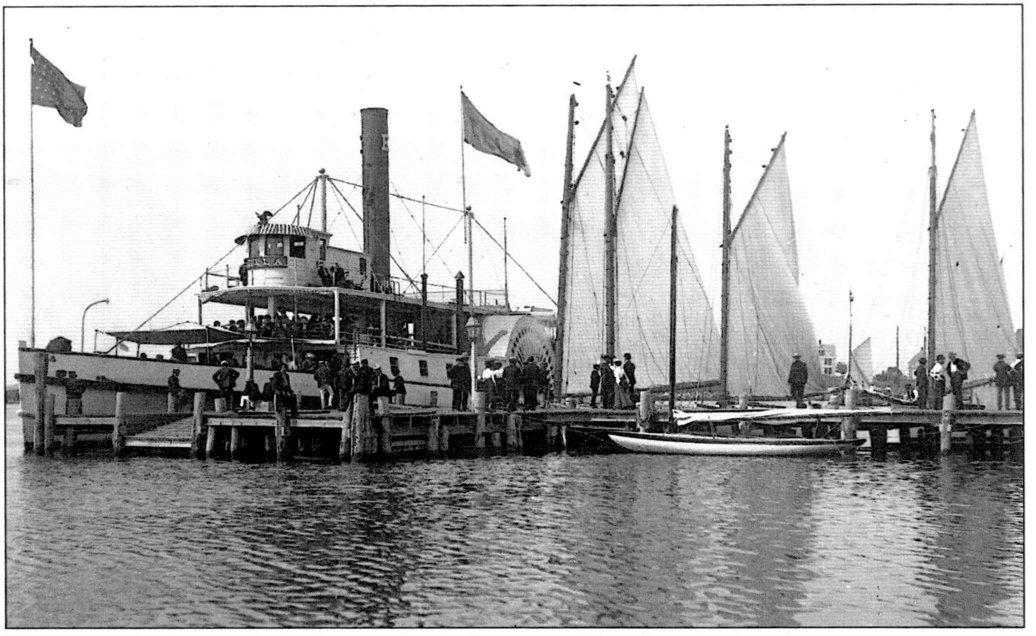

The snap of a Union Jack, the crack of a banner, and a chorus of rippling canvas greets the passengers of the sidewheel steamer *Ella* on Watch Hill Dock in the Cove. Note the letter "E" attached to the smokestack. (GHU-Burdick.)

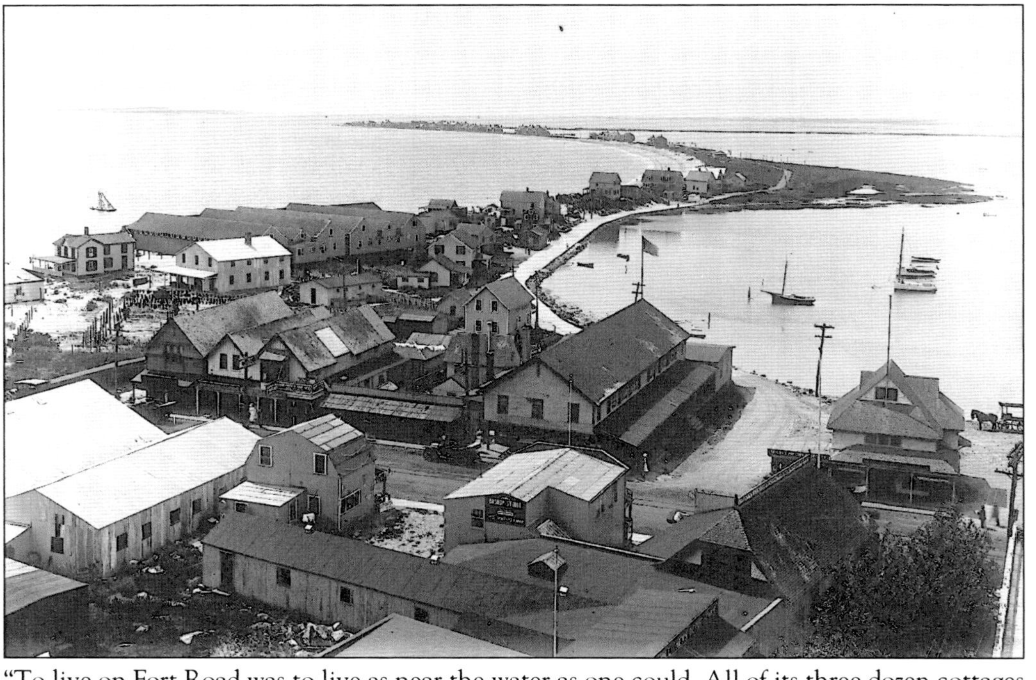

"To live on Fort Road was to live as near the water as one could. All of its three dozen cottages were actually a stone's throw from the ocean and were protected by low seawalls, which could be washed by a heavy sea at high tide . . . and this nearness to the sea was their fatal charm" (*Fort Mansfield*). (WHS.)

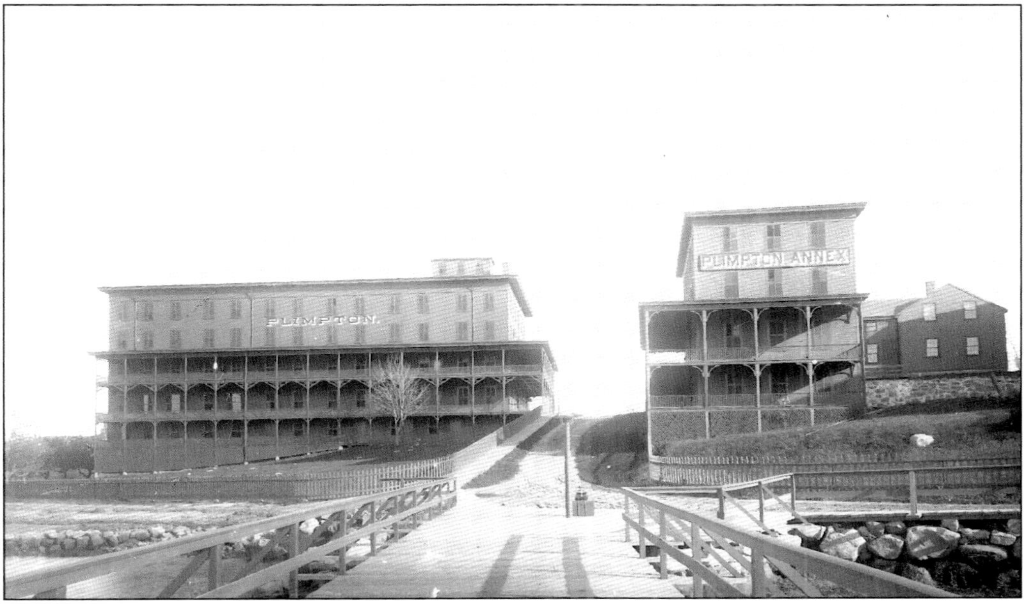

Built in 1865, the Plimpton House and its sister hostel, the Plimpton Annex, loom over their namesake dock on Watch Hill Cove. What intrigued the guests of the day? "In addition to water from a living spring on the Plimpton grounds, supplying ten thousand gallons per day, the hotel is supplied by the White Rock water – both being absolutely pure." (*Seaside Topics*, July 1905). Note the absence of telephone poles and trolley tracks. (DB.)

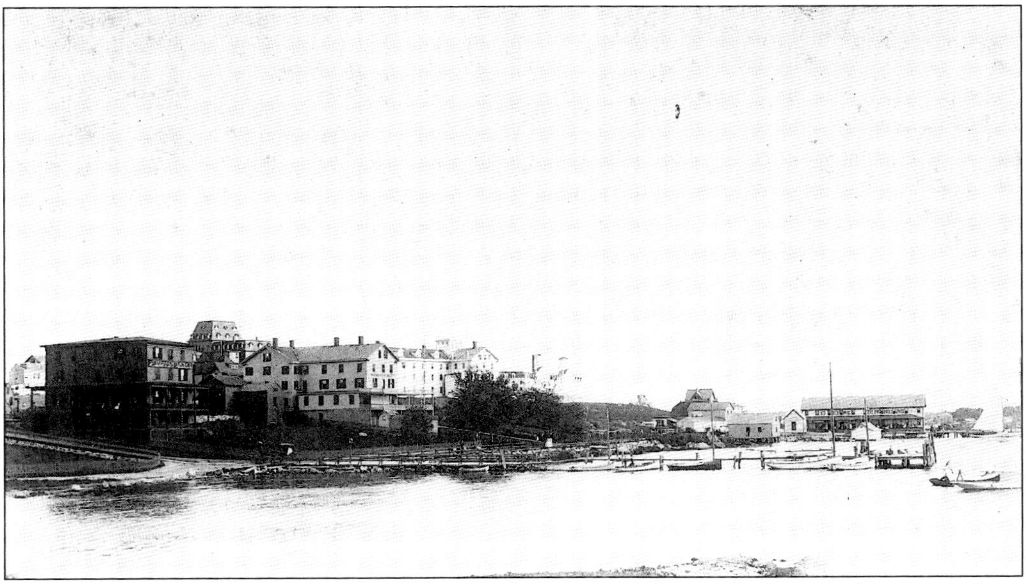

The Plimpton Annex and the rambling Plimpton Dock grace the northeastern shore of the cove. An early 1900s advertisement reads "Hotel Plimpton and Annex . . . June to September . . . All Latest Improvements Including Private Baths . . . Electric Lights and Elevators . . . Accommodations for 300 . . . Cuisine First Class . . . All Popular Amusements." (GHU-Burdick.)

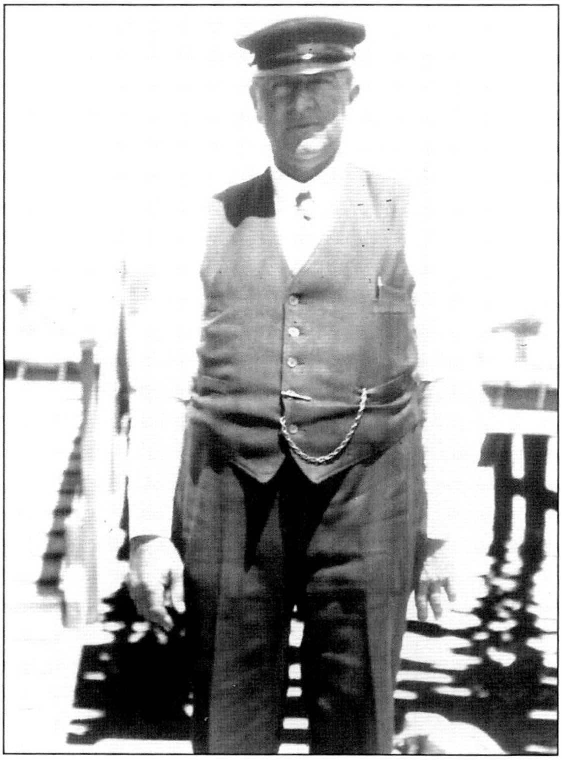

An unknown purser poses in front of a Watch Hill Cove dock. An advertisement from 1887 prominently noted that Watch Hill was readily accessible by both train and steamer from major metropolitan areas. According to the advertisement, "The distance from New York is about one hundred and twenty-five miles. The distance from Boston is about a hundred miles." (DB.)

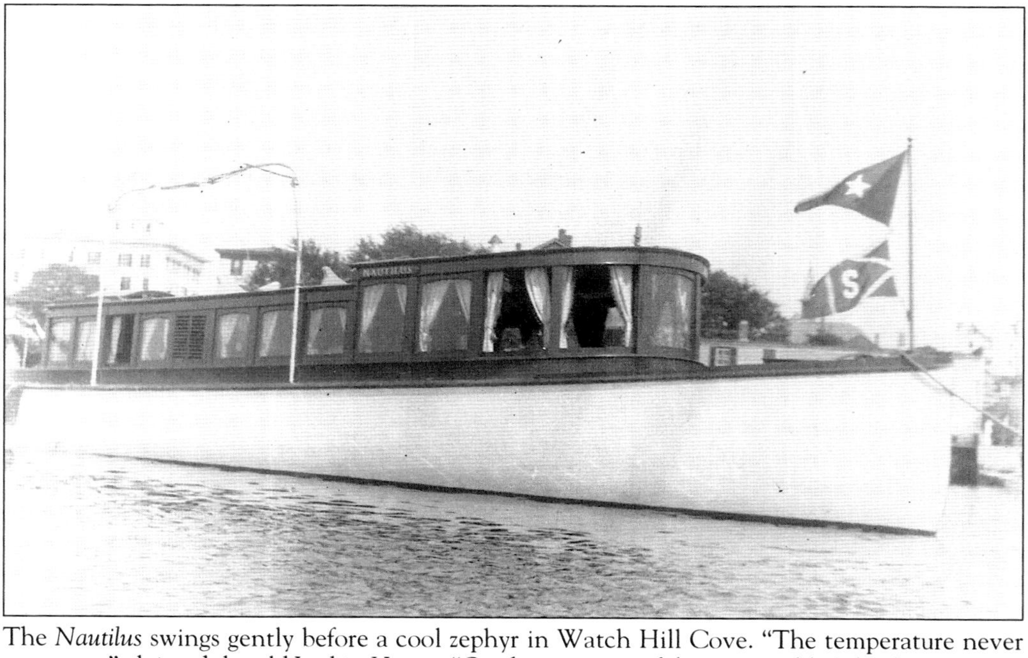

The *Nautilus* swings gently before a cool zephyr in Watch Hill Cove. "The temperature never oppresses," claimed the old Larkin House, "On the morning of the memorable 7th of September, 1881, when the thermometer ranged from 95 to 106 in the New England and Middle States . . . it barely reached 80 at Watch Hill. Mosquitoes unknown." (DB.)

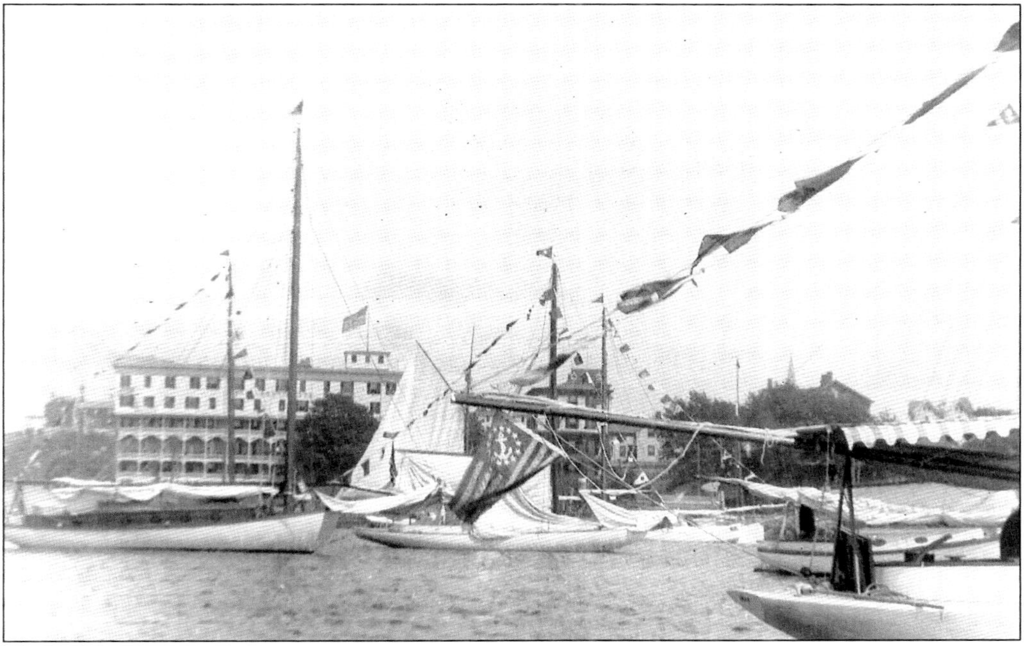

A rainbow of color dances on Watch Hill Cove before the looming presence of the Plimpton House. A light southwest breeze and the "dressed" ships presuppose a Fourth of July celebration on the cove. Note that the catboat in the right foreground is not properly "dressed" as the pennants do not fall from the leach of the boom to caress the surface of the cove itself. (DB.)

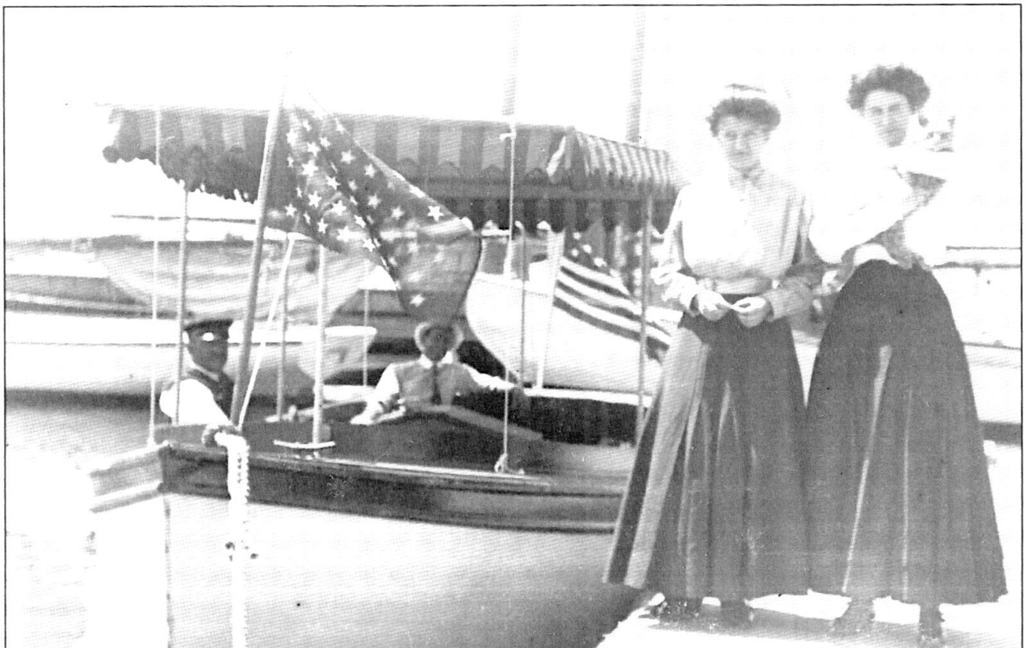

Old Glory is on the stern jackstaff and a Union Jack is on the fore, as two warmly clad ladies pose with a patient-looking feline. (DB.)

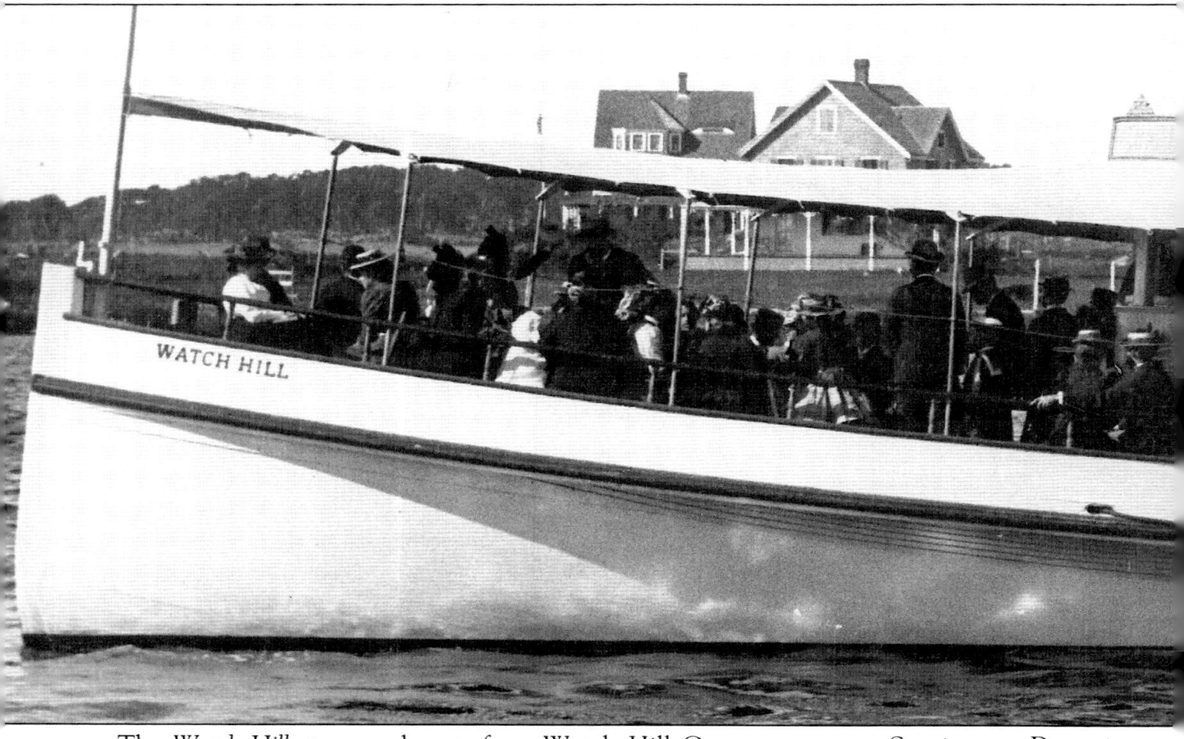

The *Watch Hill* steamer departs from Watch Hill Cove en route to Stonington. Departing hourly, a single round trip fare cost 25¢. Imagine just throwing the cargo and trunks up on the roof in today's day and age! (GHU-Burdick.)

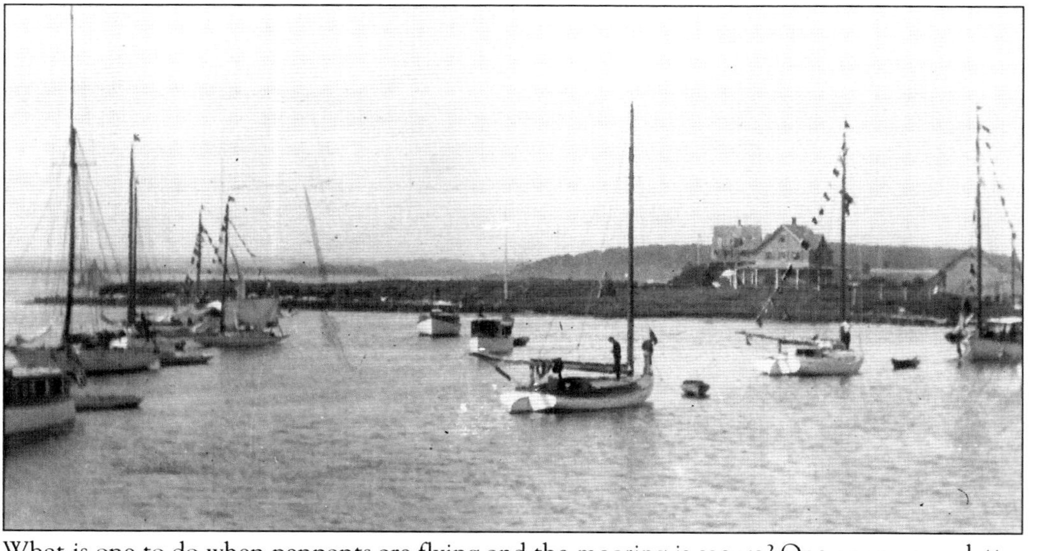

What is one to do when pennants are flying and the mooring is secure? One anonymous letter writer from Watch Hill in the 1880s speculated that "off we go up the Westerly Road and through the fields, out Ninigret Avenue that is to be, over hummock and hollow, till we reach the top of Money Hill where Captain Kidd long ago buried his pots of gold" (*Historical Souvenir of Watch Hill*). (DB.)

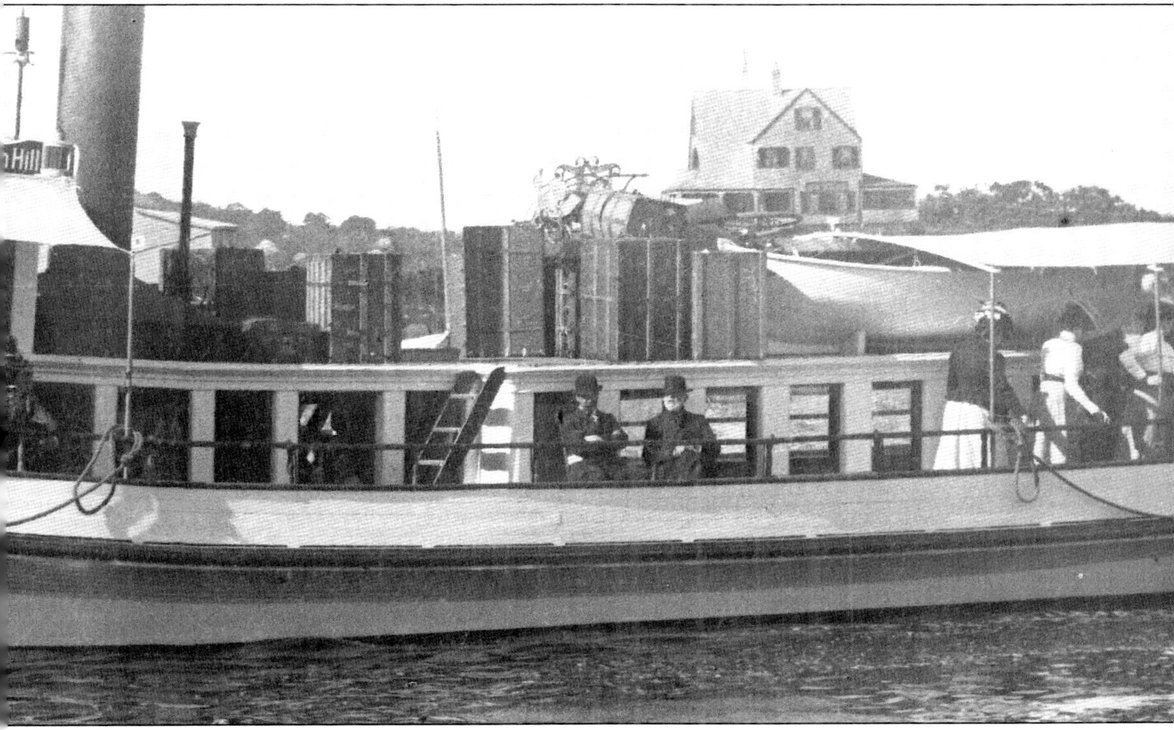

" . . . little Kathy's ears buzzed with the crescendo of hawking that arose as the first mooring lines were made fast. Plimpton House! Watch Hill House! Come to the Ocean House! Larkin House here!" Such are the memories of a little girl who once rode the *Watch Hill* steamer (*The Westerly Sun*, August 1957). (GHU-Burdick.)

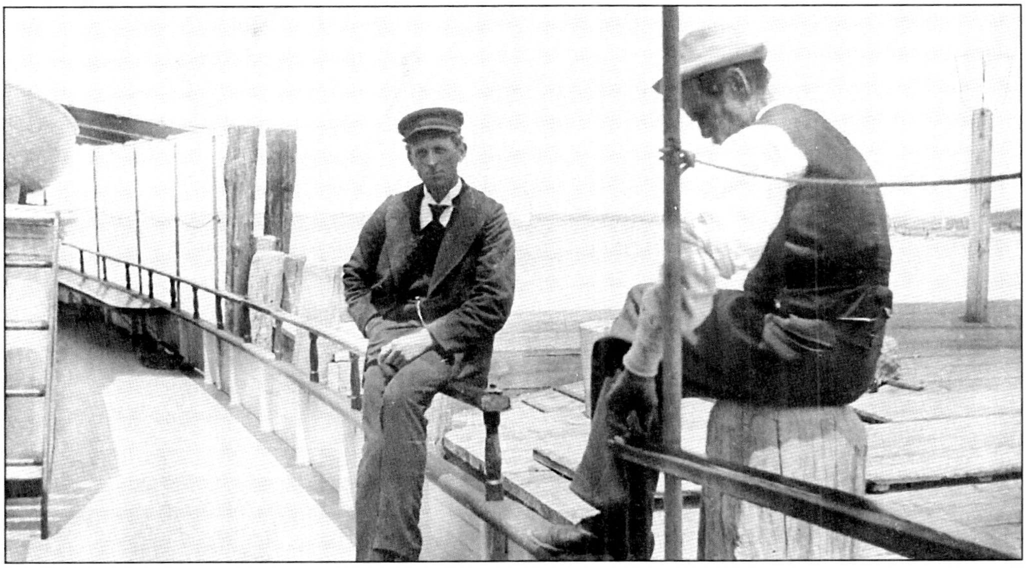

Wanton Weeks Hoxie, to the right, chats with a purser on the *Watch Hill* steamer at the Watch Hill Dock in 1901. Wanton owned a fish market on the cove side of Bay Street at the turn of the century. (JM.)

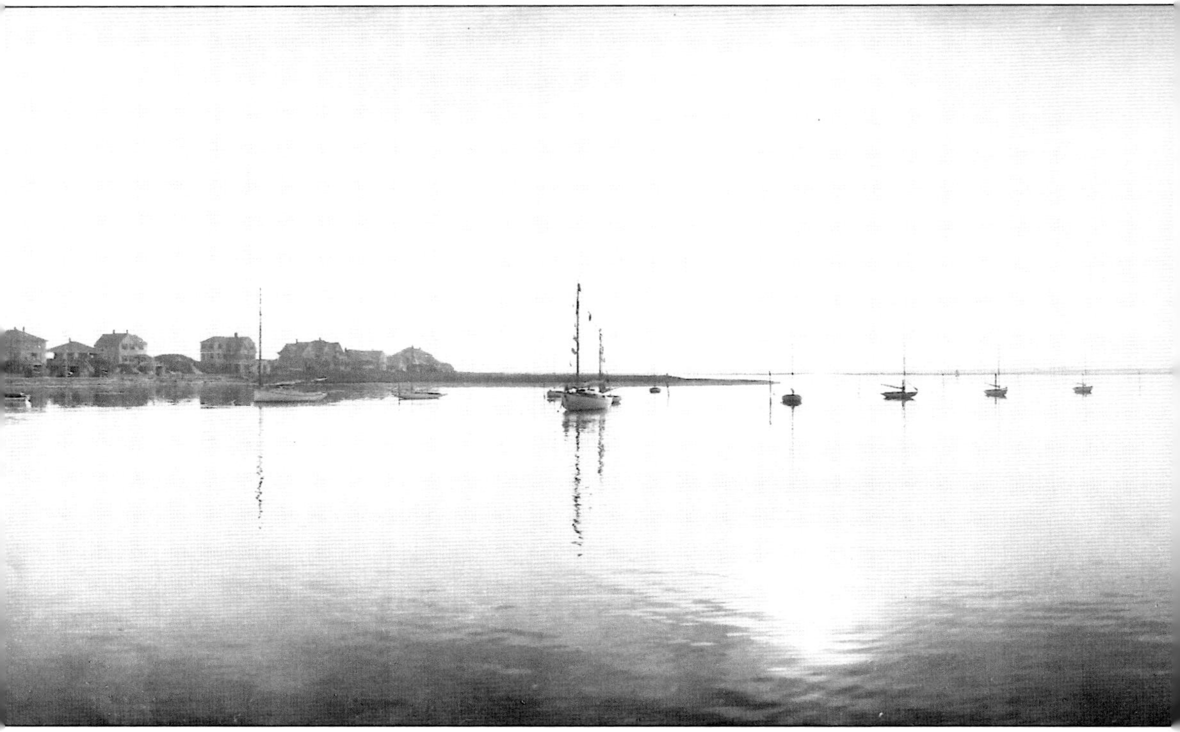

"But Twilight's watching gave this hill, The same name that you call

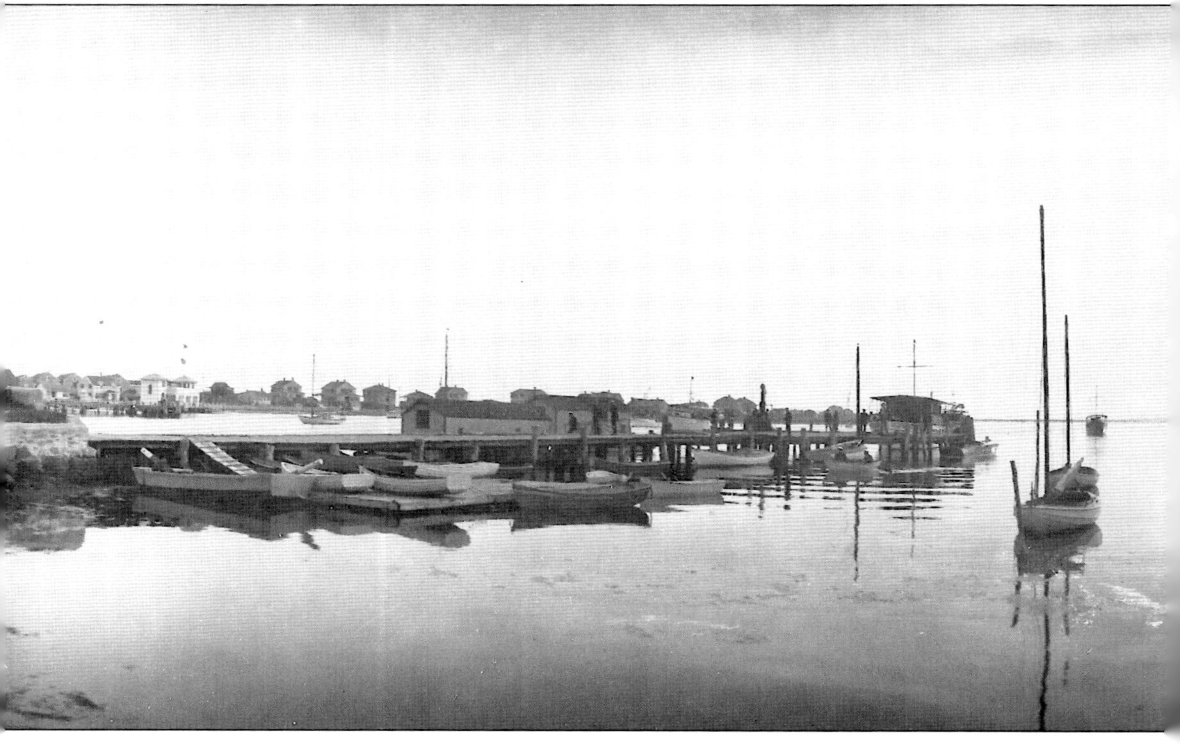

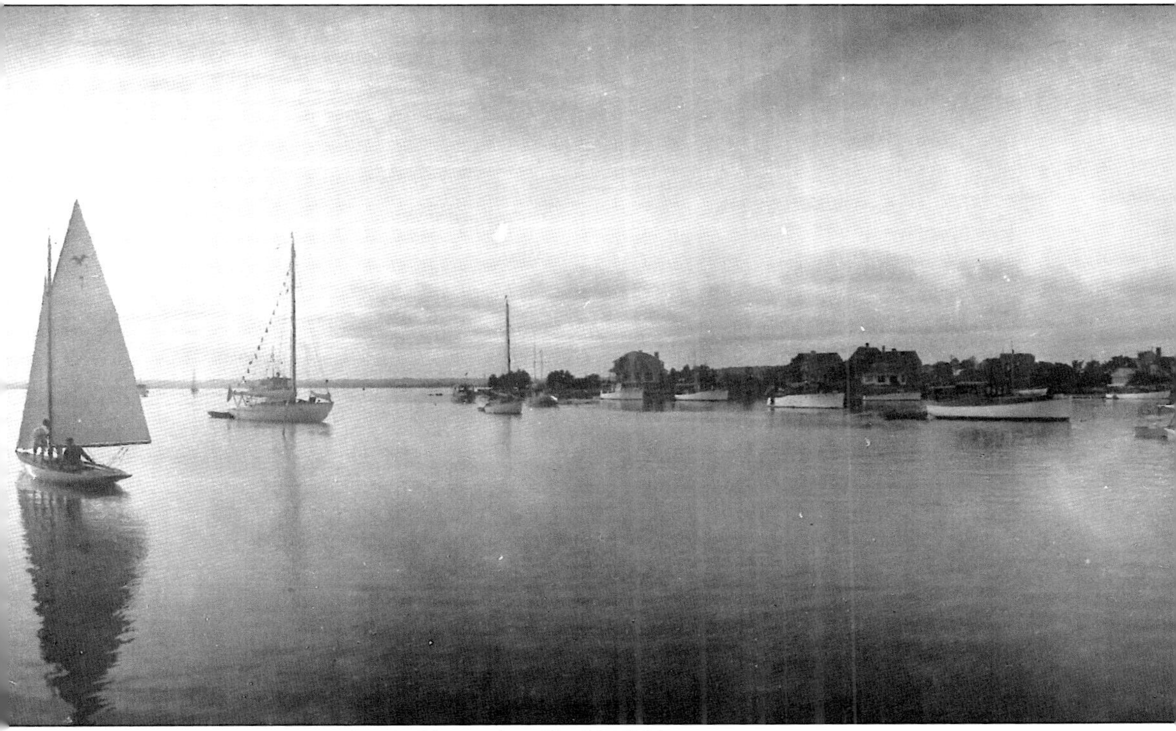

it still, 'Watch Hill' " (A *Tale of Old Watch Hill*). (GHU.)

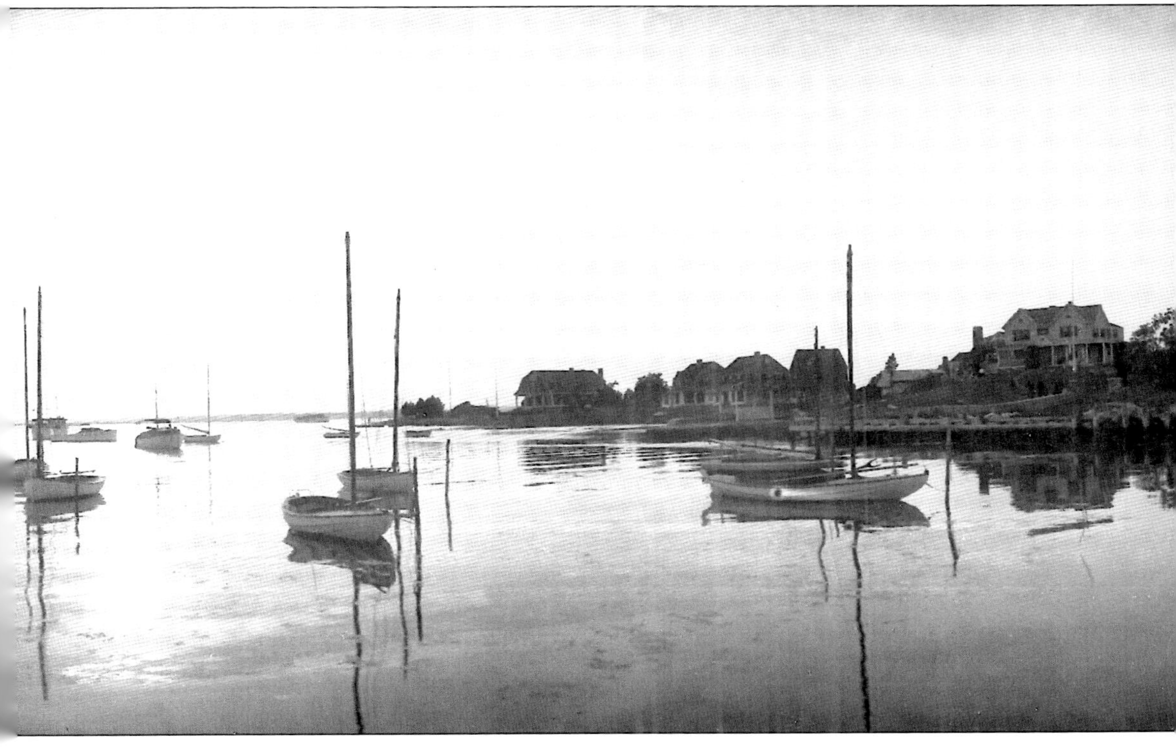

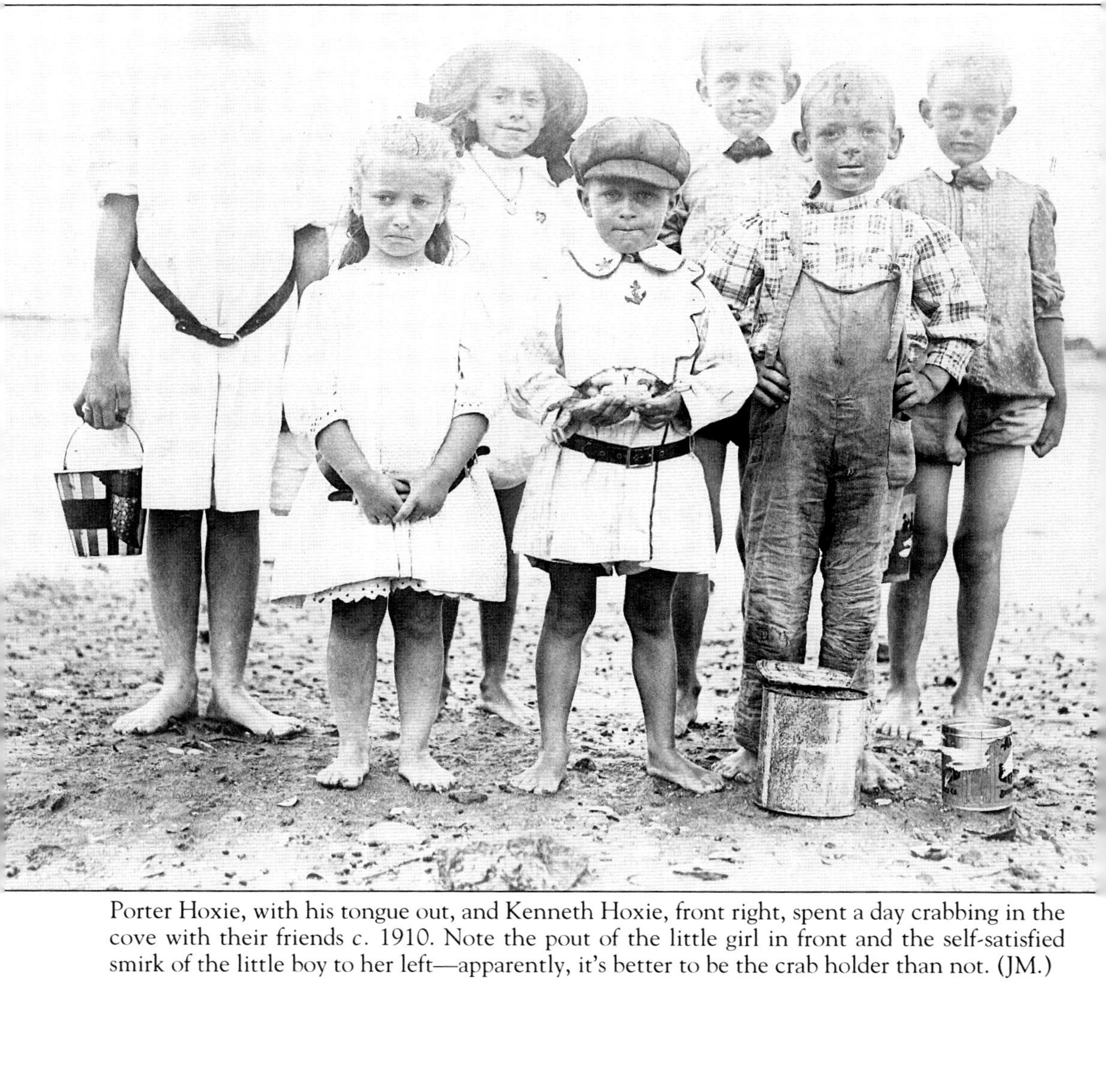

Porter Hoxie, with his tongue out, and Kenneth Hoxie, front right, spent a day crabbing in the cove with their friends *c.* 1910. Note the pout of the little girl in front and the self-satisfied smirk of the little boy to her left—apparently, it's better to be the crab holder than not. (JM.)

Three

A Street by the Bay

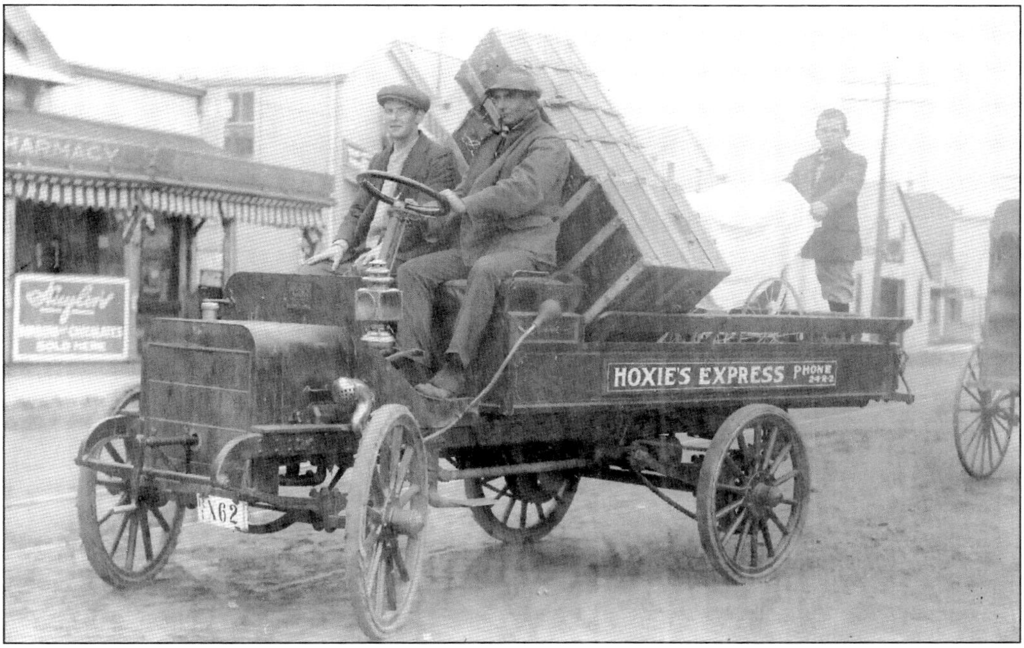

On Bay Street *c.* 1910, George Hoxie poses at the wheel of the Hoxie Express while his son Porter hangs onto the precious cargo of trunks of finery that are being transported for newly arrived summer residents. The New London Steamboat Company hired Hoxie to be on hand when the *Block Island* steamer arrived off Lighthouse Point. He would take in the mooring lines, tie up the vessel, and secure and care for baggage. It was said that Hoxie would "run like a deer from Bay Street" the minute he heard the *Block Island* steamer's whistle blowing across the Sound. His was no easy task as the steamer would average nearly 600 passengers a trip with an occasional trip accounting for as many as 1,100 or 1,200 passengers. George Hoxie, "known as a Watch Hill institution himself," held many positions during his lifetime tenure as a Watch Hill resident. He was a "dockmaster, fire chief, taxi king, chapel sexton, express man, and Cottage Opener Extraordinary" (*Seaside Topics*, July 1951). (JM.)

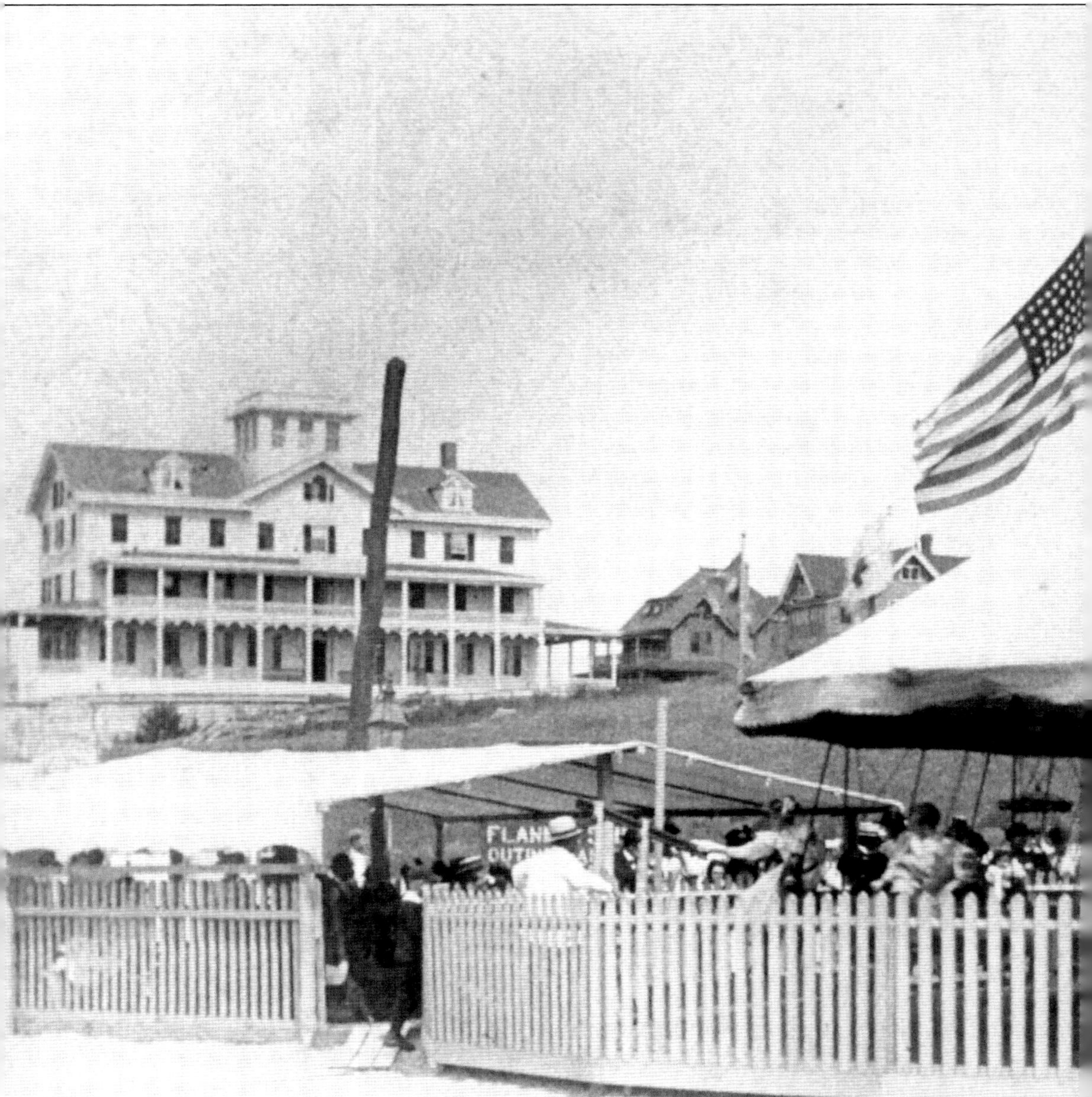

Neither the tempest nor the blowing sands nor a century of commercial development can daunt or eliminate a legend. Built during the late 1860s, the Watch Hill flying-horse merry-go-round has become a landmark unto itself on the sands of Napatree. "For more than one hundred years, summer in Watch Hill has begun and ended with the opening and closing of the little flying-horse merry-go-round. Each year the marble-eyed, leather-saddled wooden horses, with outstretched forelegs and real manes and tails, have captivated riders" (*Tidings*, August 1995).

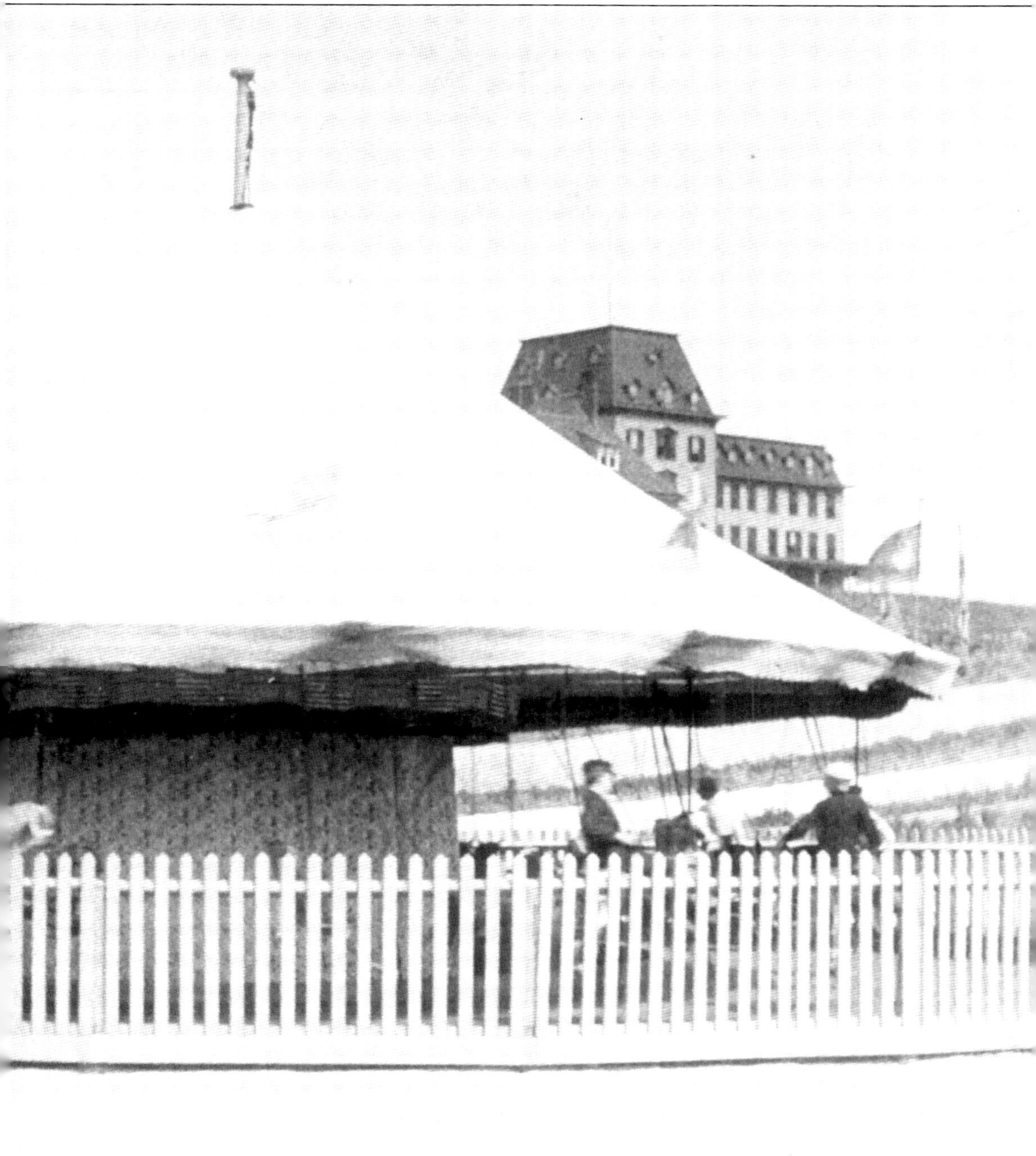

From whence did this venerable landmark come? Legend has it that the Watch Hill flying-horse merry-go-round was left behind by either a band of gypsies or a long forgotten traveling carnival that did not have the capacity to either repair or maintain the artful flying horses. More than 80,000 young riders a year take reins in hand as they gallop to the strains of carnival music in their quest to snare the elusive brass ring. (GHU.)

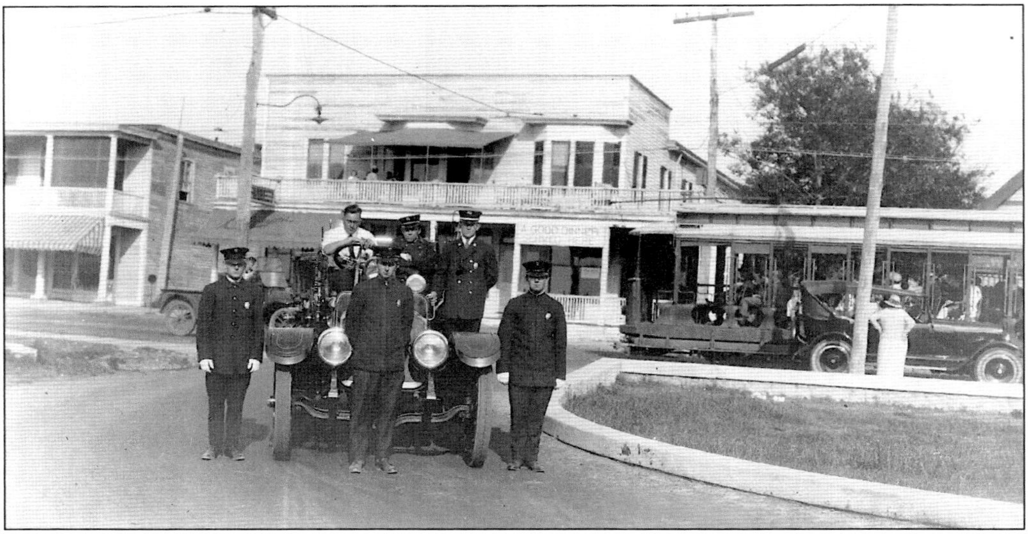

The Watch Hill Fire Department poses in front of what is today the Olympia Tea Room on Bay Street *c.* 1928. Kenneth Hoxie is standing to the left of the fire truck, Reggie Peck is sitting in the center, and Porter Hoxie is standing to his right. Note the Westerly trolley in the background en route to the north end of Bay Street. (JM.)

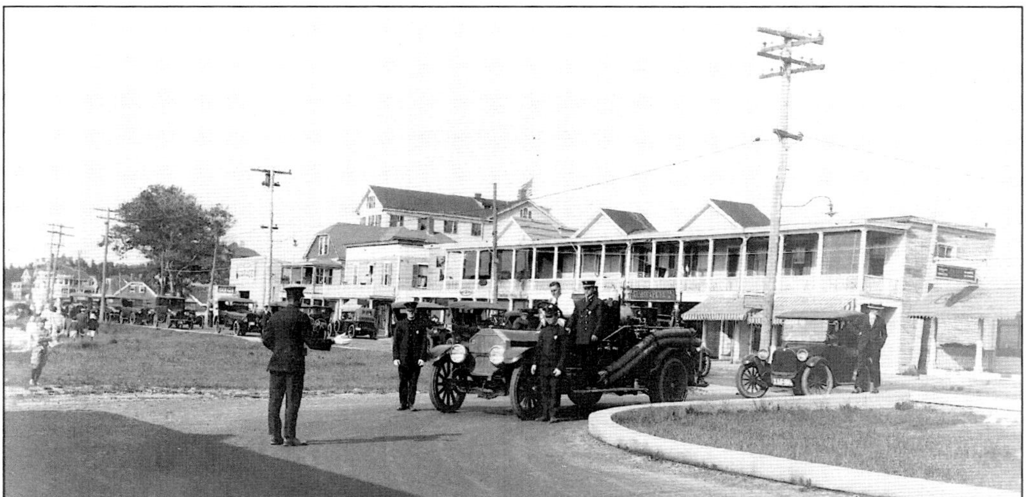

Writing about the great conflagration of 1916, Reggie Peck noted that "the fire, which started on an upper floor of the Watch Hill House, was fanned by a strong east wind, and from lack of proper equipment, the volunteer firemen were unable to stem the tide." This fire "awoke the voters" and a LaFrance pumper was purchased that "more than paid for itself" (*Early Land Holders*). (JM.)

Winslow York, the Watch Hill postmaster, poses in front of the Watch Hill Dock. The early post office of Watch Hill shared a small building with the steamer ticket office at the head of the dock. Once it outgrew this shared arrangement, the postal business was moved to the west side of Bay Street. (DB.)

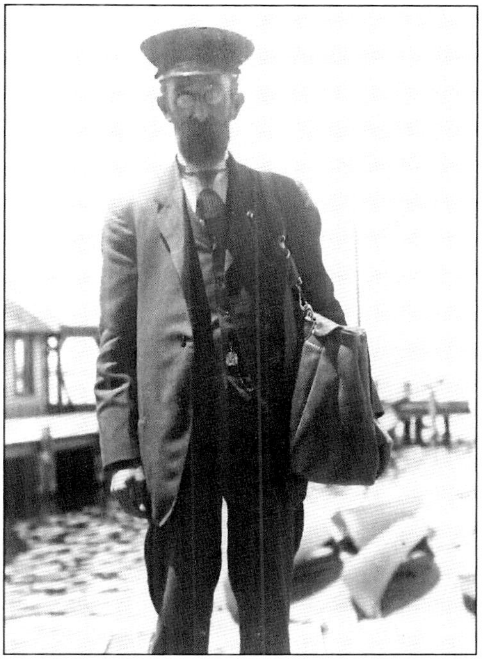

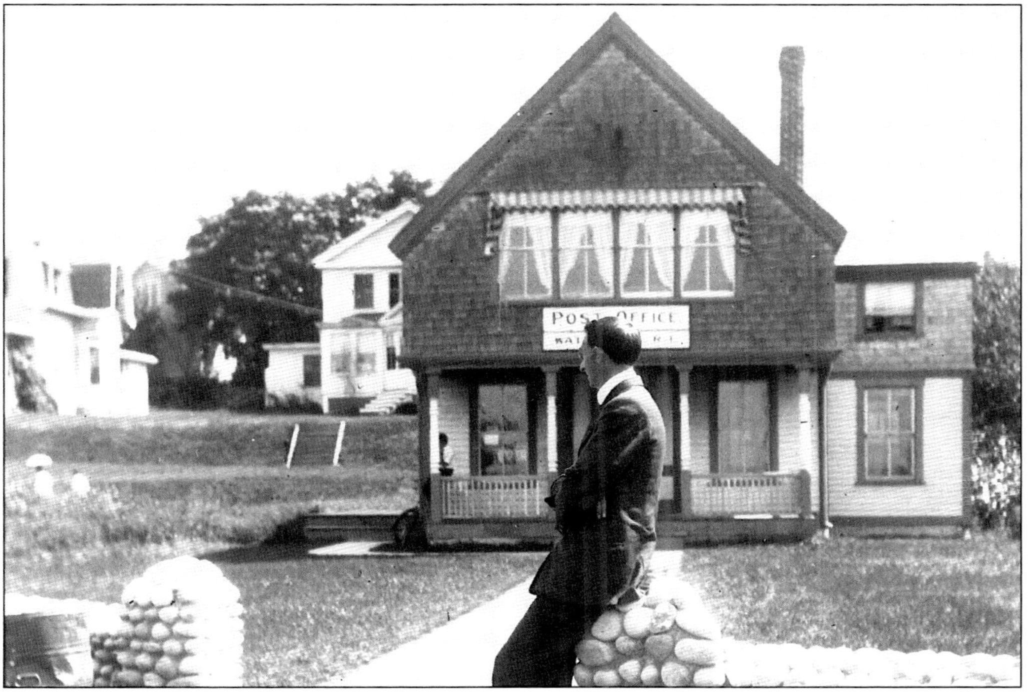

A Westerly Historical Society paper noted that the park commission bought "the land and buildings on the west side of Bay Street from Frank Larkin's line to the property of William H. Peck" between 1909 and 1910. As part of this process of cleaning up the cove waterfront, the post office was moved, once again, to this site near the present Watch Hill Inn. It is now a private residence. (DB.)

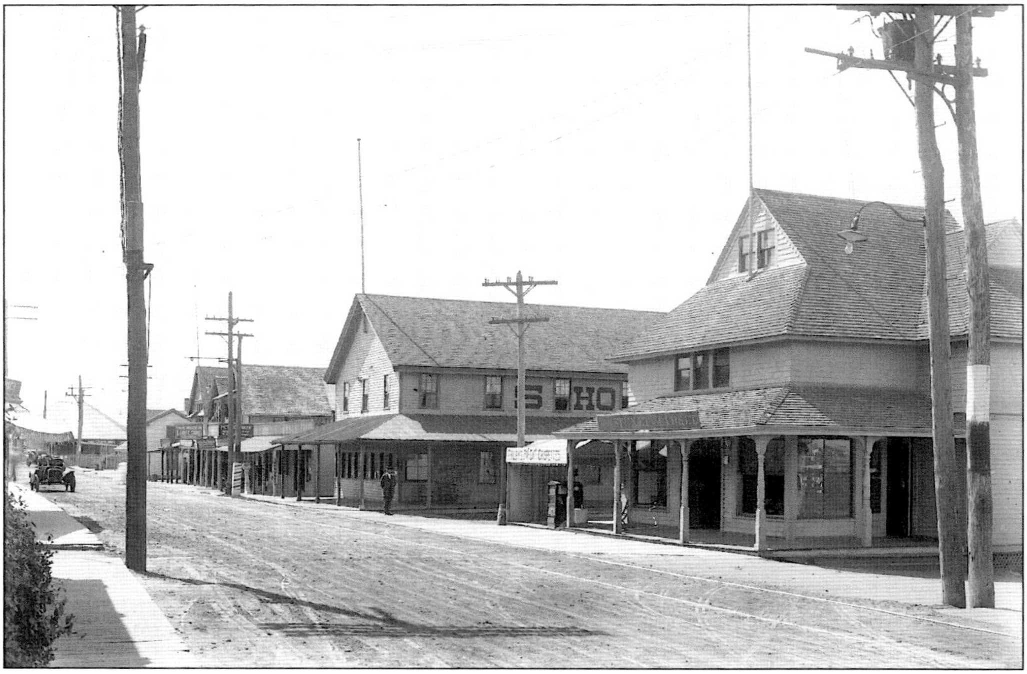

Looking south on Bay Street during September 1909, one can just make out the distinctive roof of the carousel. The strip of shops south of the Mastuxet Market include the present-day St. Clair Annex, famous for its homemade ice cream and frozen yogurt. (WHS.)

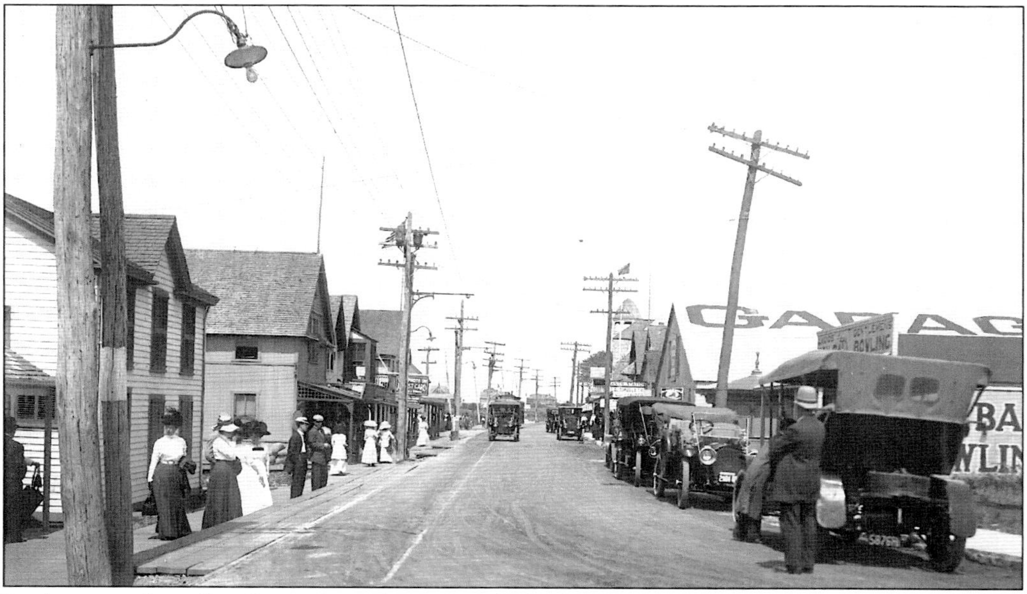

Looking north on Bay Street from the carousel, this bustling intersection with Larkin Road was a popular amusement center during the 1920s. Note the "WLIN" of the Larkin bowling alley sign to the right of the automobile. One resident recalls that he "bowled there so often that he knew the alley well and it was easy to make 10 strikes in rapid succession" (*Seaside Topics*, September 1942). (WHS.)

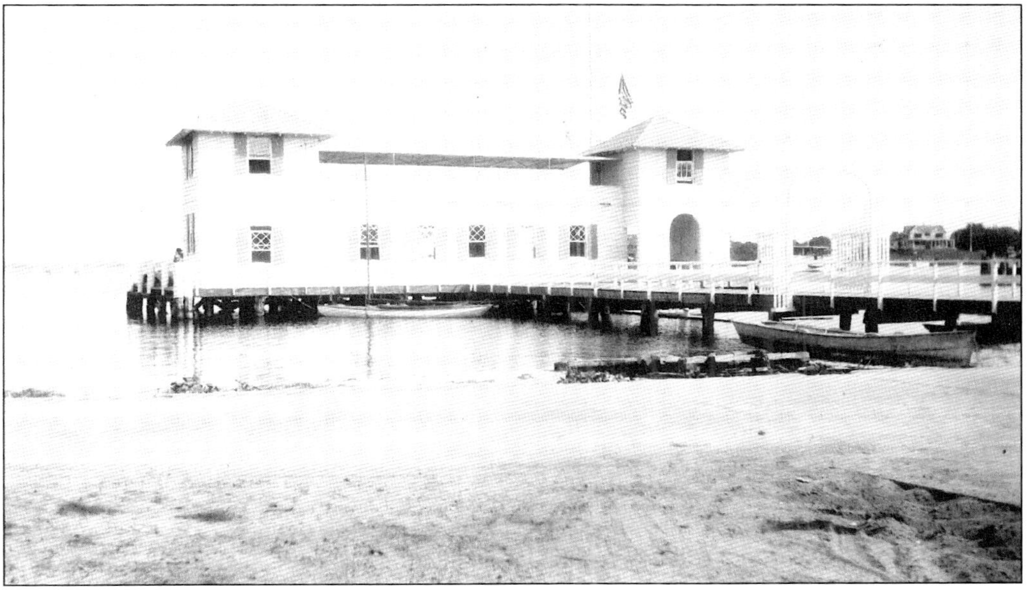

The "old" Watch Hill Yacht Club clubhouse was a familiar sight on the cove. "On September 21, 1938," noted the 75th anniversary book published by the Yacht Club, "Watch Hill was hit by the Great Hurricane. One of the many casualties was the Club House, which was washed off the dock into the Bay. The docks and flagpole remained." (GHU.)

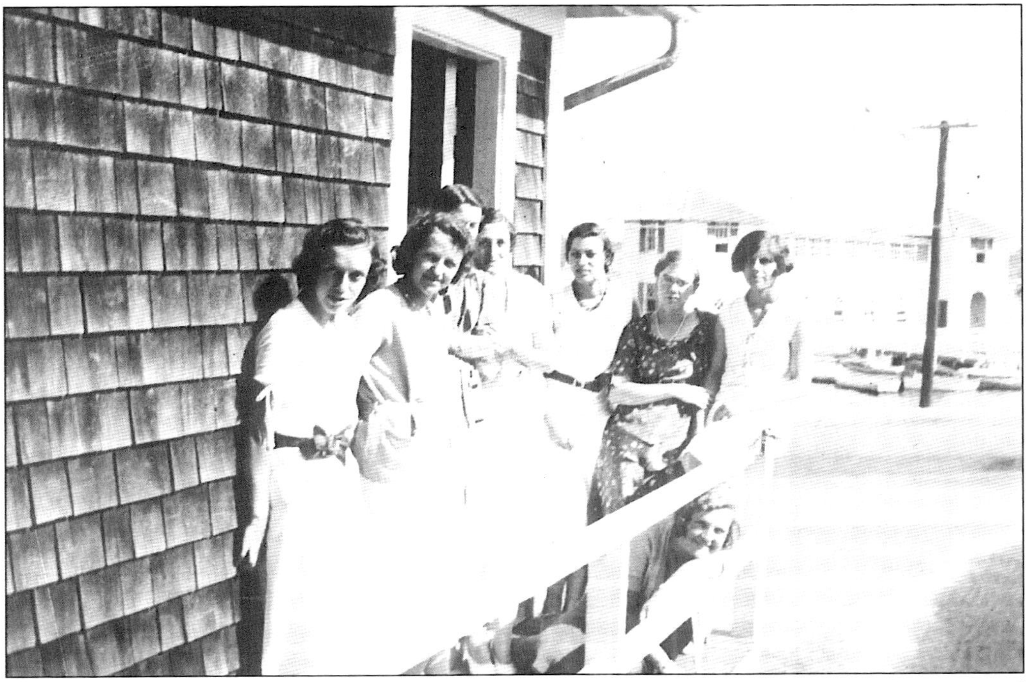

"I was born in Watch Hill, with the bay on one side of me and the ocean on the other." So said Doris Nash, far right, a native "Watch Hiller." Living year-round on Fort Road on Napatree, Doris' granddaughter recalls family tales about the need to wrap seaweed around the foundation of their Fort Road house to keep out the winter chill. (SC.)

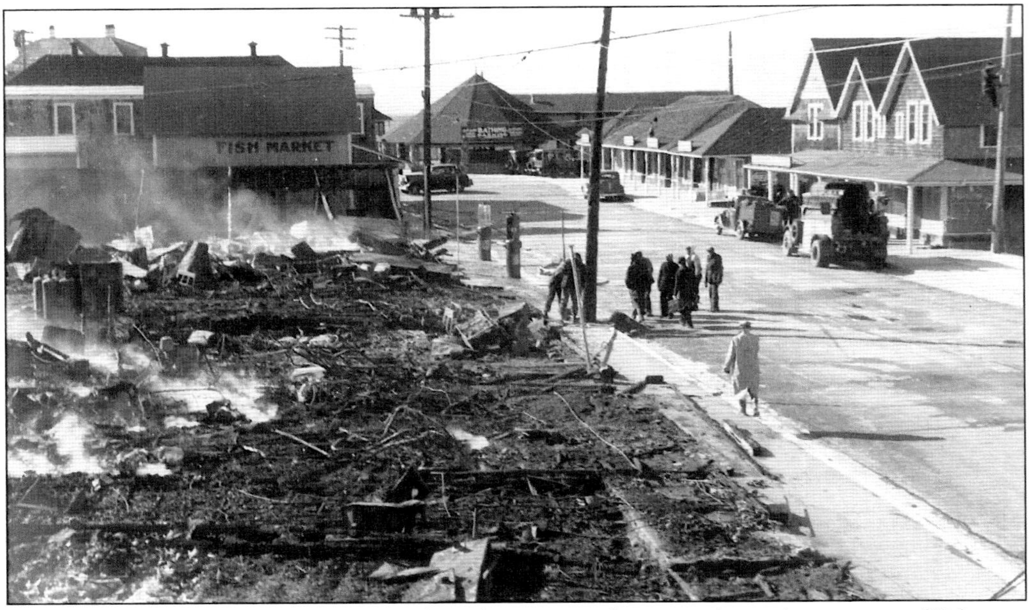

As a child, Jane Hoxie Maxson remembers the ringing phone on the early morning of February 15, 1938, that alerted her father, Porter, a fireman, about the great fire at Sisson Block. The fire destroyed five stores, a garage, and two small cottages in the heart of the business section on Bay Street, with estimated damage of approximately $25,000. (JM.)

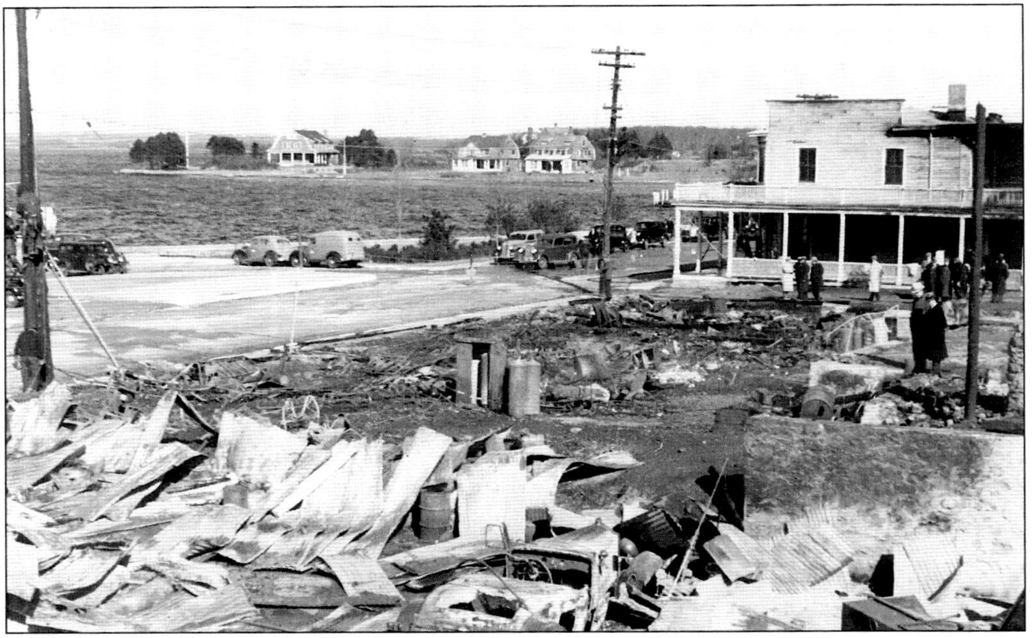

A Packard Sedan, the sole car in the Bayside Garage during the Sisson Block fire, is immolated. A newspaper clipping reported that "while the fire was at its height, the corrugated iron walls of the Bayside Garage collapsed with a roar and . . . fresh sparks went up into the air and were carried a considerable distance" (*New London Day*, February, 1938). Patrol crews were sent to chase these sparks down. (JM.)

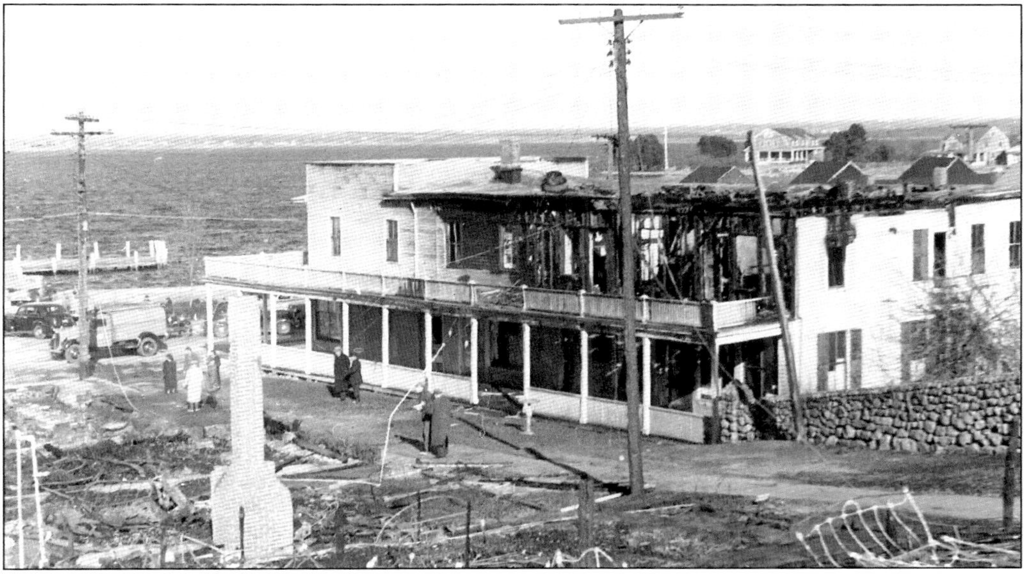

The Columbia Hotel building, the site of the Olympia Tea Room today, was occupied on the ground floor by the Olympia Candy Kitchen, Farquhar Smith's florist shop, and Ruisi's barber shop, all summer establishments. These first floor shops were thoroughly gutted and one side and the rear end of the upper story of the building were completely destroyed by the Sisson Block fire. (JM.)

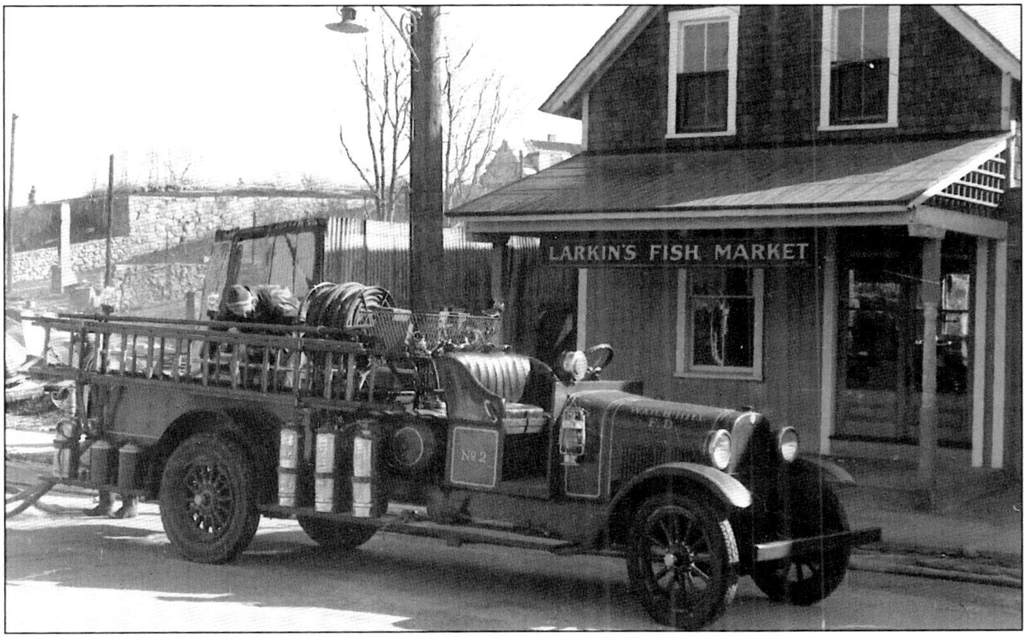

Fire Chief George Hoxie believed that the Sisson Block conflagration was caused by defective wiring in the Var Brothers Drug Store. Fire fighters from Watch Hill, Westerly, and nearby Misquamicut battled to control flames, which were fanned by ocean winds, from 3 a.m. until 7:30 a.m. Note that the Larkin Fish Market, in the background, narrowly escaped disaster. (JM.)

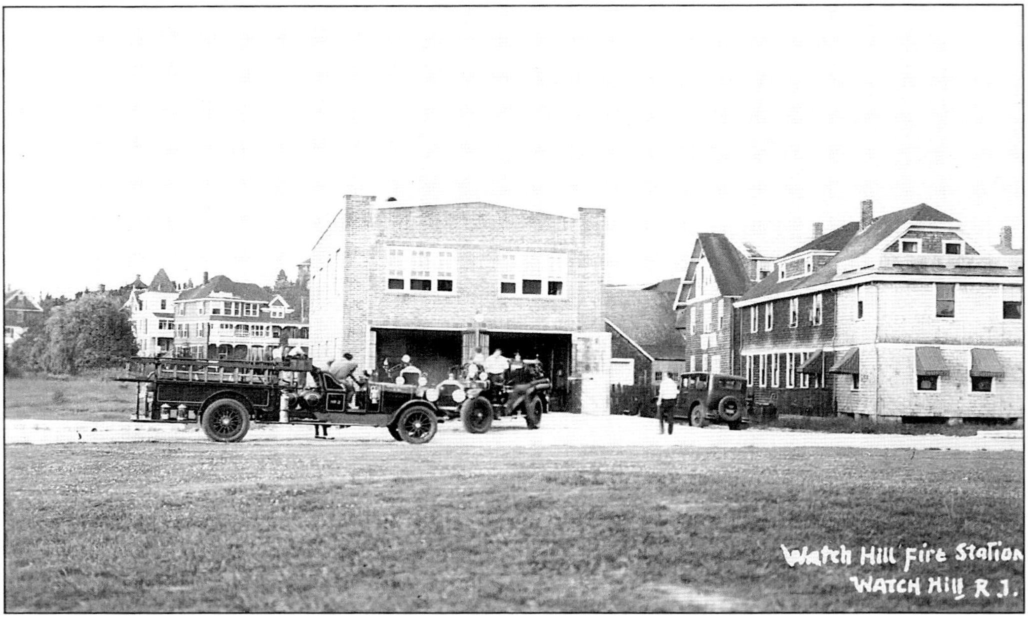

Three fire engines are visible in this photo of the two-bay fire station that was located just off the shore of the northeast corner of the Watch Hill Cove. This site of the second Watch Hill fire station is now the site of the Old Firehouse Antique Store. (JM.)

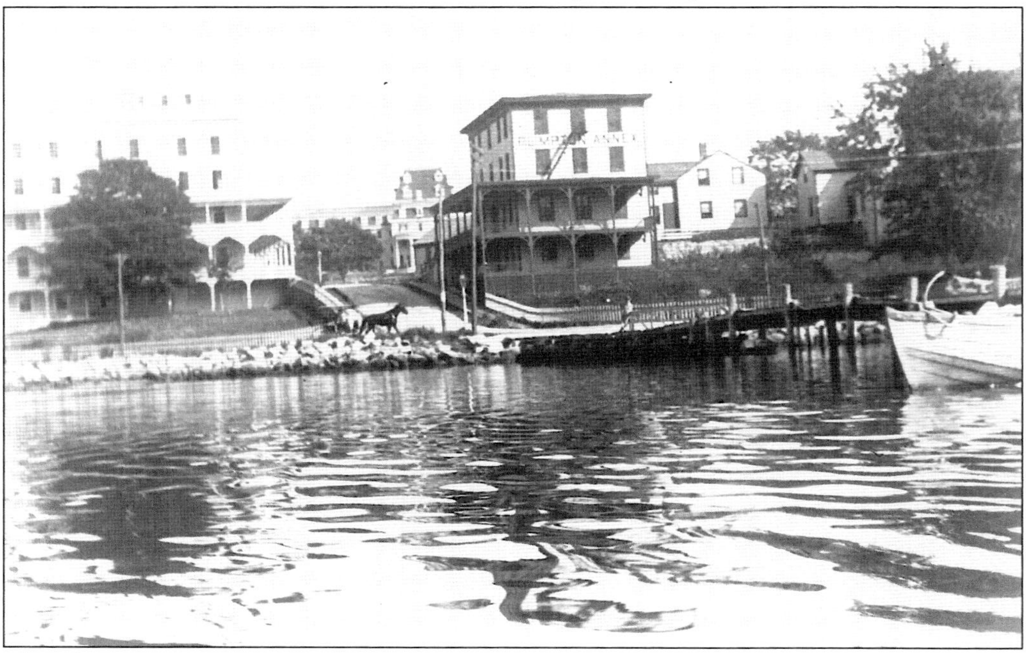

The Plimpton House, to the left, and its annex, to the right, face the cove at the corner of Plimpton Road and Bay Street. "Hotel Plimpton and Annex," proclaims an advertisement from the early 1900s, "located on high ground overlooking the Little Narragansett Bay and the Atlantic Ocean, contains 125 rooms." It is interesting to note that many newspaper articles of the day referred to the Plimpton as the "Plympton." (DB.)

The Plimpton

WILLIAM HILL, - Proprietor.

Wednesday, July 10, 1889.

Consomme a la Colbert. Scotch Mutton Broth.

Filet of Cod, Sauce d'Homade.

Sliced Tomatoes. Potato Souffle.

Boiled Fowl and Salt Pork, Egg Sauce.

Corned Beef. Boiled Buffalo Tongue.

Ribs of Beef au Jus.

Young Turkey, Cranberry Sauce.

Spare Ribs Pork, Brown Sauce.

Fricasse of Chicken a la Chevalier.

Scallops d'Bœuf au Marachale.

Boston Queen Puffs, Golden Sauce.

Mashed Potatoes. New Peas. Turnips.

New Boiled Potatoes. Squash. Rice.

Sago Pudding, Hard Sauce.

Apple Pie. ~~Blackberry~~ Cherry Pie. Cocoanut Pie.

Wine Jelly. Orange Sherbet Assorted Cake.

~~Orange~~. Apple Meringue. Watermelon.

Tea. Edam Cheese. Pineapple Cheese. Coffee.

Apollinaris, 25 cents, Ginger Ale, 15 cents.

Park & Tilford's Champagne Cider, Quarts 50 cents, Pints 25 cents.

Barton & Guestier's Floirac, Quarts $1 50, Pints 75 cents.

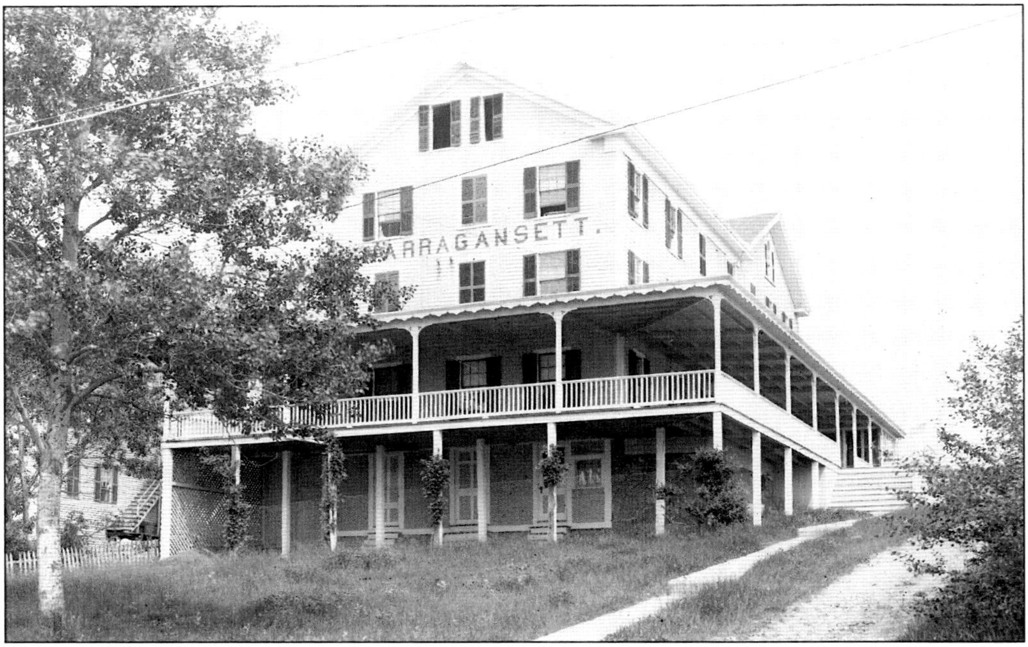

The rustic Narragansett House looms large above Bay Street in the early 1900s. Once the site of an inn that was run by Captain Nathan Nash in the 1840s, this structure was expanded and later improved to become a full-service family hotel. A newspaper article from the early 1900s notes that the Narragansett had "a fine reputation for real home comforts" (*Seaside Topics*, July 1905). (WHS.).

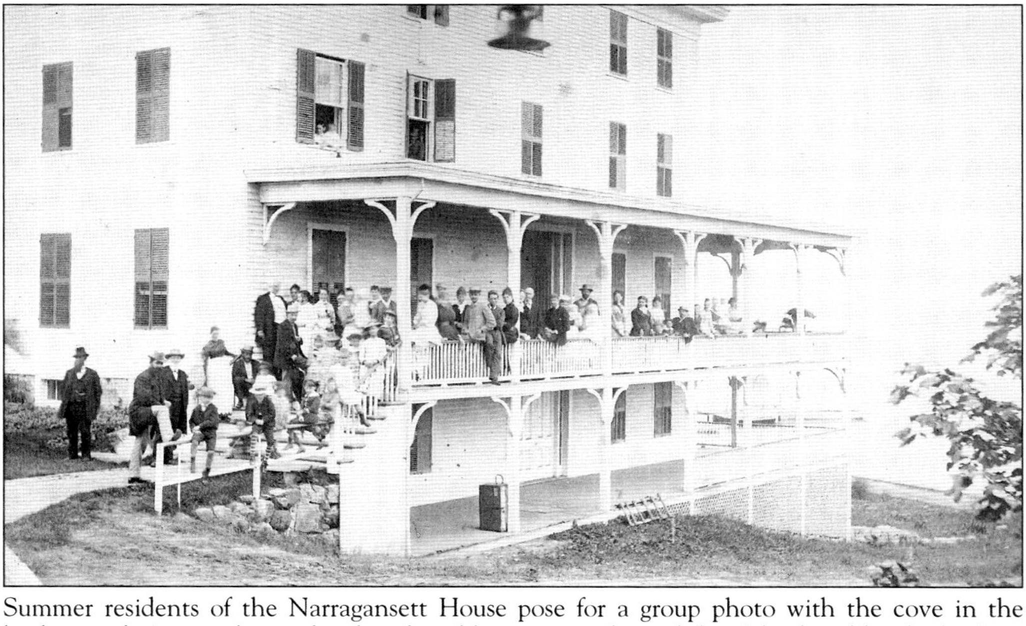

Summer residents of the Narragansett House pose for a group photo with the cove in the background. An article in a local trade publication proclaimed that "this hotel has had a first-class family occupation during the season ever since Watch Hill became a summer rest for weary cityites" (*Seaside Topics*, July 1905). (WPL.)

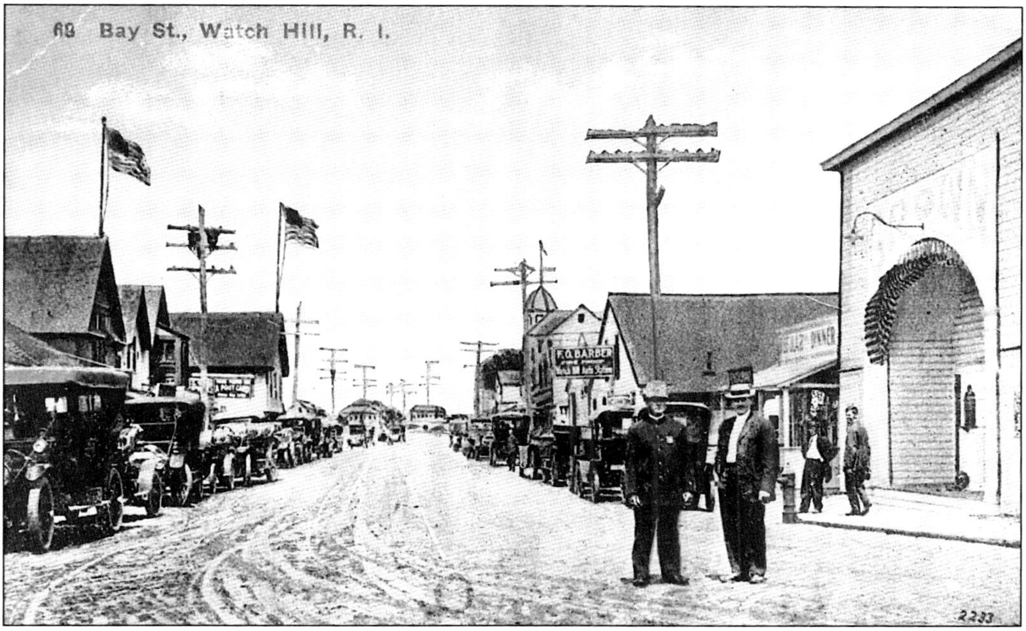

The landmark Crown Theater, located kitty-corner across Bay Street from the carousel, was constructed in 1912. Over the next 39 years, it would change its name to the Ninigret Theater until its ignominious conversion into a grocery market in 1951. Jane Hoxie Maxson of Wakefield recounts her mother's tale of the evening that Douglas Fairbanks Jr. sat in a seat near her at the Crown. (GHU.)

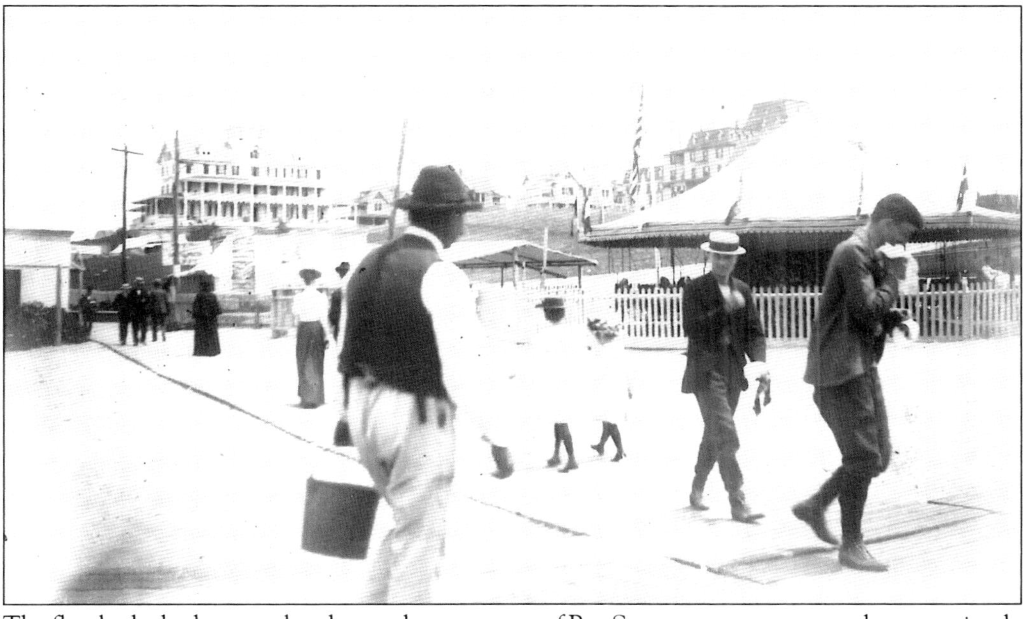

The flag-bedecked carousel at the southwest corner of Bay Street was once powered, appropriately enough, by a horse. "According to legend, when the horse eventually died, his tail was cured and inset into the rump of one of the carousel horses as a permanent memorial. Sadly, we have lost track of which horse it was" (*Around and Around*). (DB.)

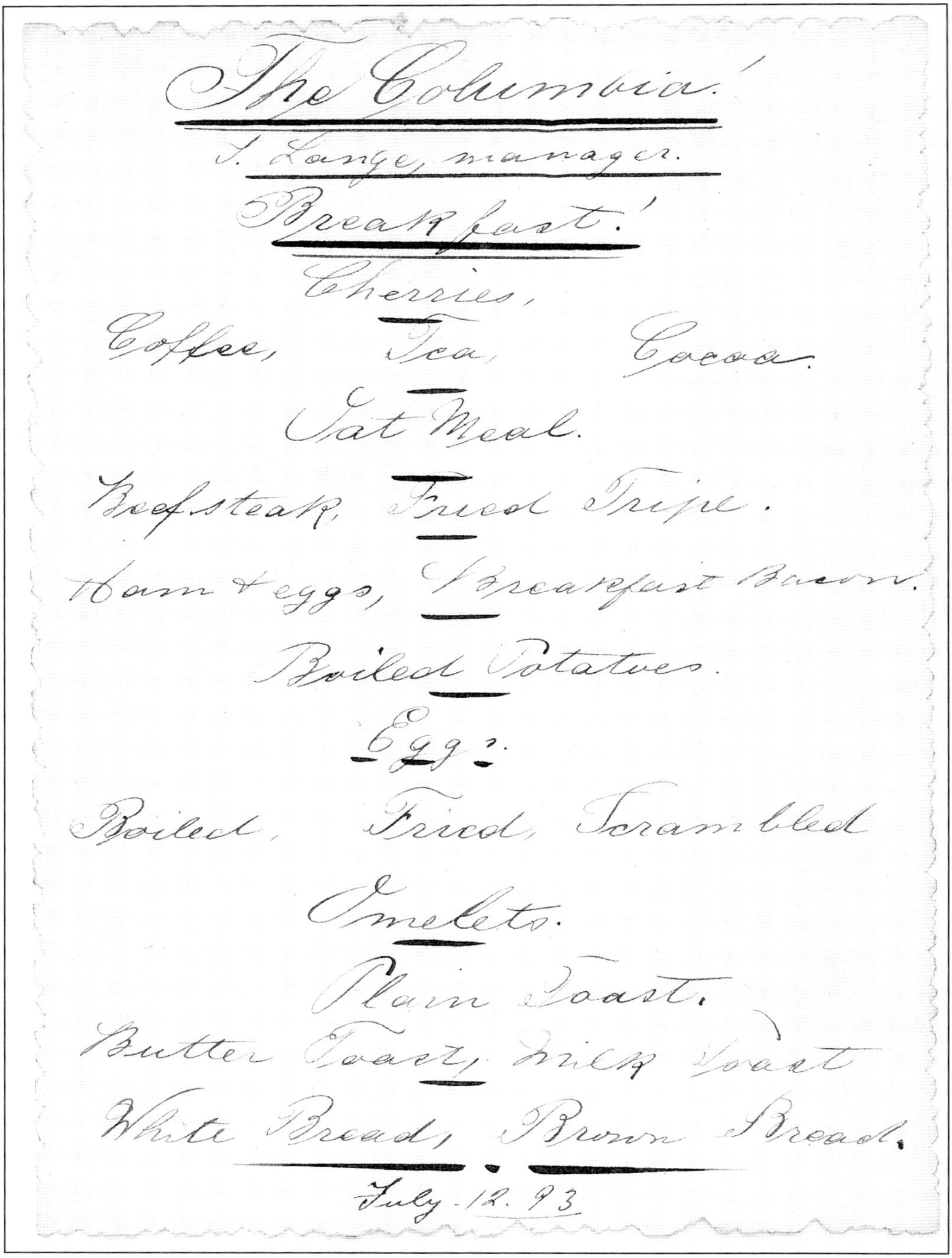

The Columbia!

I. Lange, manager.

Breakfast!

Cherries,

Coffee, Tea, Cocoa.

Oat Meal.

Beefsteak, Fried Tripe.

Ham & eggs, Breakfast Bacon.

Boiled Potatoes.

Eggs:

Boiled, Fried, Scrambled

Omelets.

Plain Toast.

Butter Toast, Milk Toast

White Bread, Brown Bread.

July. 12. 93

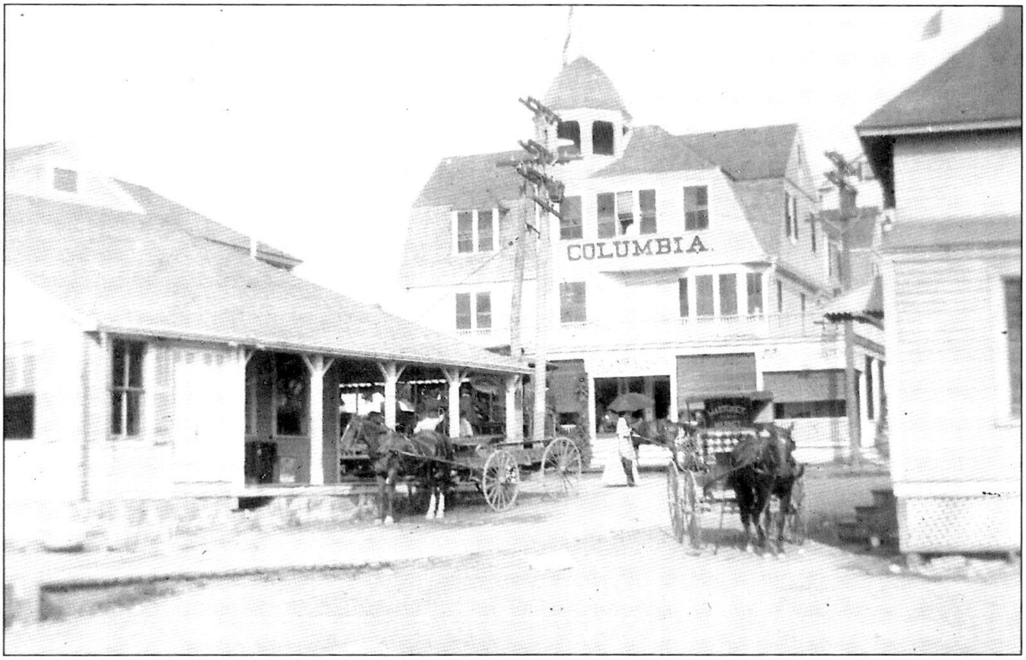

The Columbia House, located on the east side of Bay Street, was the last of the rambling wooden hotels built at Watch Hill around the turn of the century. Replete with an open-air porch and a distinctive cupola, this inn did not have the benefit of the magnificent scenic views that were the domain of its larger and older competitors. (GHU.)

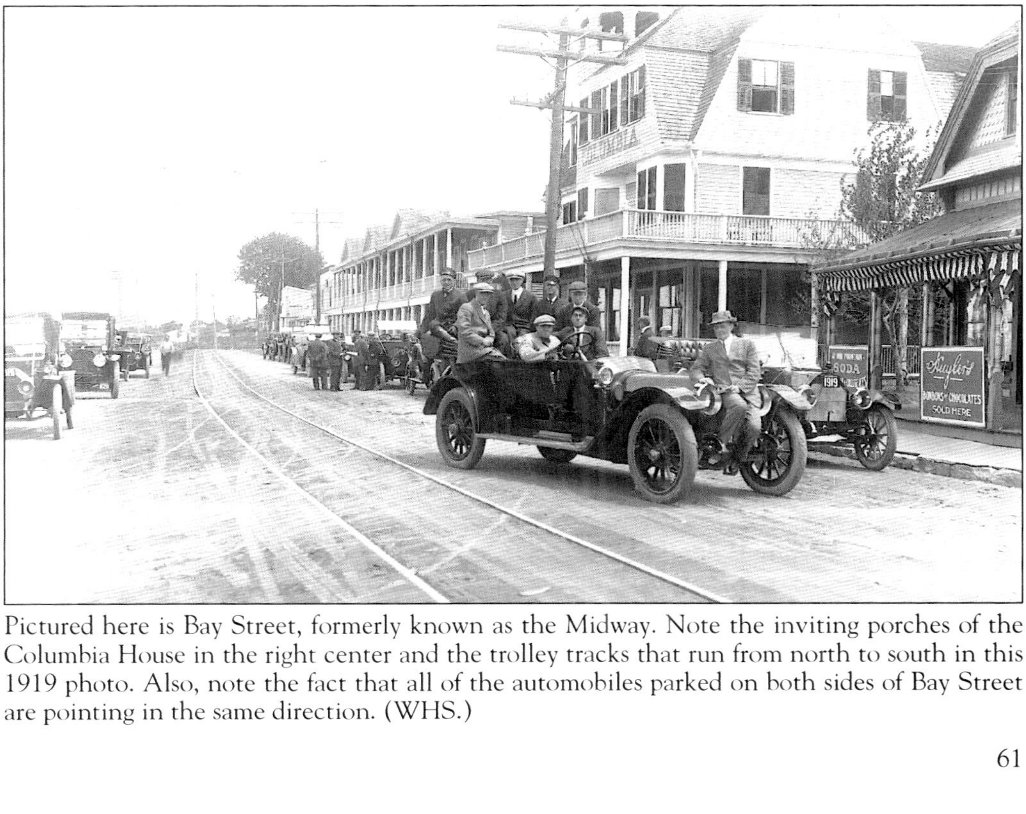

Pictured here is Bay Street, formerly known as the Midway. Note the inviting porches of the Columbia House in the right center and the trolley tracks that run from north to south in this 1919 photo. Also, note the fact that all of the automobiles parked on both sides of Bay Street are pointing in the same direction. (WHS.)

1894

The COLUMBIA,

WATCH HILL, R. I.

Hotel open from June 15th until October 1st. . . .

"Whoe'er has traveled life's dull round,
Whate'er his various tour has been,
May sigh to think how oft he found,
His warmest welcome at an inn."

—William Shenstone (1714–1763)

The Columbia

Is one of the best located hotels at Watch Hill, as it is nearest to Wharfs, Post Office and Stores.

The Rooms are large, pleasant, and nicely furnished, (hair mattresses on all beds.)

The table is under the special care of the Proprietress, and neither trouble nor expense will be spared to make this Hotel first-class in every respect.

For families who desire to stay by the week, month, or season, special arrangements will be made.

Among the attractions at Watch Hill are Bathing, Boating, Fishing, and Driving.

The Bathing Beach is but a short distance from the Columbia.

Accessible via. New London, Stonington, Westerly, and Block Island Steamers.

The Columbia will be open June 15, 1894.

For terms, address

(MISS) J. LANGE,
WATCH HILL, R. I.

Four

ABOUT THE HILL

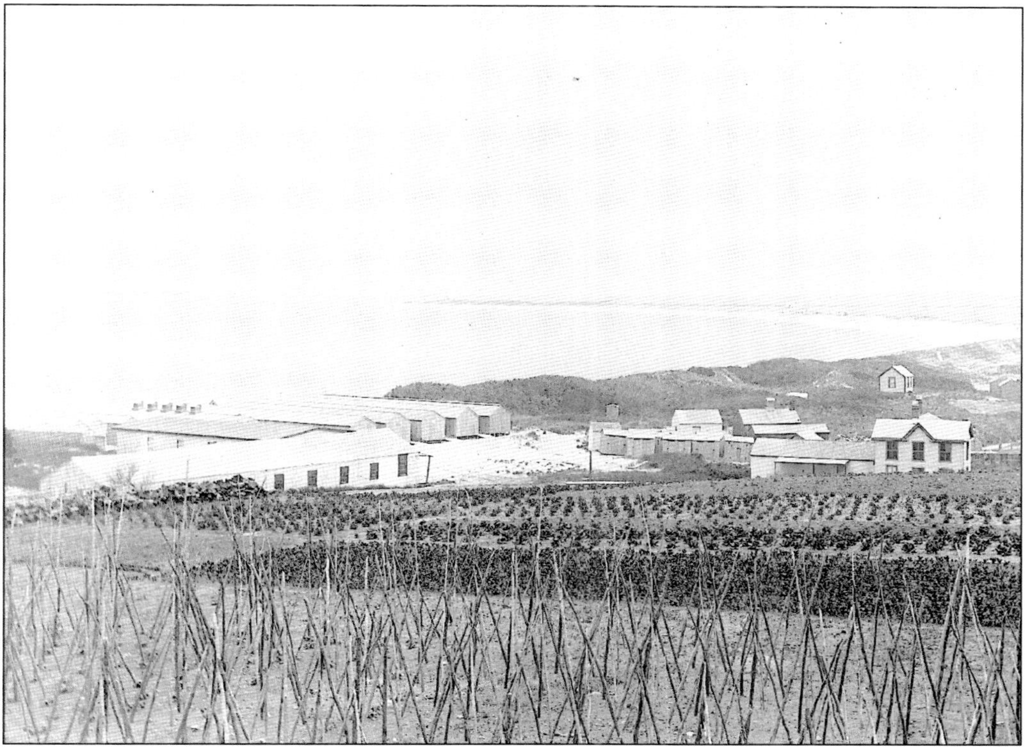

Captain Larkin's vegetable garden had a commanding view of Fishers Island Sound, Napatree, Little Narragansett Bay, and the cove during the 1870s. Note the former thickness of the Napatree peninsula and the high ridge of dunes that once tapered out towards the Nap. Also, note that Sandy Point was connected to Napatree at a distinct right angle that ran from south to north. Notable structures include the eight Larkin bathhouses to the left and the lonely Peninsula House, halfway out on the sands of Napatree. The Peninsula House was floated across Little Narragansett Bay from Osbrook Point. Some of these structures and most of this geography was irrevocably altered by the terrible fury of the Hurricane of '38. (WPL.)

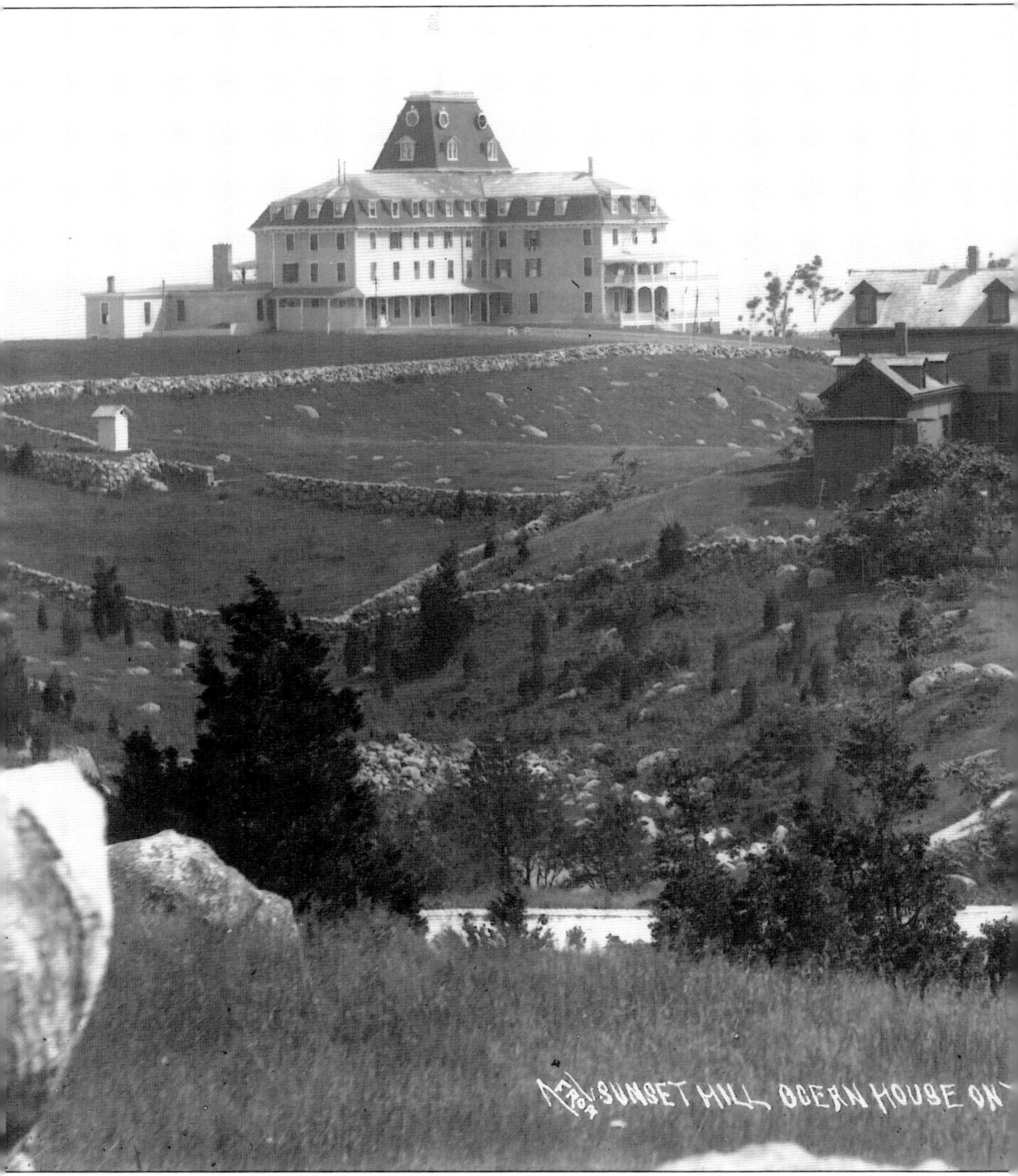

Looking southeast from the heights of Sunset Hill in 1895, a contemporary viewer would be immediately struck by the Hill's barren rock-strewn topography and its dearth of shrubs and trees. It is interesting to note that the Ocean House, the hotel on the left, cleared its lawn of every rock of every size to build the magnificent stone walls that encircled its lofty campus; yet, the grounds of the Watch Hill House, the hotel on the right, are still studded with a large

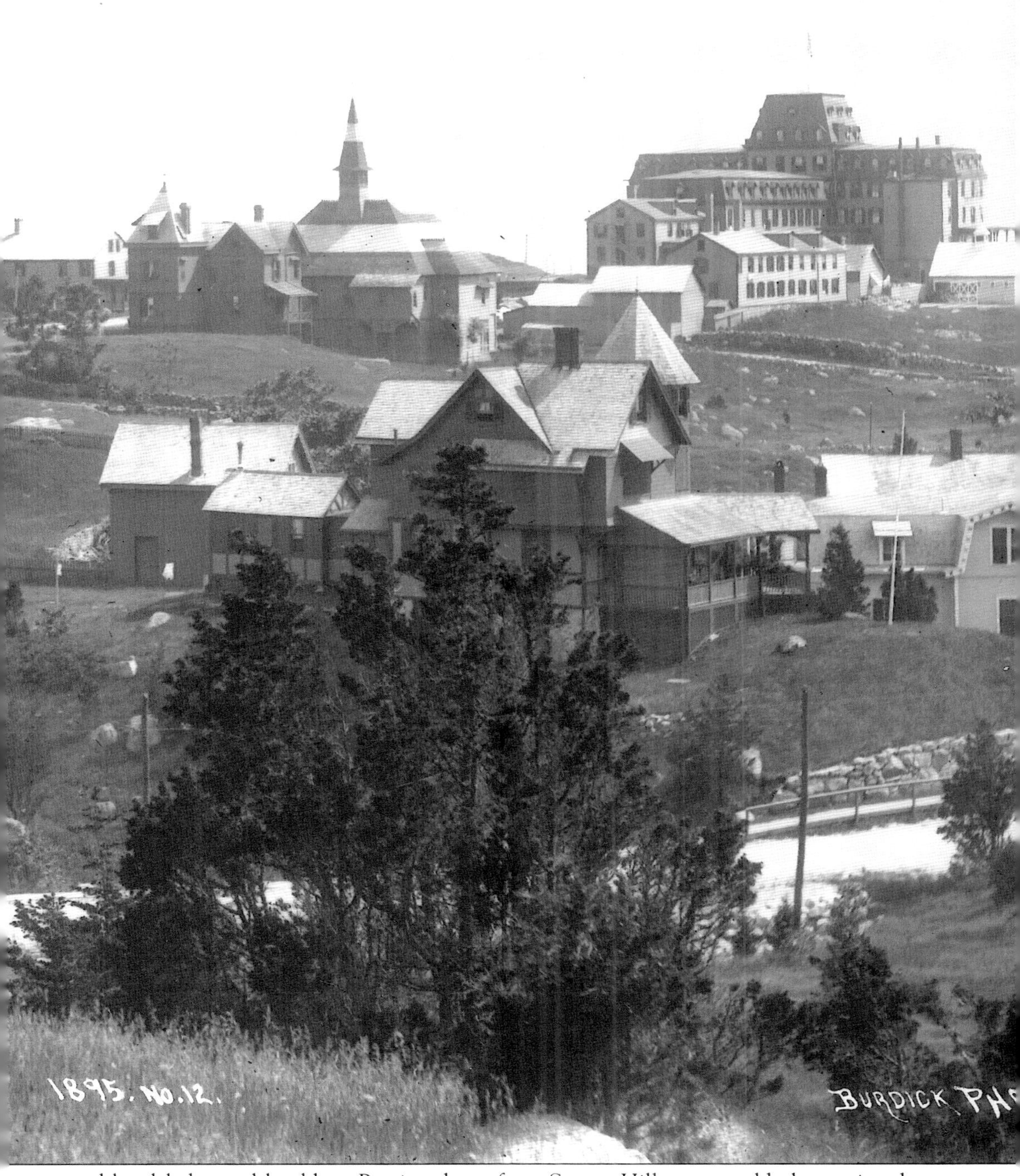

ground-level ledge and boulders. Peering down from Sunset Hill, one would also notice the unpretentious steeple of the Watch Hill Chapel poking up between the two hotels. Note that the flag atop the Ocean House is blowing to the south while the flag atop the Watch Hill House is luffing to the southwest. (GHU-Burdick.)

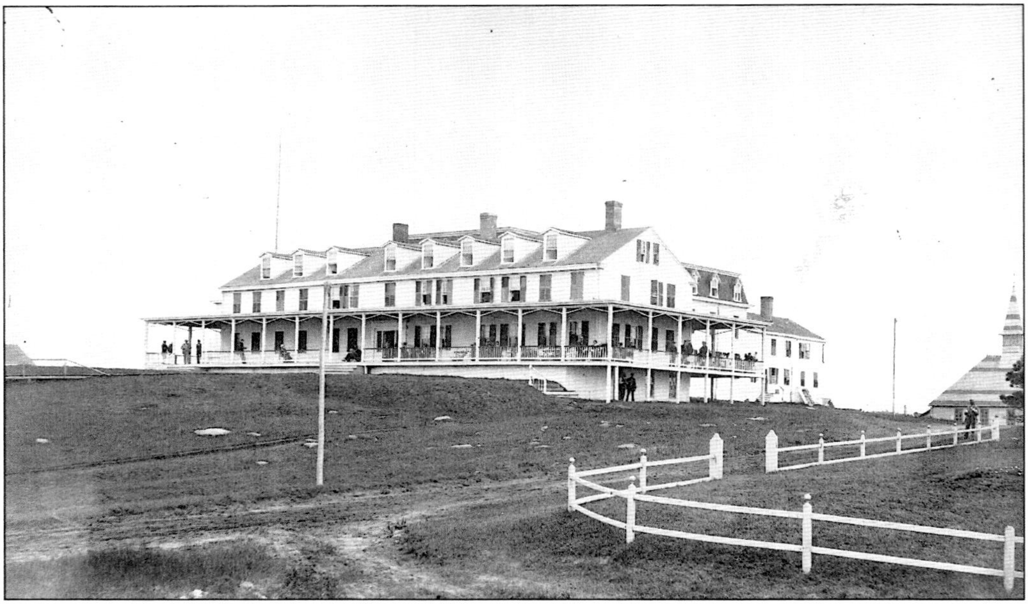

The Watch Hill House was built in 1835 for its owner and operator, Jonathan Nash. In turn, hotel operations were eventually handed over to his son, George Nash. The large front wing of this hotel, which loomed over East Beach from the heights of Lookout Hill, was moved closer to East Beach in 1881 as an annex. In 1906, it was moved back across Bluff Avenue toward the chapel. (WPL.)

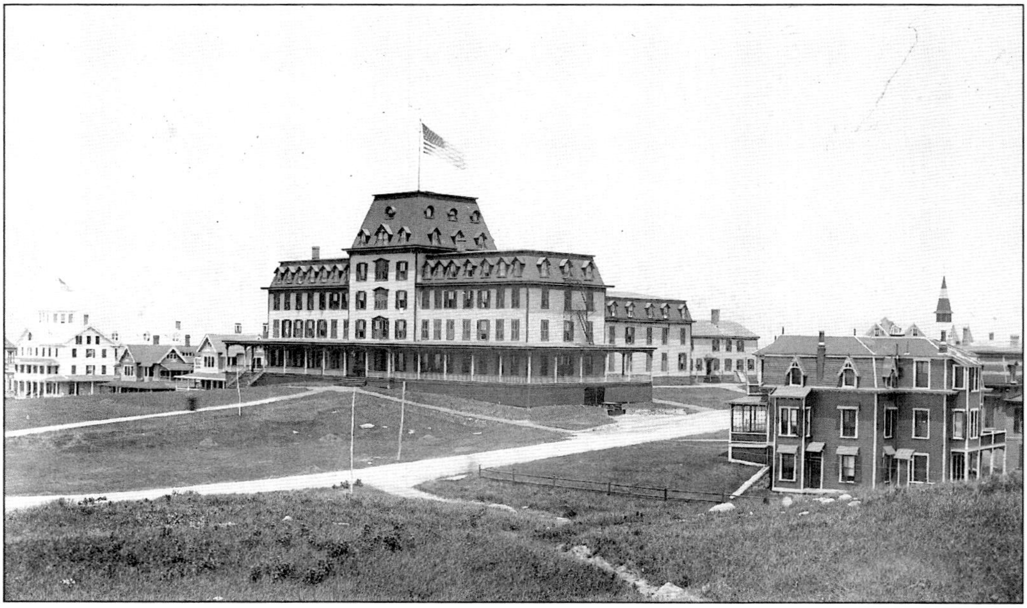

A "new" Watch Hill House, built in 1877, lauded the fact that its 165 rooms made it the largest hotel at Watch Hill. From spacious piazzas, one could enjoy a panoramic view of the mouth of the Pawcatuck River, Little Narragansett Bay, Fishers and Block Island Sound, East and Napatree Beach, and Lighthouse Point. Ads boasted that there were no "inside rooms, every room commanding fine views of the water." (WPL.)

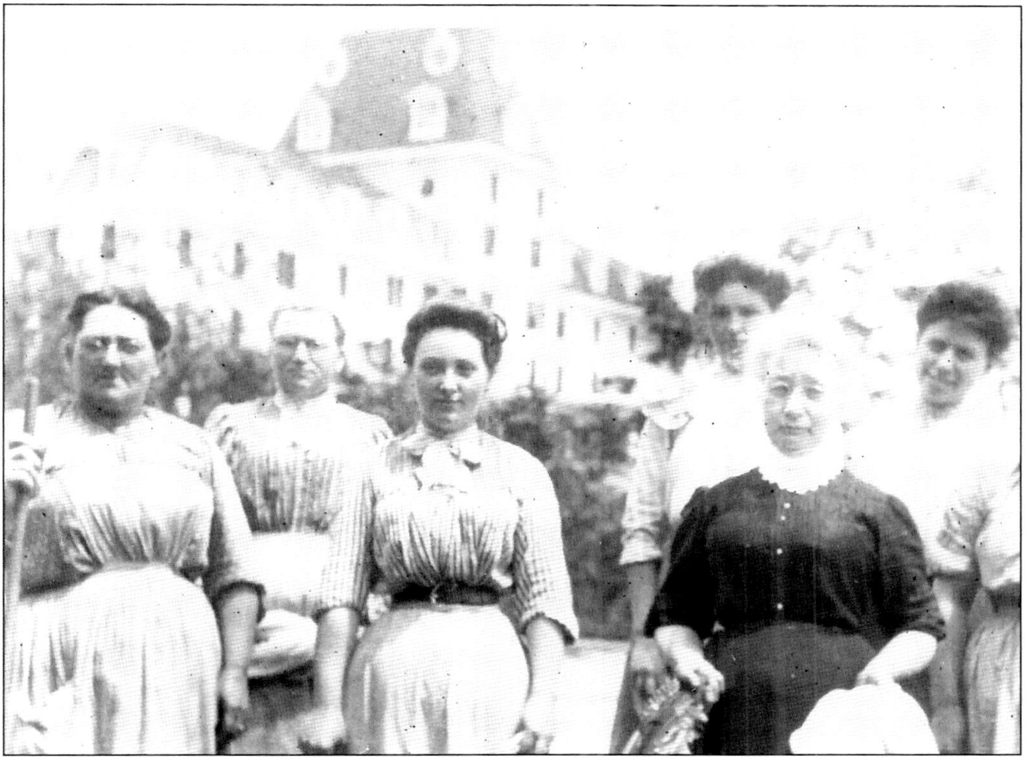

Watch Hill House maids pose cheerfully in front of "their" hotel. A contemporary report observes that "the most fastidious may find clean rooms, the best of beds, well supplied tables and excellent service" (*Westerly's Oldest Witness*). (DB.)

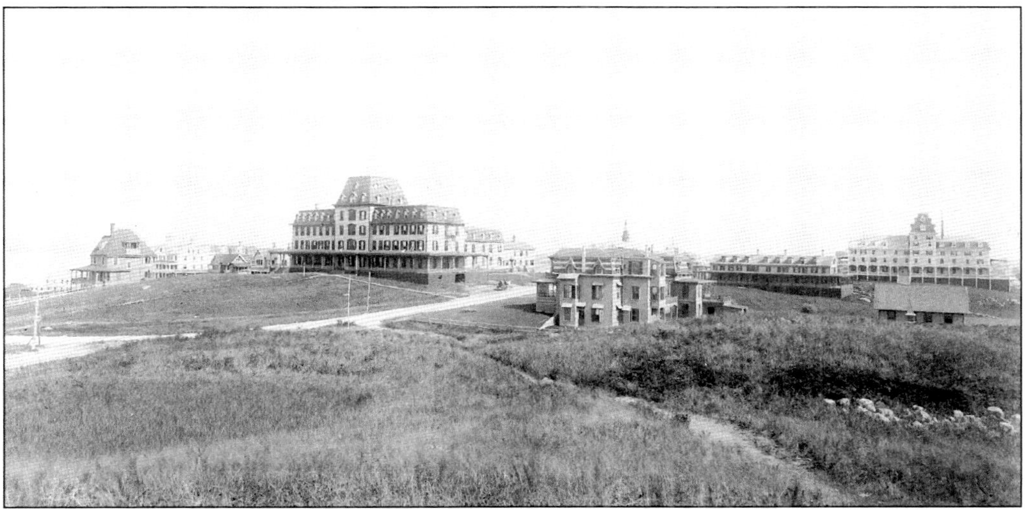

Standing by the Larkin House, a late-1800s panorama depicts, from left to right, the lone chimney of By-the-Sea, a local cottage; the white cupola of the Atlantic House; the five-storied Watch Hill House; the Watch Hill Chapel; and the vast expanse of the Ocean House. Both the Atlantic House and the Watch Hill House would ultimately succumb to raging fires. (WPL.)

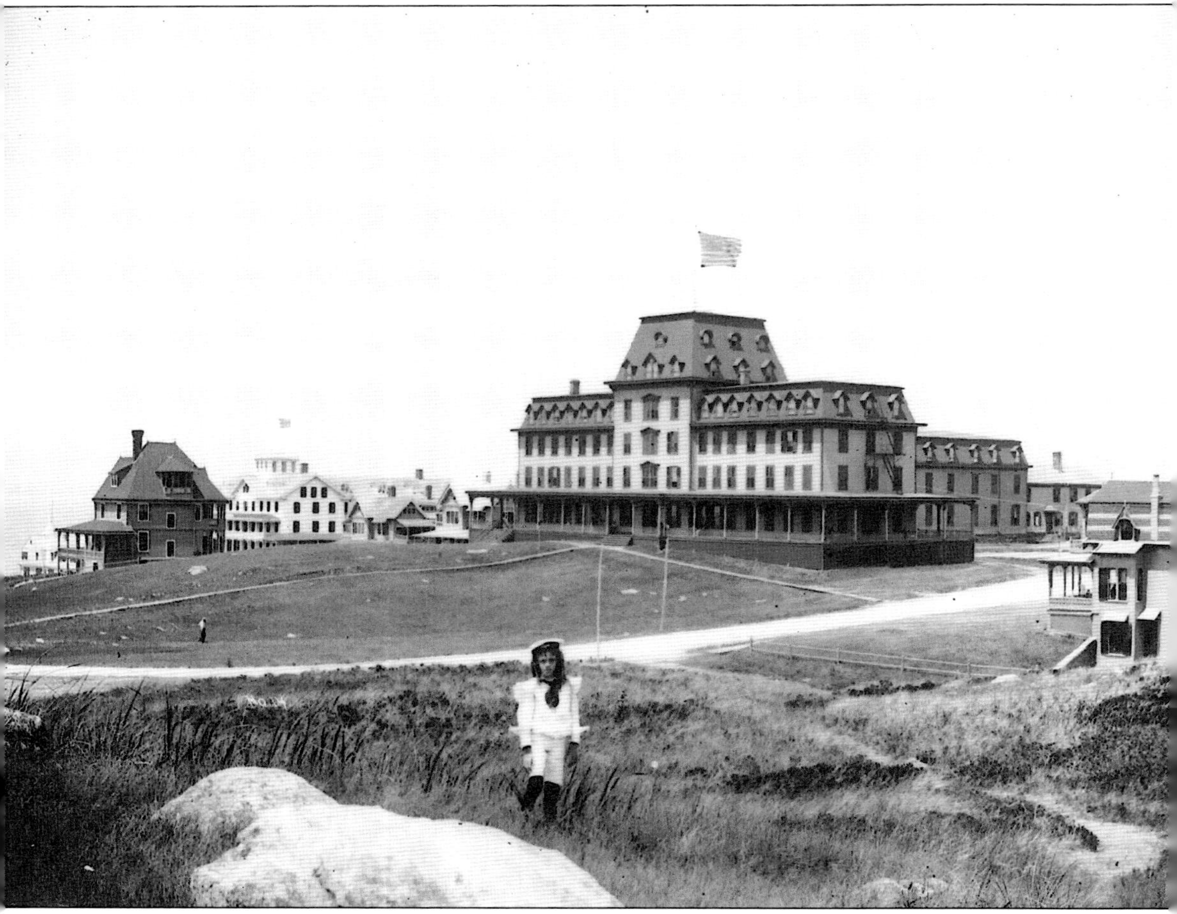

"It's gone," said Watch Hill Fire Chief Walter Nash, "it's gone." So saying, the exhausted fireman fell asleep in his clothes in his family's living room after spending the night battling the great fire that burned the Watch Hill House to the ground on the evening of October 19, 1916. This tale of the fire that ultimately destroyed the Watch Hill House, the Atlantic House, and several Watch Hill cottages is recalled by Walter's great-granddaughter, Susan Carr of Westerly. Before its destruction, however, the Watch Hill House stood proudly upon its hill before the sea. (GHU-Burdick.)

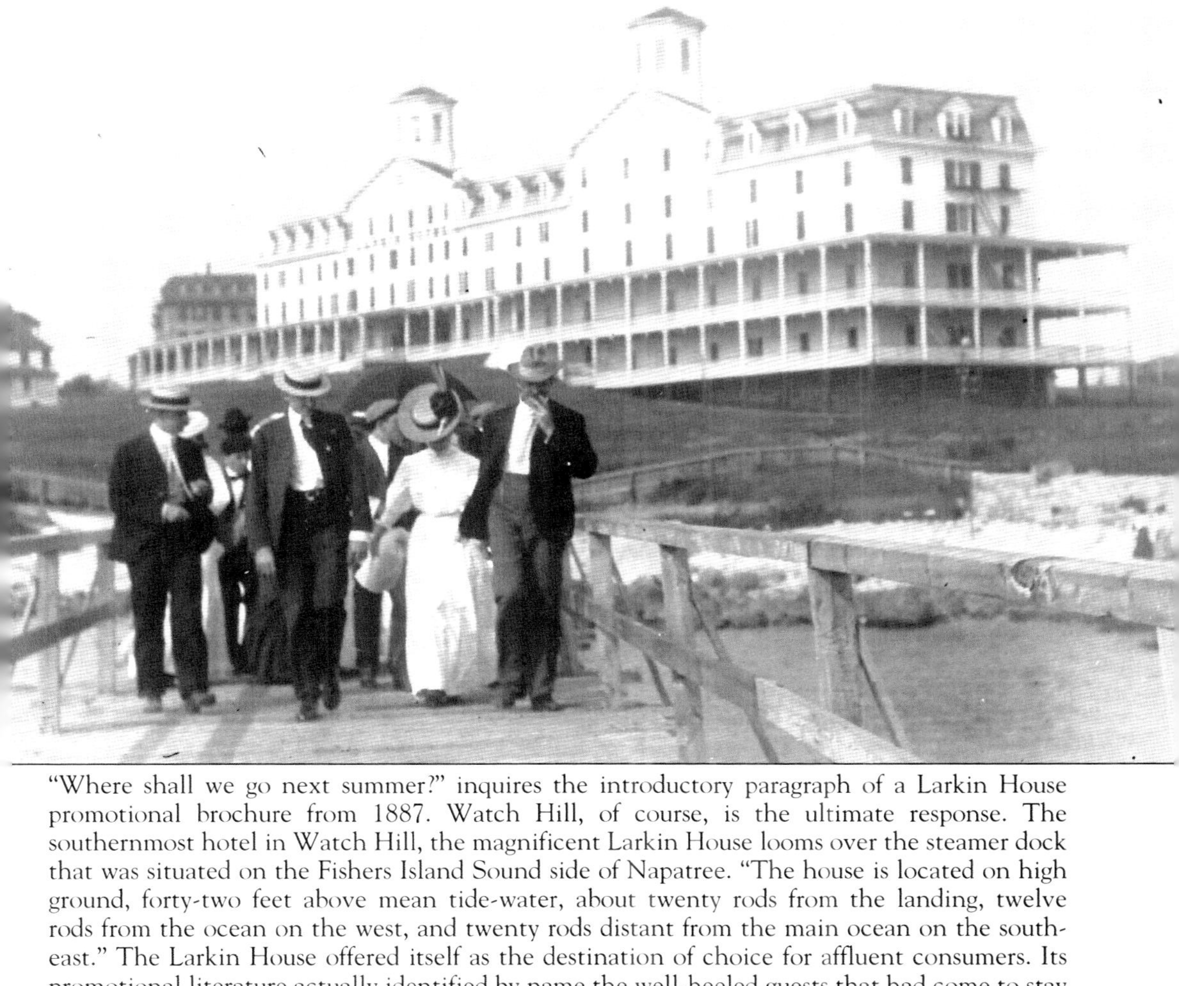

"Where shall we go next summer?" inquires the introductory paragraph of a Larkin House promotional brochure from 1887. Watch Hill, of course, is the ultimate response. The southernmost hotel in Watch Hill, the magnificent Larkin House looms over the steamer dock that was situated on the Fishers Island Sound side of Napatree. "The house is located on high ground, forty-two feet above mean tide-water, about twenty rods from the landing, twelve rods from the ocean on the west, and twenty rods distant from the main ocean on the south-east." The Larkin House offered itself as the destination of choice for affluent consumers. Its promotional literature actually identified by name the well-heeled guests that had come to stay from cities such as New York, Chicago, and Hartford. (DB.)

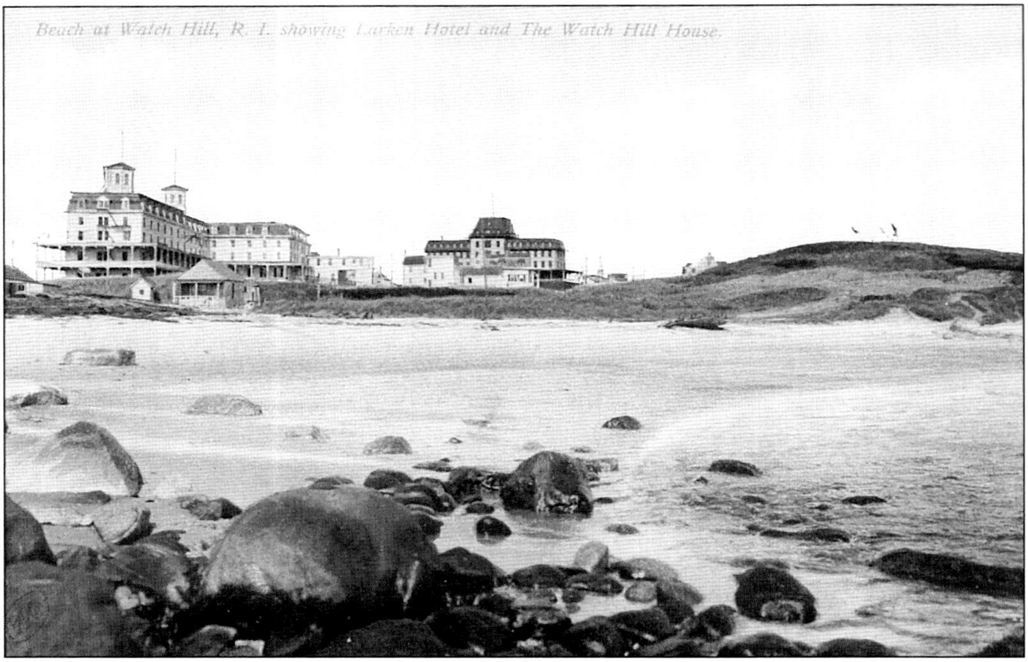

Standing on the eastern shore of Lighthouse Point before the turn of the century and looking north toward Watch Hill, the Larkin House and its twin cupolas would be visible to the left, the Watch Hill House and its lone flag pole would be visible in the center, and the "Watch" Hill itself would loom up to the right. (BAFR.)

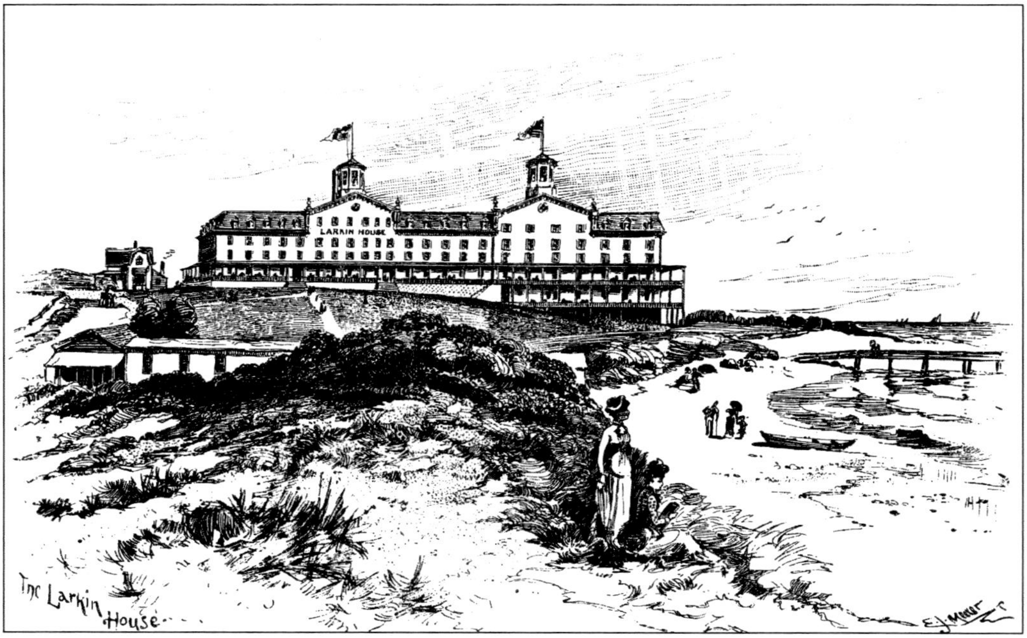

Shown here is a fanciful sketch of the Larkin House from a vantage point looking eastward from the dunes of Napatree. The sketch depicts a southerly breeze, which is a rare commodity on Fishers Island Sound. (BAFR.)

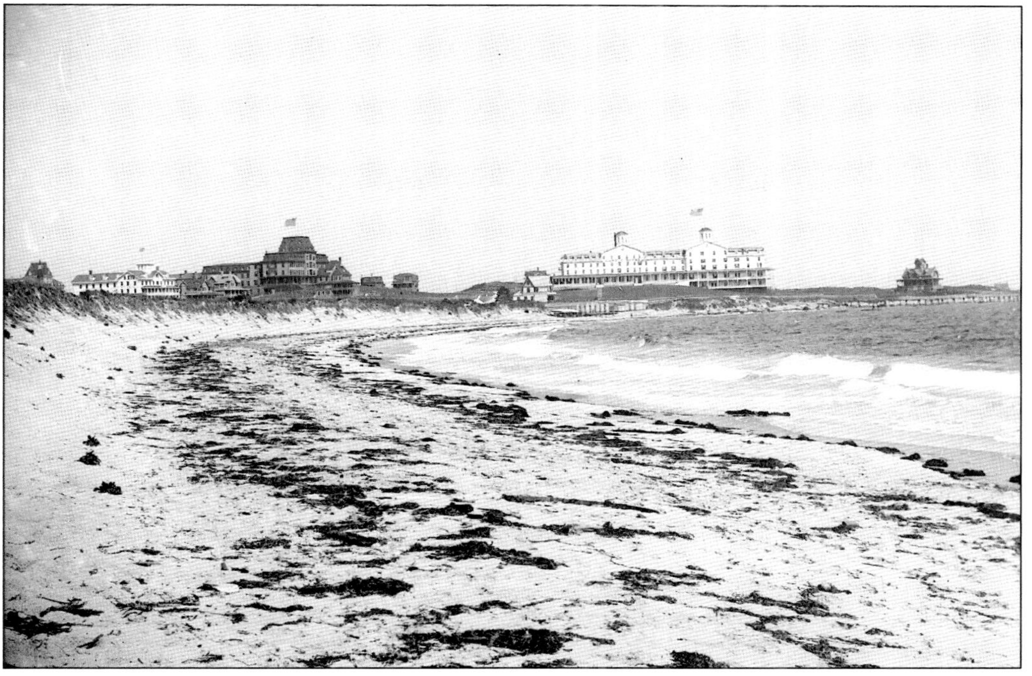

Situated on Lighthouse Point, the Larkin House and its twin cupolas commanded an unobstructed view of the vast Atlantic Ocean. What would such a magnificent sight cost a would-be traveler? "Rates: $3.00 to $4.00 per day. Single rooms, $17.50 to $28.00 per week. Double rooms $35.00 to $56.00 per week. Special rates for families for the season." (GHU-Burdick.)

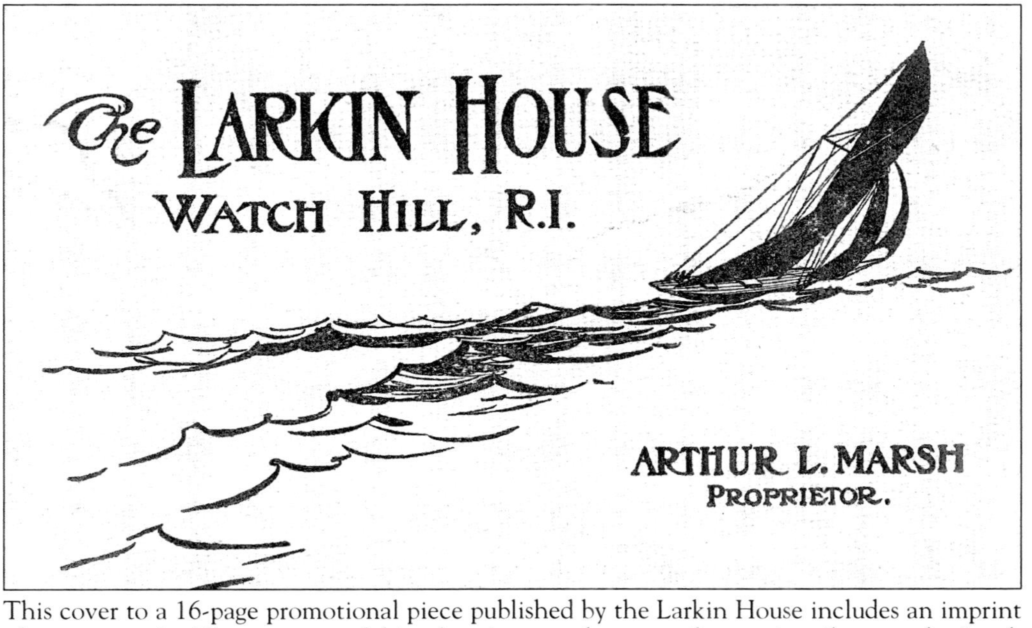

This cover to a 16-page promotional piece published by the Larkin House includes an imprint of a racing yacht. The contents of this advertisement, however, focus primarily upon the "cool, bracing air" and the "perfectly safe bathing beach." (JM.)

13th Annual 13th

Minstrel Concert and Cake Walk

to be given
by the . . .

Waiters of the Larkin House

in the

Dance Hall, Thursday Evening,

AUG. 17, 1899

Admission, 50 Cents. Children, 25 Cents.

Doors open at 8. Performance at 8.30.

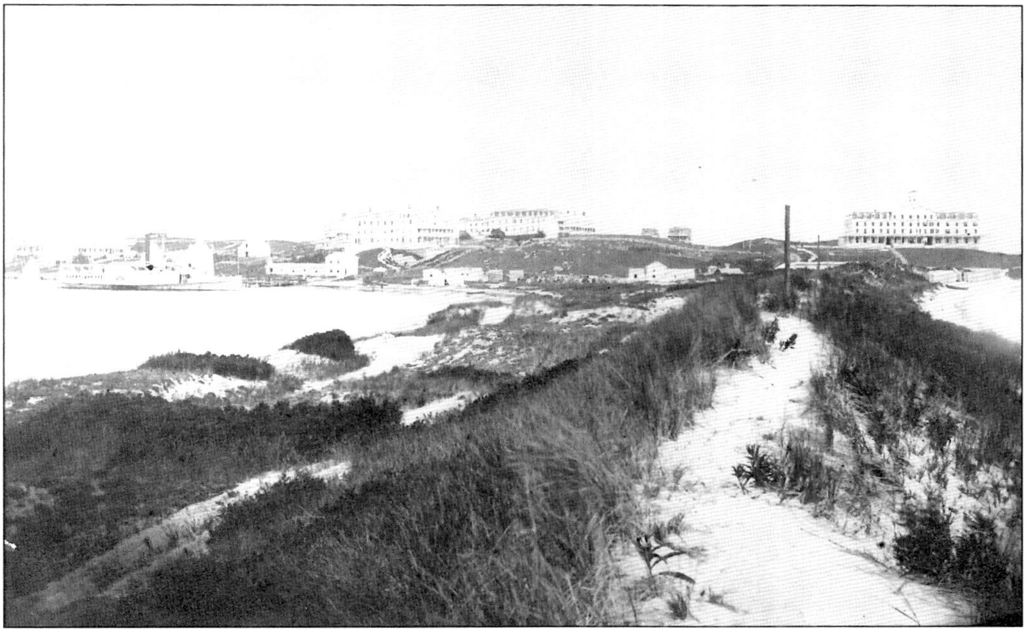

The Larkin House, the hotel on the right, sits high on its perch above Lighthouse Point before its substantial expansion in 1876. One cupola became two cupolas when the Larkin House was expanded "by an addition 100 feet by 42 feet on the south." Promotional literature noted an additional expansion in 1887 that included "an additional 111 feet by 25 feet on the north, securing an enlarged hall, dining room, kitchen, baker's and pastry rooms." (WPL.)

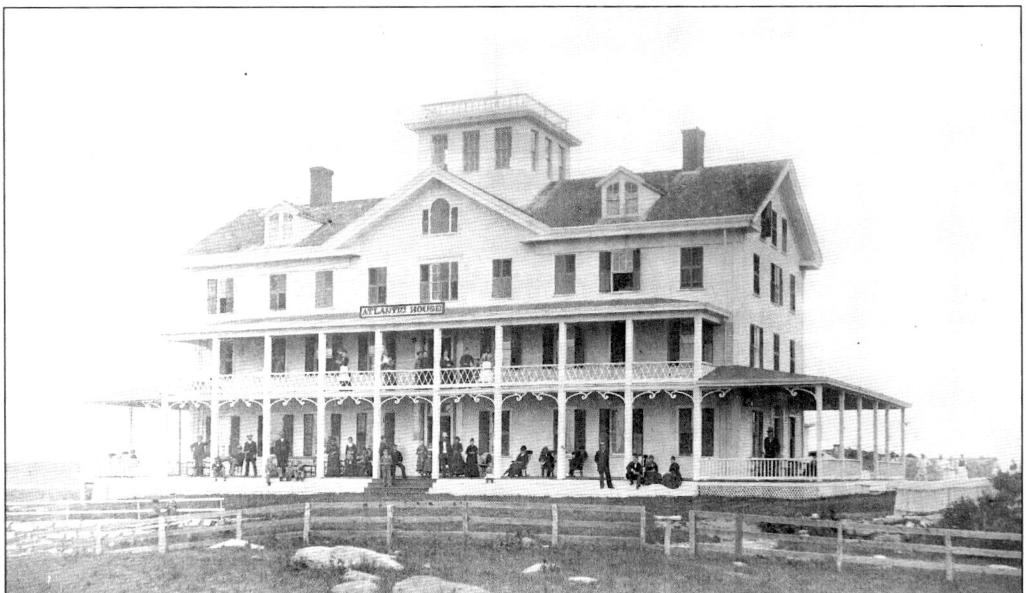

The Atlantic House, though smaller than its competitors of later years, was built in 1856. Facing Fishers Island Sound, this hotel "enjoyed the cream of the trade until about 1869." The great conflagration of 1916 burned the Atlantic House to the ground (*Early Landholders*). (WPL.)

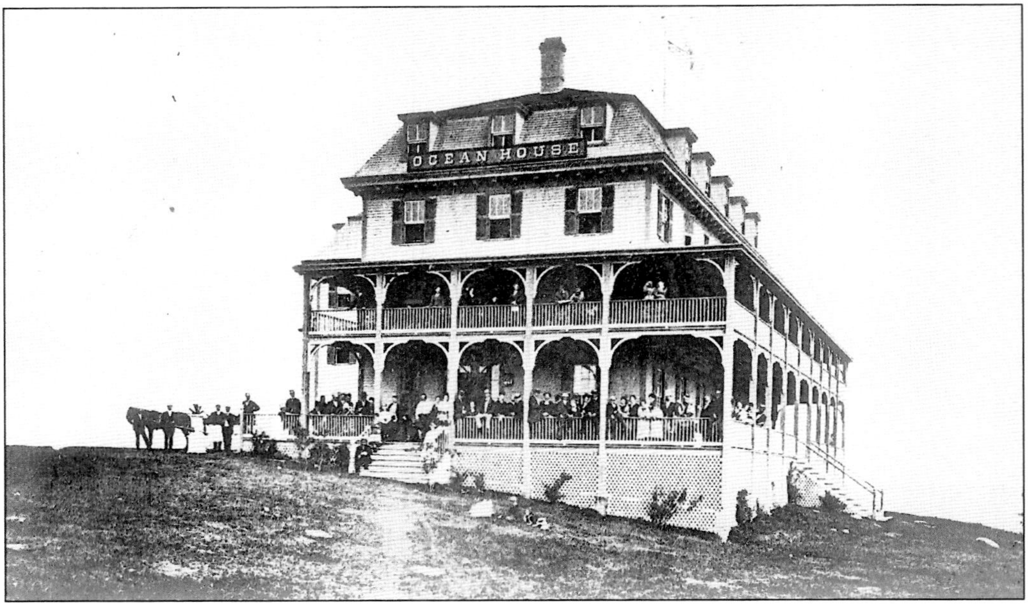

The Ocean House was built in 1868 by George Nash, son of Jonathan Nash, the original owner and operator of the Watch Hill House. Located on Plimpton and Westerly Roads, this picture captures the Ocean House before it was expanded by various additions. "It has a most commanding situation overlooking the wide sweep of the ocean and facing the west where magnificent sunsets . . . are to be seen" (*Watch Hill Life*, 1898). (DB.)

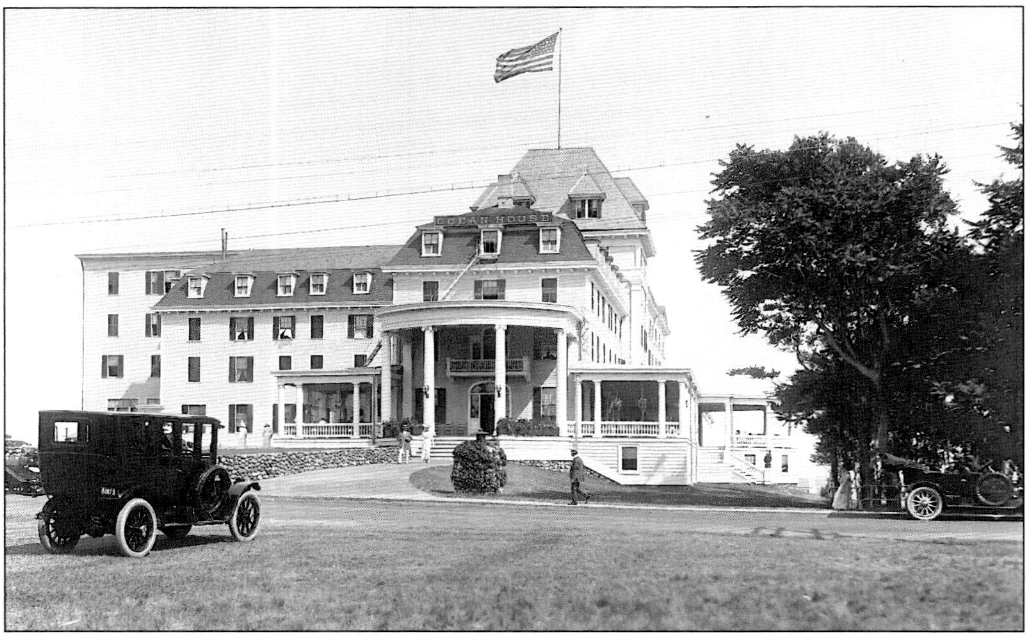

A 50-room addition was added to the Ocean House in 1897. By 1911, the hotel was a sprawling and expansive structure. Well known for its inviting decor, "the interior of the house, the rotunda and the music room are very attractive in their furnishings and everything that is possible is done for the convenience of the guests" (*Watch Hill Life*, 1898). (WHS.)

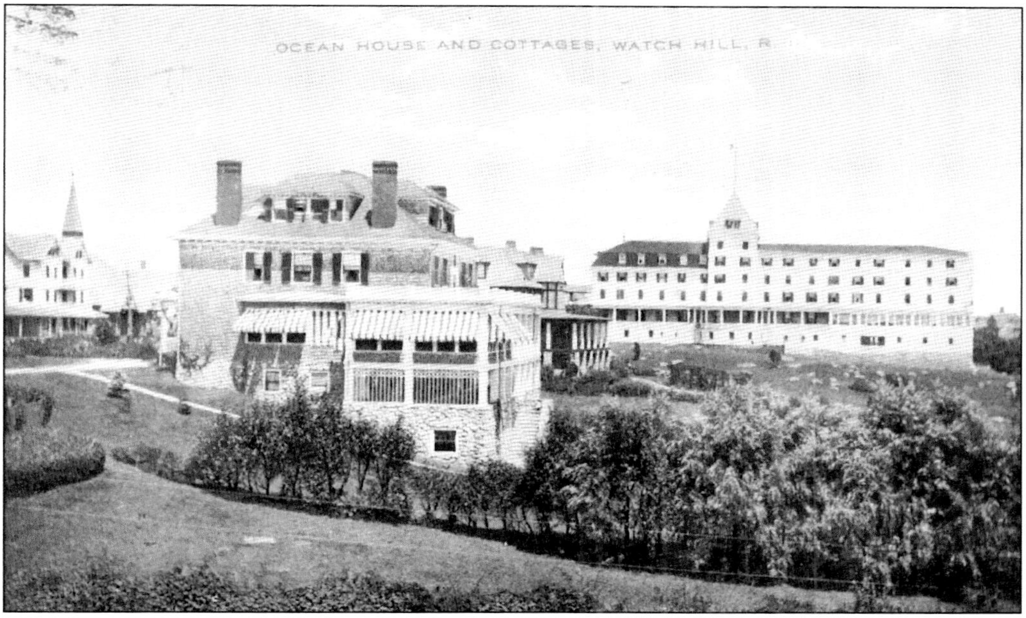

The Ocean House, to the right, owned various cottages in Watch Hill that it let to summer tourists. "The Ocean House cottages are grouped about the hotel and are always in demand. None of them have ever been unoccupied an entire season" (*Seaside Topics*, 1905). The Ocean House still serves summer residents to this very day. (BAFR.)

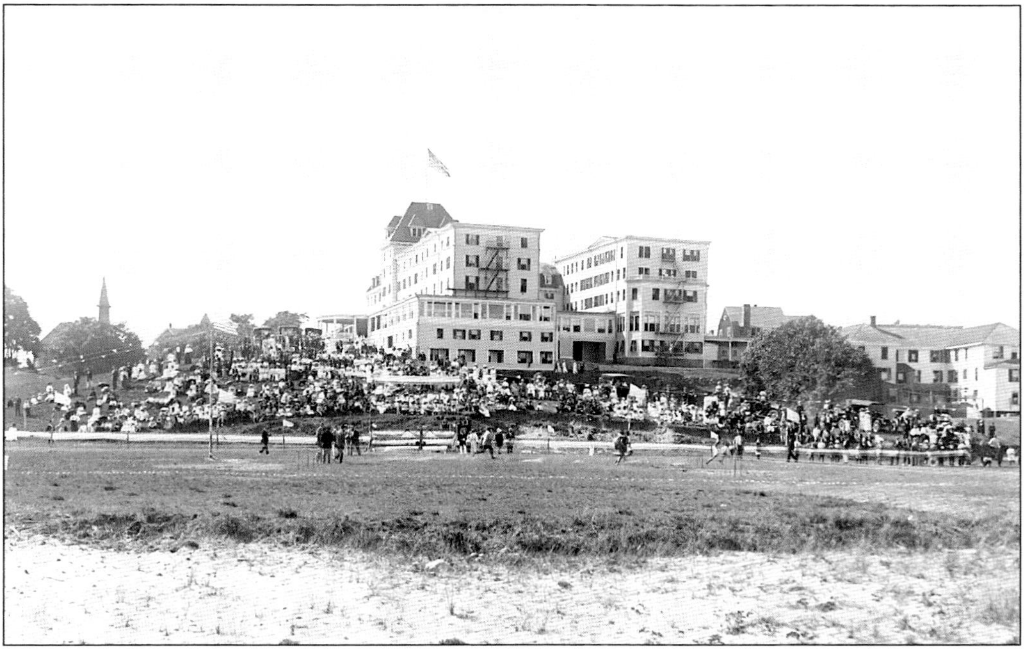

Note the crowd at this Field Day competition during August 1911. The annual event took place on the baseball field that sat below the Ocean House. In addition to baseball, "the list of events consists of a 100 and 150 yard dash, a 100 and 150 yard hurdles, an obstacle race . . . and tug of war between a Watch Hill House and an Ocean House team" (*Seaside Topics*, 1905). (WHS.)

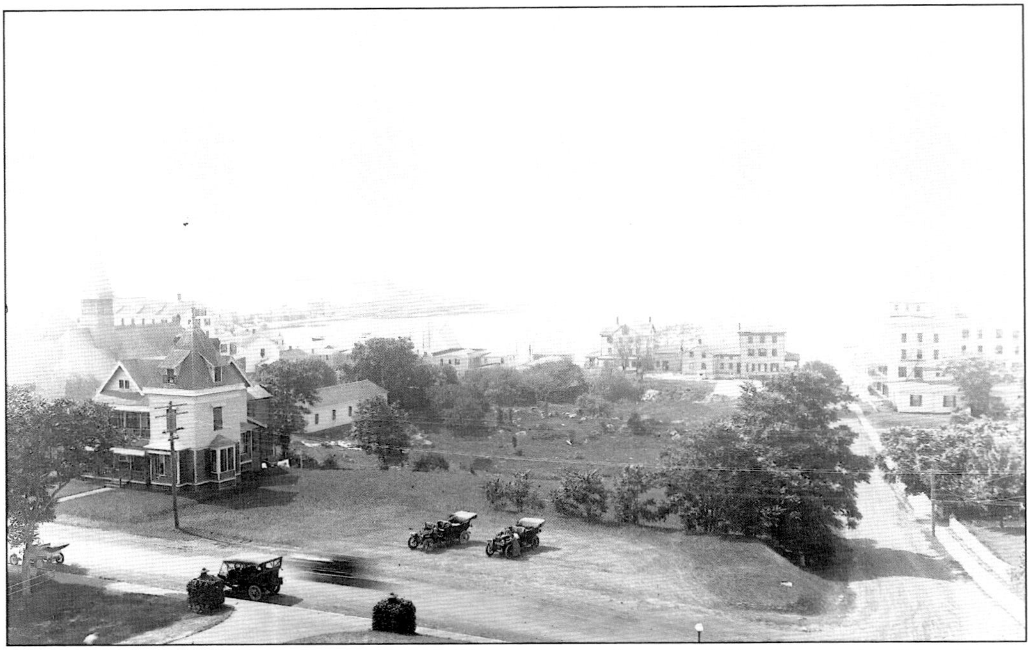

Looking west from the roof of the Ocean House during August 1910, the steeple of the Watch Hill Chapel is visible to the left and the Plimpton House and Plimpton Annex are visible to the right. Note the luffing gaff-rigged catboat sails at mid-center, the significant width of Napatree, and the houses that grace Fort Road all the way out to the Nap on Napatree. (WHS.)

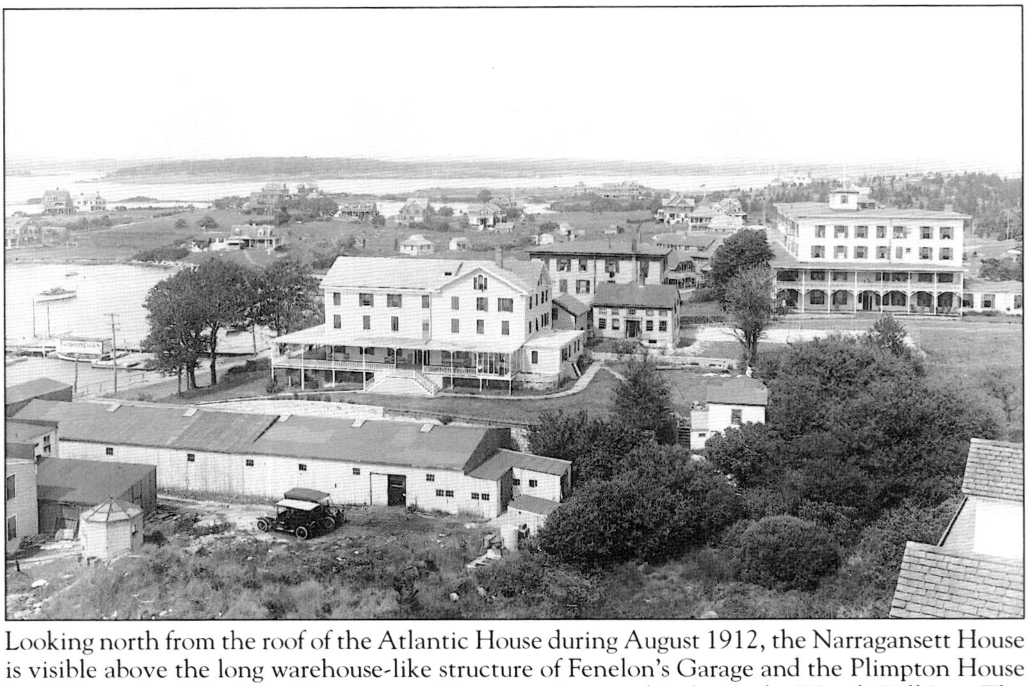

Looking north from the roof of the Atlantic House during August 1912, the Narragansett House is visible above the long warehouse-like structure of Fenelon's Garage and the Plimpton House is visible to the right. The Narragansett House survives to this day as the Watch Hill Inn. The circular structure at bottom left is the laundry room for the Fenelon family. (WHS.)

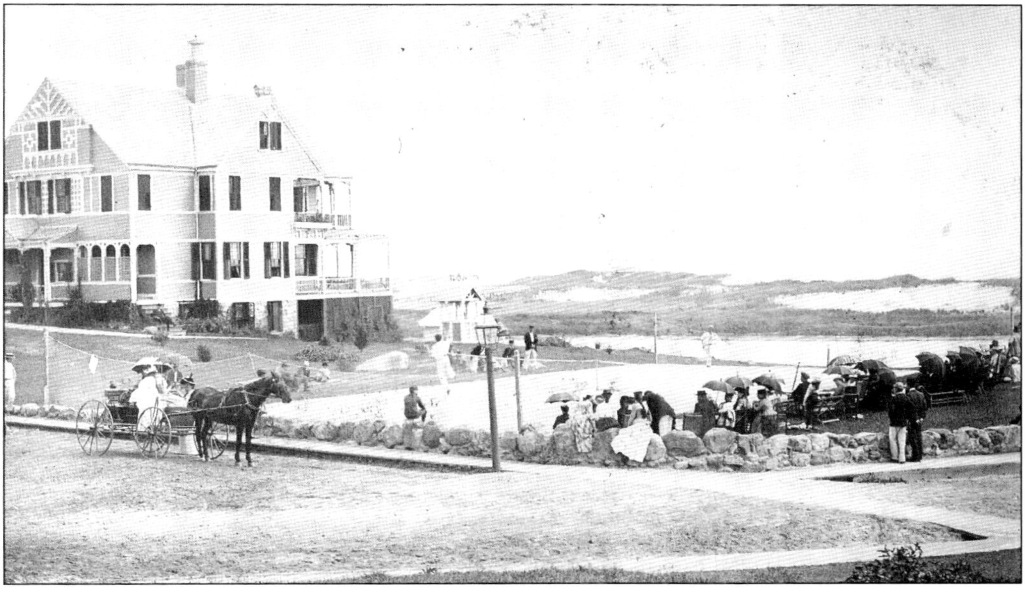

A tennis match on the courts that abut the Niantic Avenue cottage of William Anderson during September 1890 draws onlookers and well-wishers despite the rainy weather. The dunes in the background slope down to East Beach. (DB.)

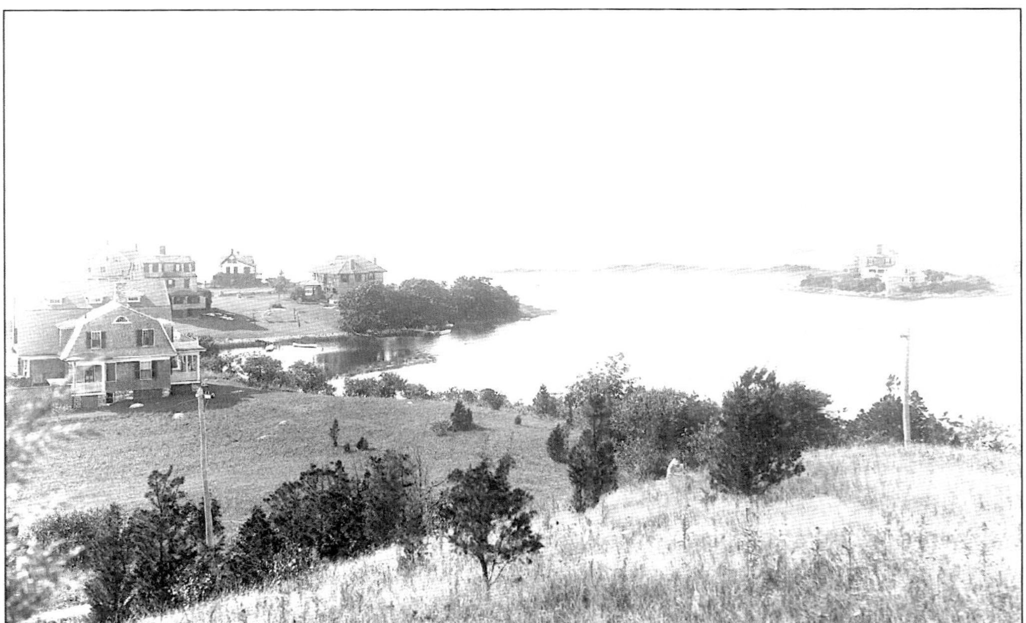

This view is looking westward from Sunset Hill over Foster Cove toward Little Narragansett Bay. "If you have a love for nature, in her brilliant twilight hues; You will find a jeweled pleasure, Sunset Hill's resplendent views" (*Seaside Topics*, 1905). (WHS.)

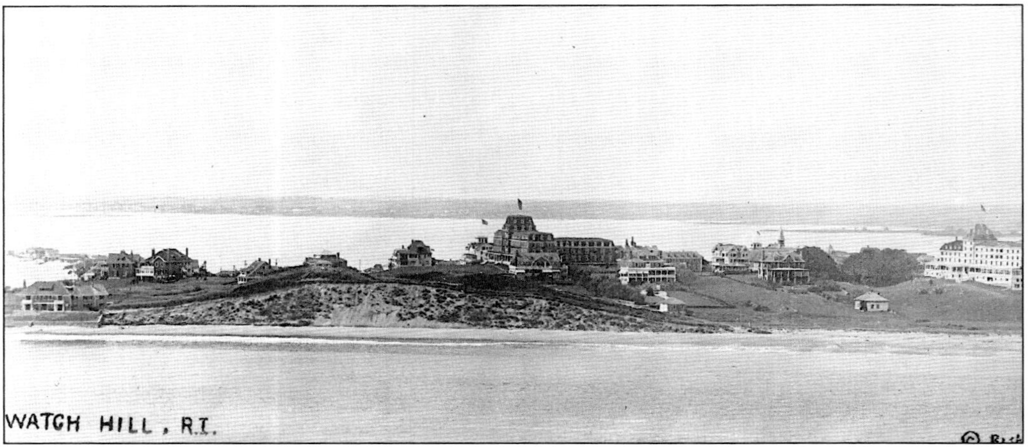

"In short, there's simply not a more congenial spot; For happy ever-aftering than here in Camelot" (*Camelot*, 1960). At one time three magnificent hotels stood atop East Beach, but such things are no more. The Ocean House, to the right, still stands; however, the Watch Hill House, mid-center, was consumed by fire in 1916 and the majestic Larkin House, which stood upon the vacant plot of acreage to the left, was torn down in 1906. The postmark from the long-ago Watch Hill Station is a lonely memento from the time when there were but two hotels on East Beach. (WPL.)

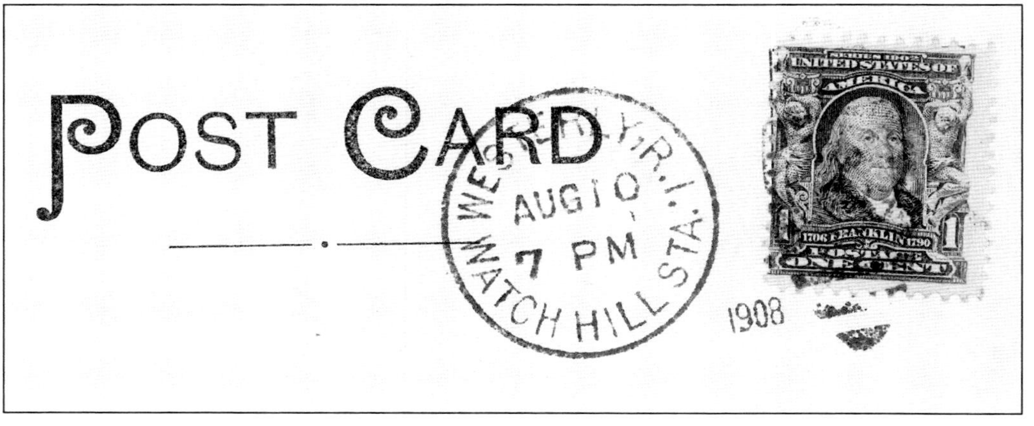

Five

BY THE SEA

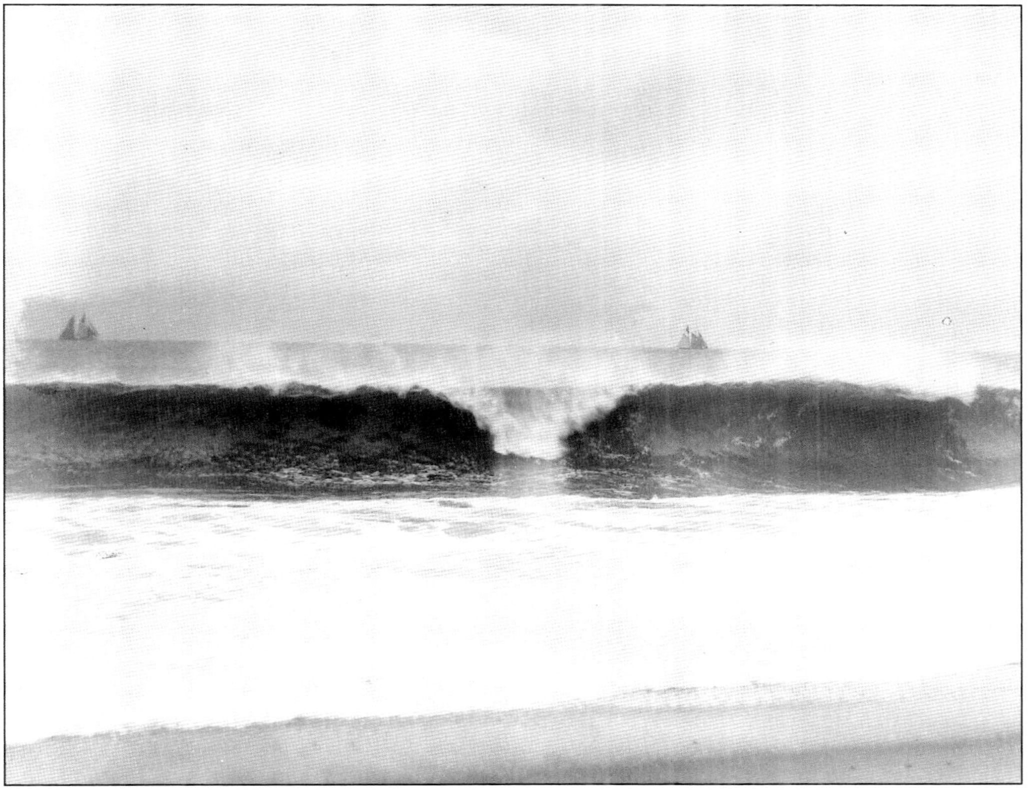

Watch Hill promotional literature from 1887 notes that "the East Beach . . . is one of the greatest attractions of the place. On this magnificent shore the surf never ceases . . . A storm on the wide waters of the Atlantic or a stiff gale on the coast, drives the huge breakers for miles along the barless coast with a fury that appalls. Then, indeed, one beholds the mighty ocean in its grandeur and power, and hears the thunder of its voice" (*Historical Souvenir of Watch Hill*). Located northeast of Lighthouse Point, East Beach was generally regarded as the more dangerous of Watch Hill's two bathing beaches. Promotional literature from 1882 provides that "on the great East Beach the breakers are generally too heavy and the undertow too dangerous to admit of bathing" (*Watch Hill, A Description . . .*). The full sail carried by the two distant schooners suggest that these breakers are rolling toward the beach in light to moderate weather. (GHU-Burdick.)

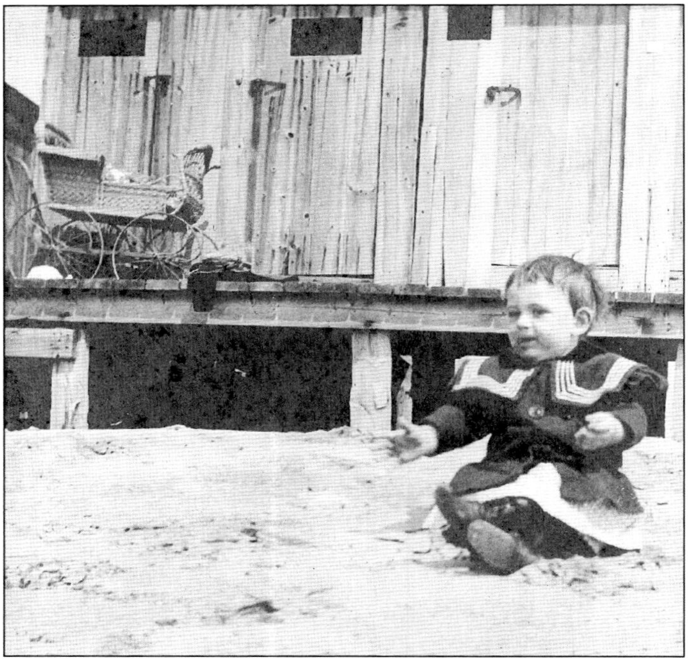

Porter Hoxie, a native "Watch Hiller," sits steadily before the "old" bathhouses on Napatree Bathing Beach in the early 1900s. Note the wicker baby carriage on the veranda of the bathhouse. (JM.)

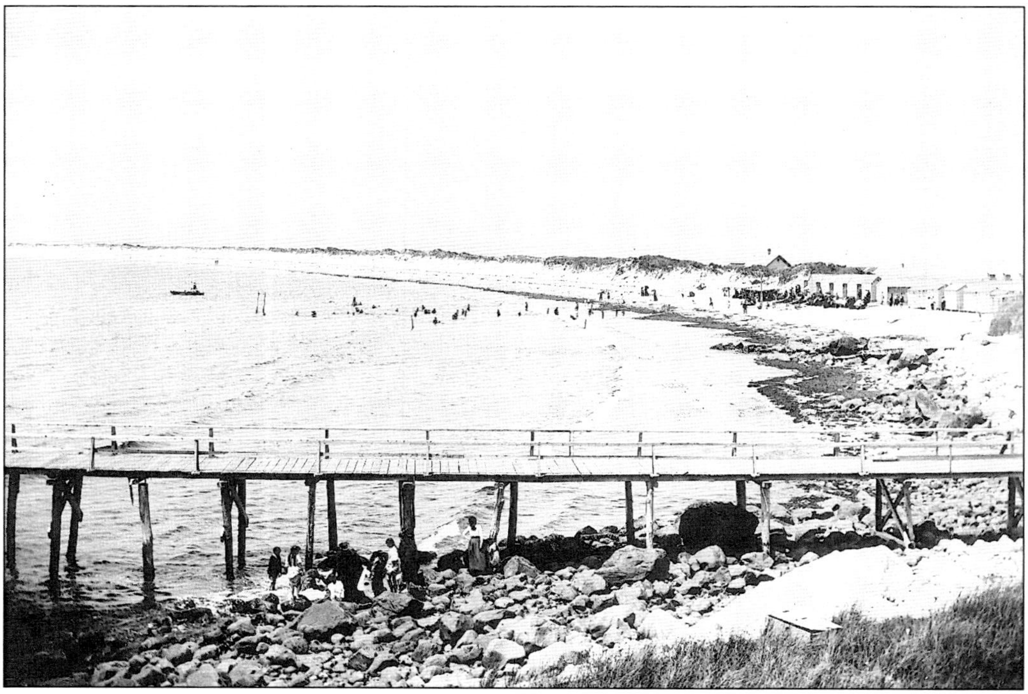

This ocean-side pier was constructed in 1881 as a landing site for the steamer *George R. Kelsey*. The *Kelsey* would take passengers from Watch Hill to Stonington, where they could connect with the steamer *Belle* for passage to Block Island on Mondays, Wednesdays, Fridays, and Saturdays. Note that the south shore of Napatree has yet to be developed with the Fort Road cottages. (GHU-Burdick.)

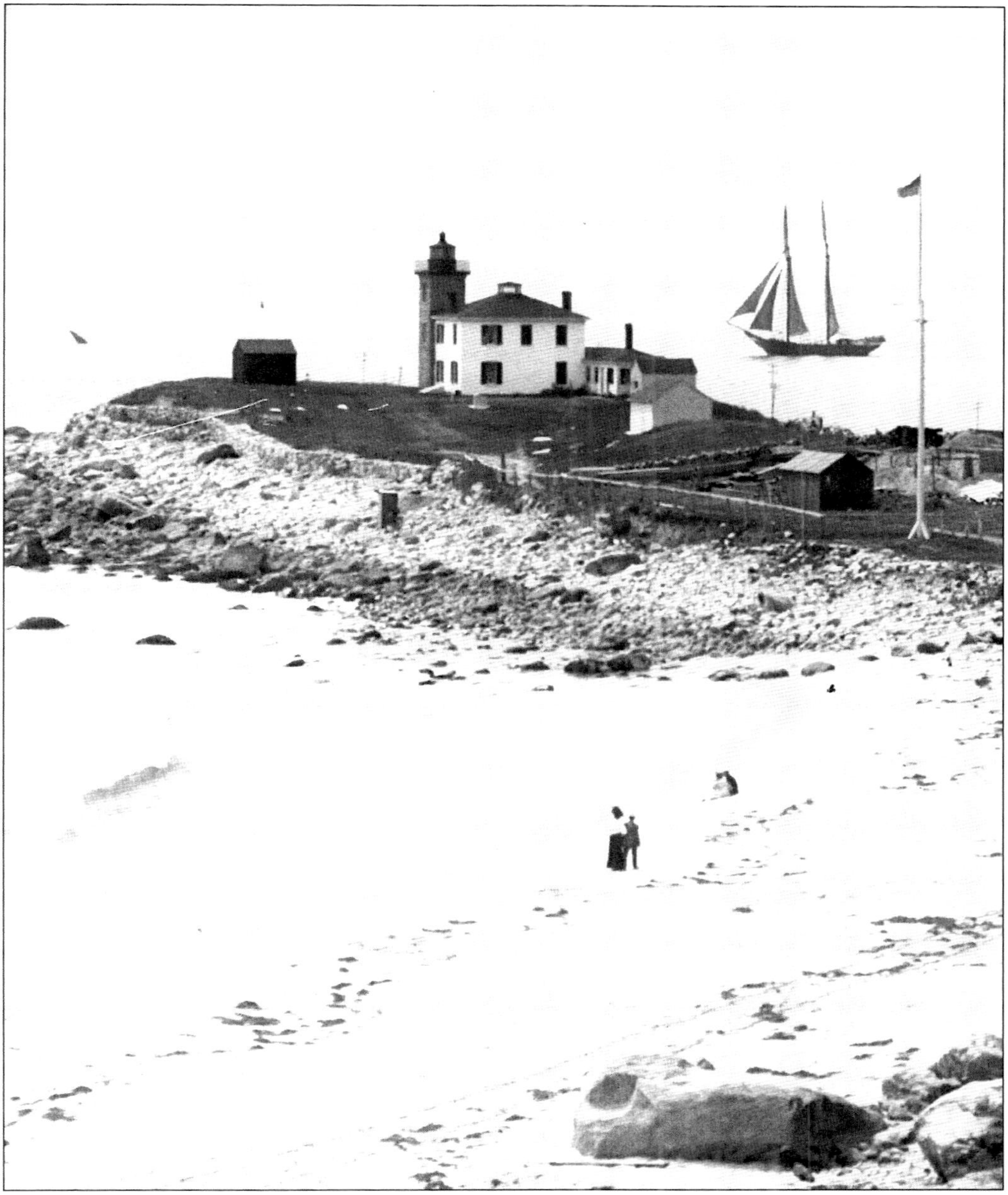

". . . You hold her hand
And she holds yours
And that's a very good sign
That she's your tootsy wootsy
In the good old summertime . . ."

—*In the Good Old Summertime*, 1949
(GHU-Burdick.)

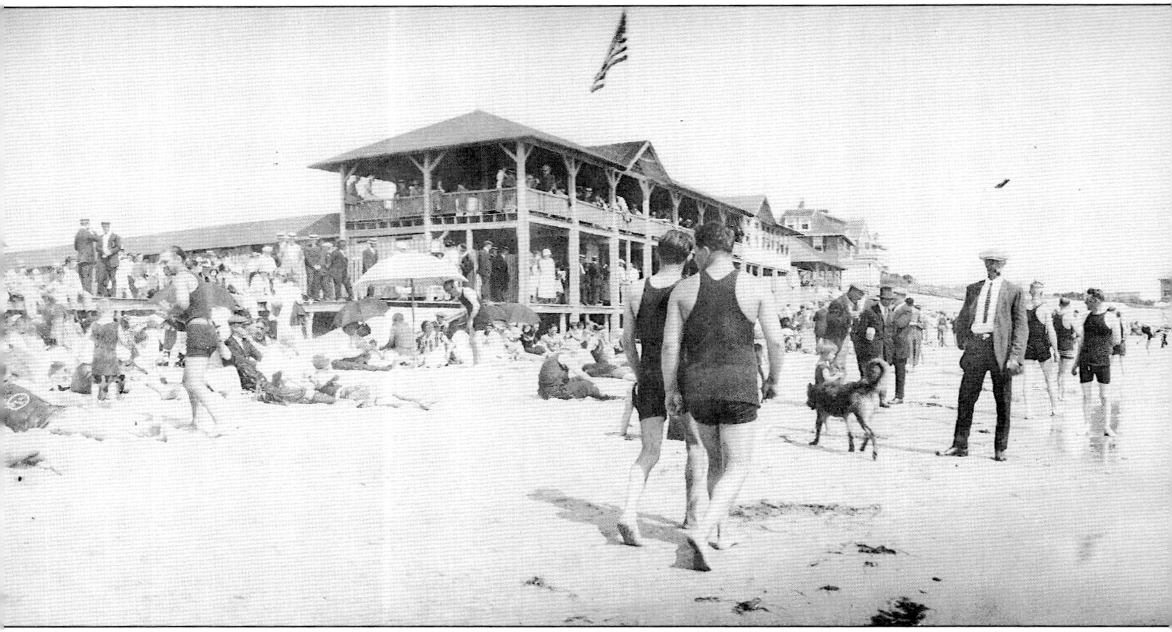

"By the sea, by the sea, by the beautiful sea; you and me,

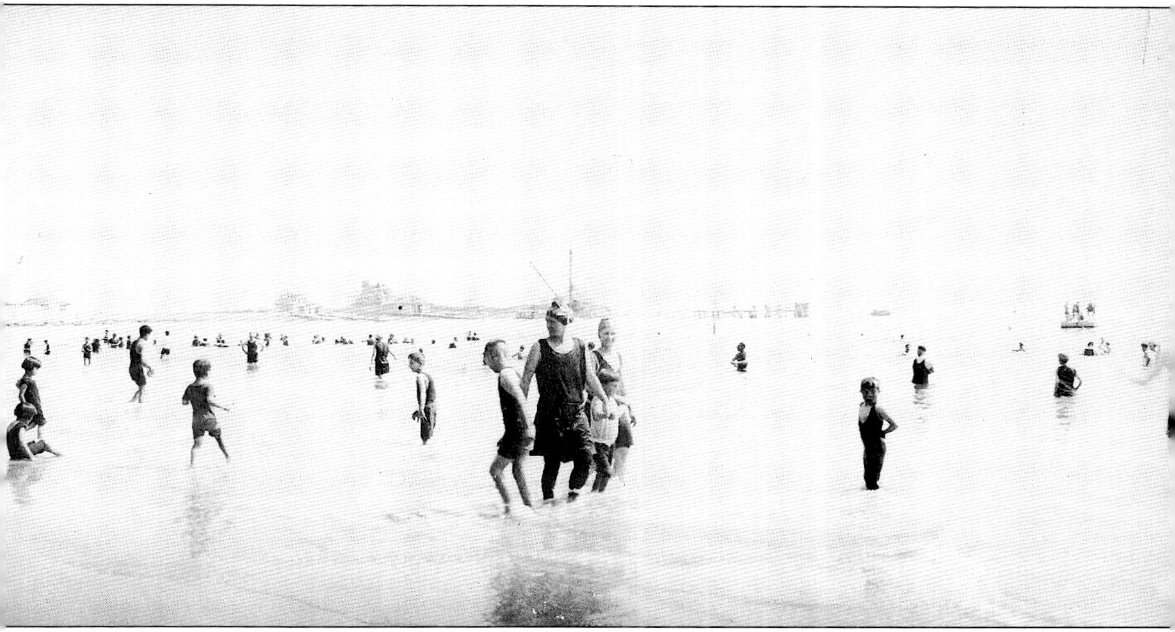

you and me, oh how happy we'll be. . ." (GHU.)

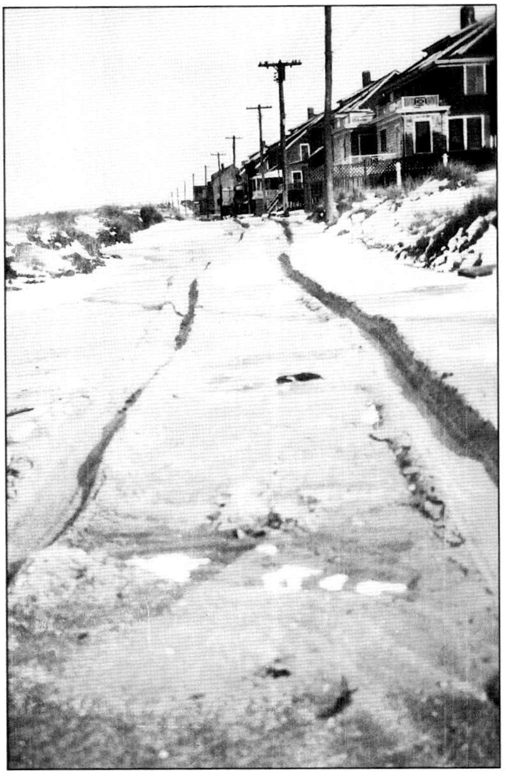

Eel grass, frozen sand, and snow are rare sights today for most visitors to Watch Hill. This scene depicts just another winter's day for the denizens of Fort Road when they peered out of their windows toward Little Narragansett Bay. (JM.)

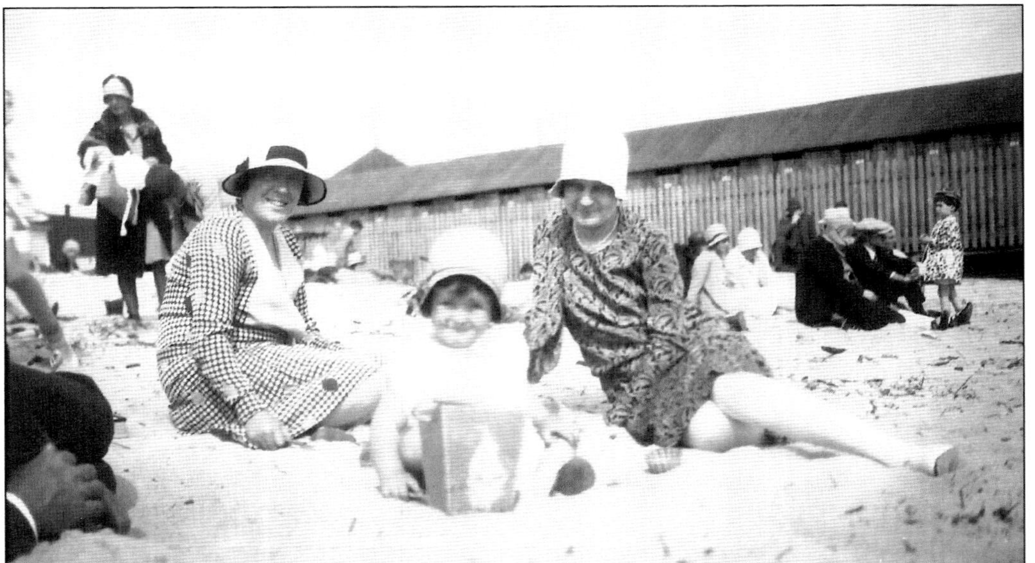

Jane Hoxie Maxson (center) and her mother, Isabelle Hoxie (on the left), relax upon their sandy perch before the old public bathhouses on Napatree Bathing Beach. It is a rare moment nowadays that one will find such attire, complete with hats, worn by the ladies at the beach. Note young Jane's wooden pail. (JM.)

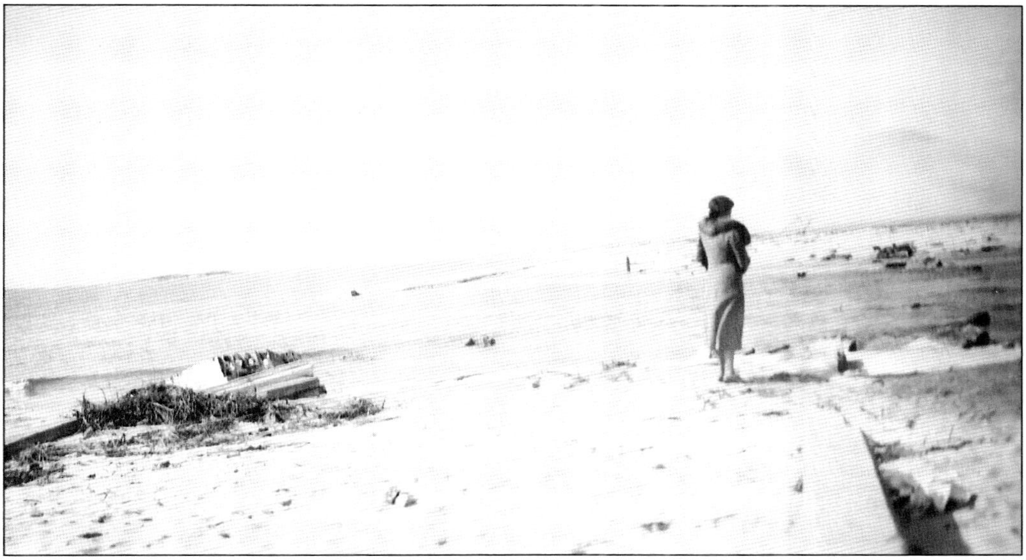

Standing near the current site of the beach cabanas, a woman peers westward over the breachway that was cut through Napatree in the wake of the devastating Hurricane of '38. Note the retaining wall at right that once abutted the cove. Old Colonial-period maps show a similar breachway that was cut through Napatree at nearly the same location—such is the way of the killer gale, such is its path. (JM.)

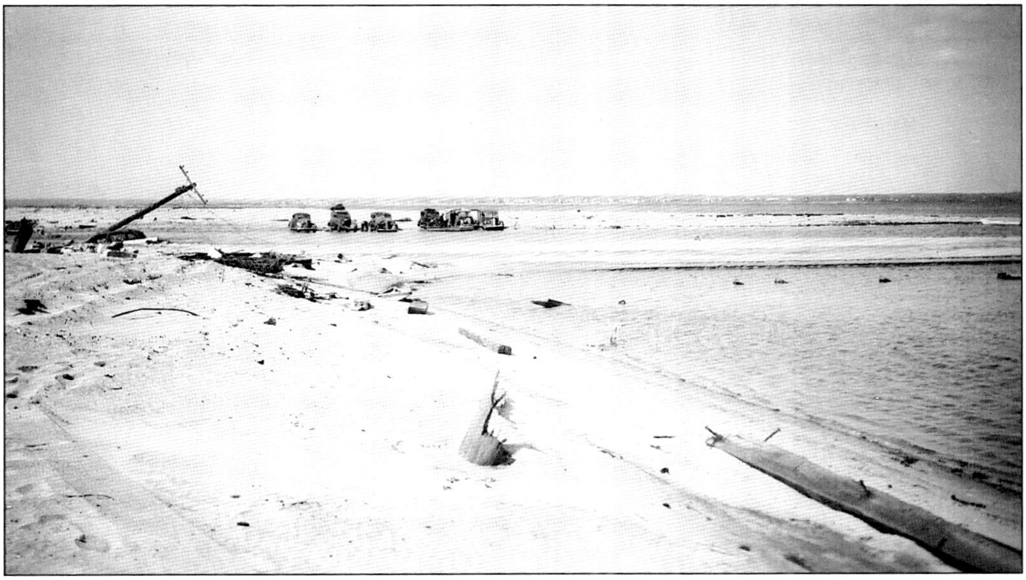

A toppled telephone pole stands sentinel over a fleet of cars from Fort Road that were used to fill in the breachway cut through Napatree by the '38 Hurricane. Lives were lost and countless structures were demolished around Watch Hill. In the midst of the storm's fury, a young girl turned to her parents and said "mummy, if I must die, I want my rosary" (*Tidings*, 1996). (JM.)

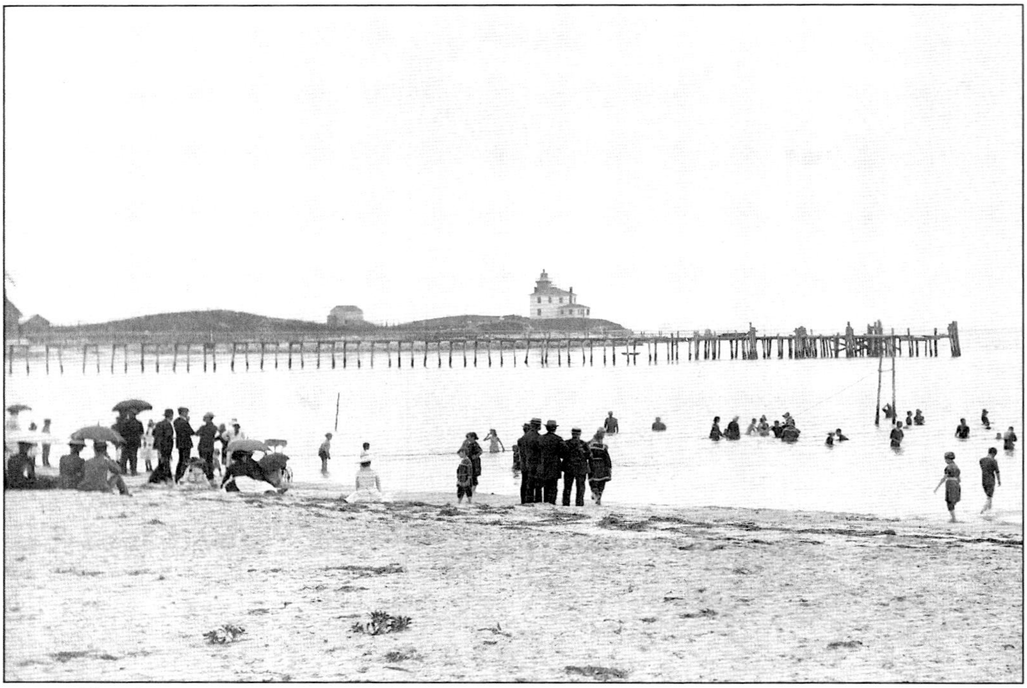

Framed by the steamer dock with Lighthouse Point in the background, the Napatree Bathing Beach was a draw for both adults and children alike in the first decades of this century. A 1905 ad noted, "Swimming taught by P.F. Cavil of the famous family of amateur and professional champions, who will train here at Watch Hill for the World's Championship Race at Newport in August." (WPL.)

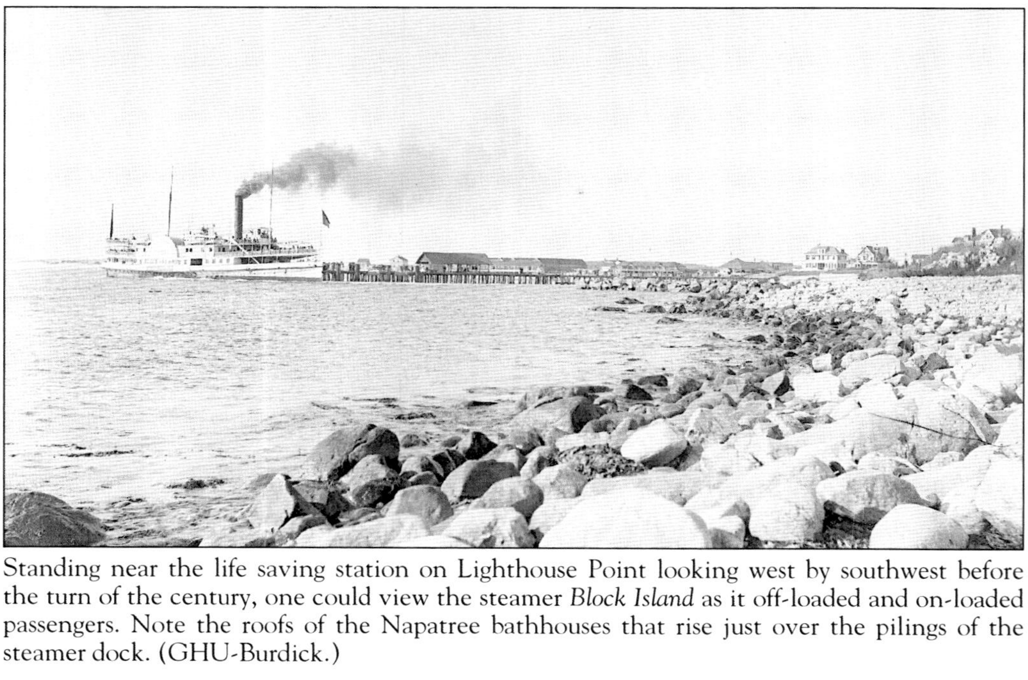

Standing near the life saving station on Lighthouse Point looking west by southwest before the turn of the century, one could view the steamer *Block Island* as it off-loaded and on-loaded passengers. Note the roofs of the Napatree bathhouses that rise just over the pilings of the steamer dock. (GHU-Burdick.)

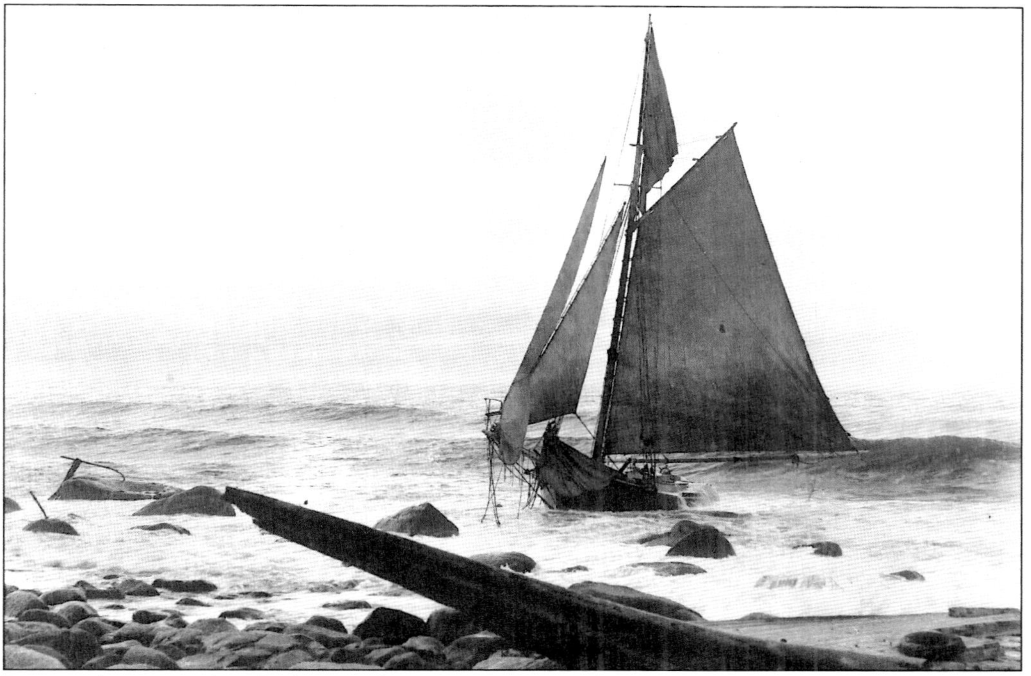

During the Age of Sail, shipwrecks were a matter of course and the spoils of such wrecks oftentimes littered both East Beach and Napatree. Lt. Oliver Hazard Perry, for instance, in the War of 1812, lost the 14-gun schooner *Revenge* on Watch Hill Reef. Likewise, the fishing smack *Annie* met her fate at Quonochontaug in 1899. (GHU-Burdick.)

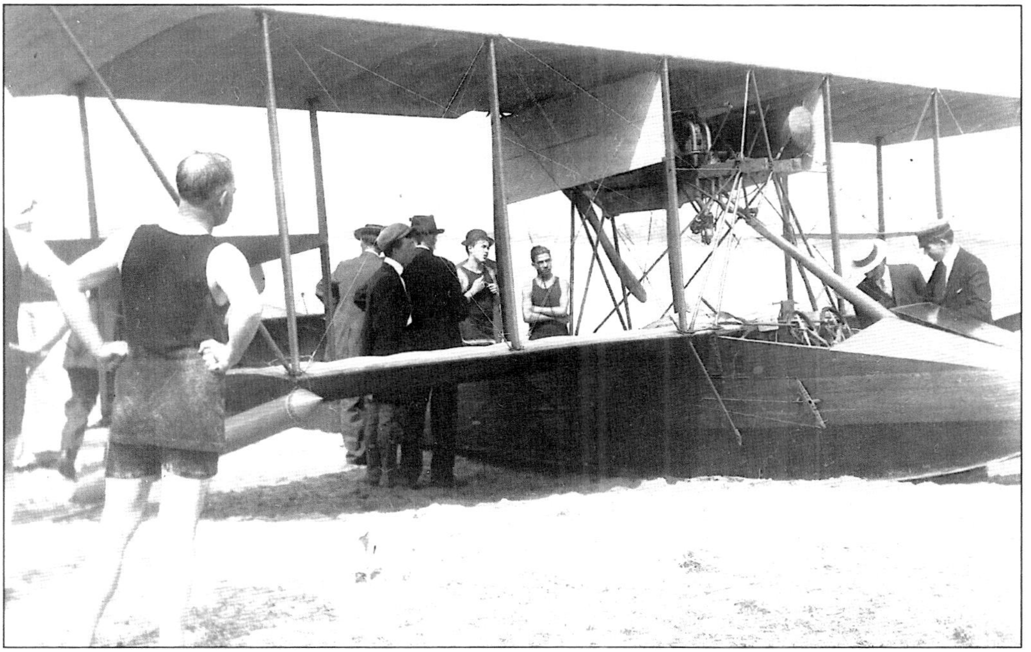

A flying craft on Napatree is observed by curious onlookers. Note the cut of the men's bathing suits. (DB.)

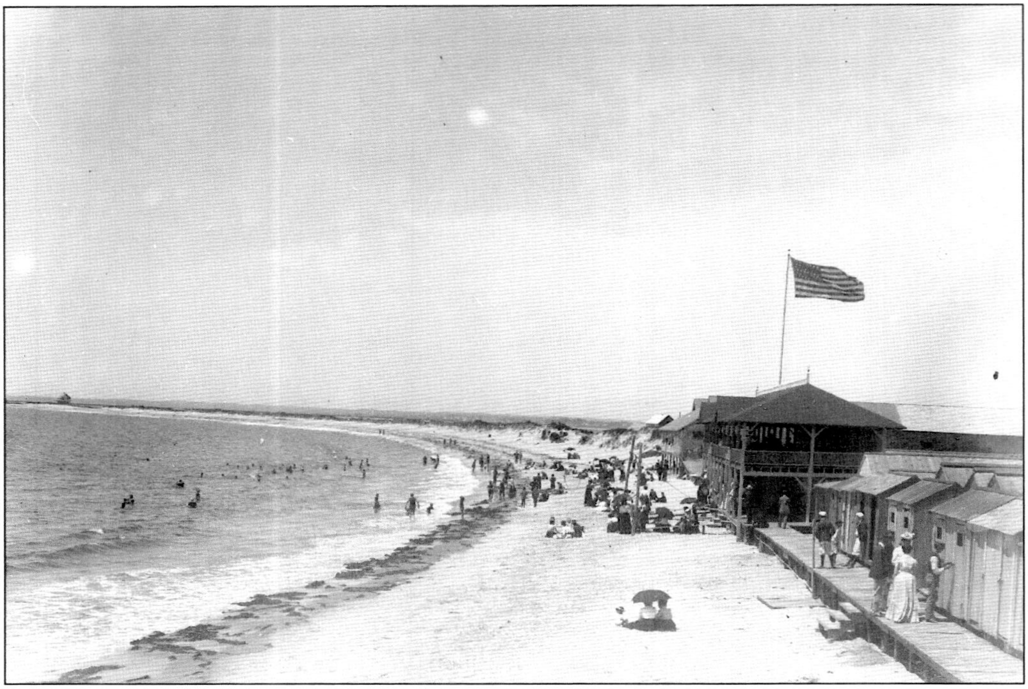

Bathhouses stretch across Napatree beneath a stiff southerly breeze in July 1900. It was said of Napatree Beach before the turn of the century that "it is so protected from the prevailing summer winds and currents that it is very rarely too strong for ladies and children. It is of such a gradual slope that bathers can go far out into the waters with safety" (*Historical Souvenir of Watch Hill*). (DB.)

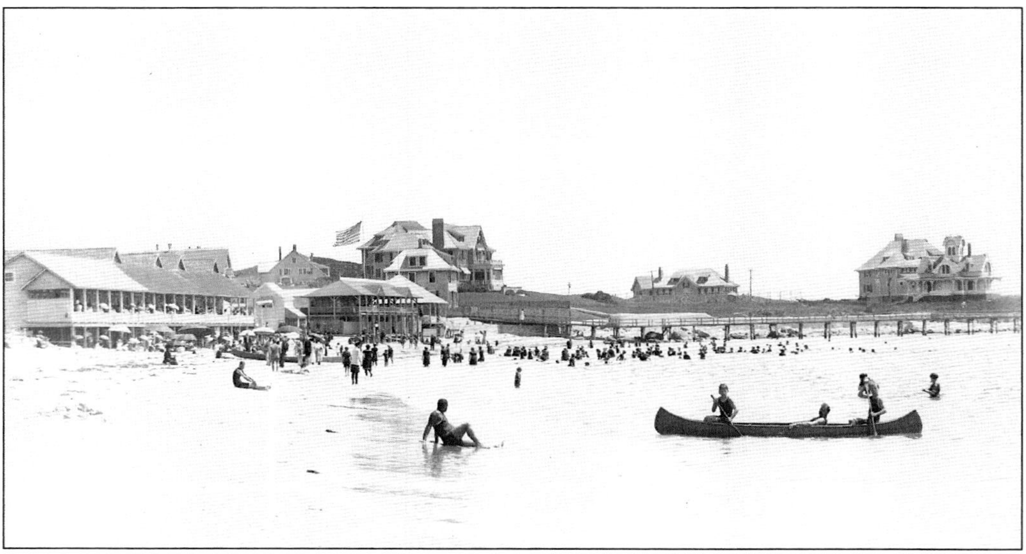

Early promotional literature also noted that "the facilities for bathing are unusually good. The lighthouse promontory against which the sea dashes from the east affords a natural breakwater to check the violence of the waves, and just southwest of this is the safe and beautiful Napatree Beach" (*Historical Souvenir of Watch Hill*). (WHS.)

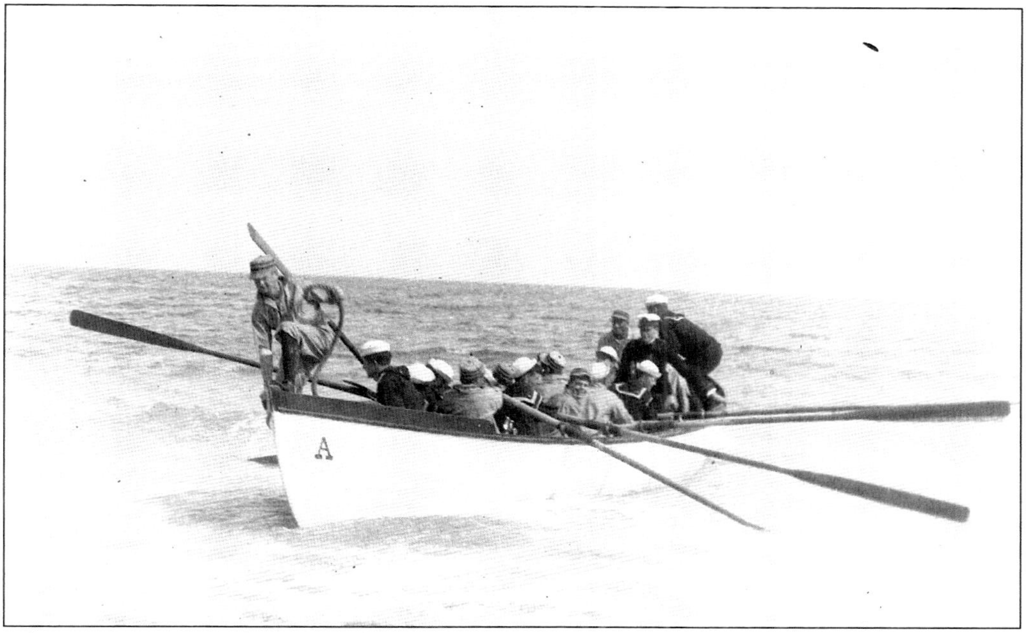

Life saving station volunteers ride a wave into Napatree. "The life-savers of the Watch Hill and Fishers Island Life Saving Stations had a rather unpleasant experience Tuesday, when they struggled all day to free the tern schooner *Grace Seymour*, which had lain helpless in Long Island Sound, about four miles south of Watch Hill, for two days" (*The Westerly Sun*, October 1909). (DB.)

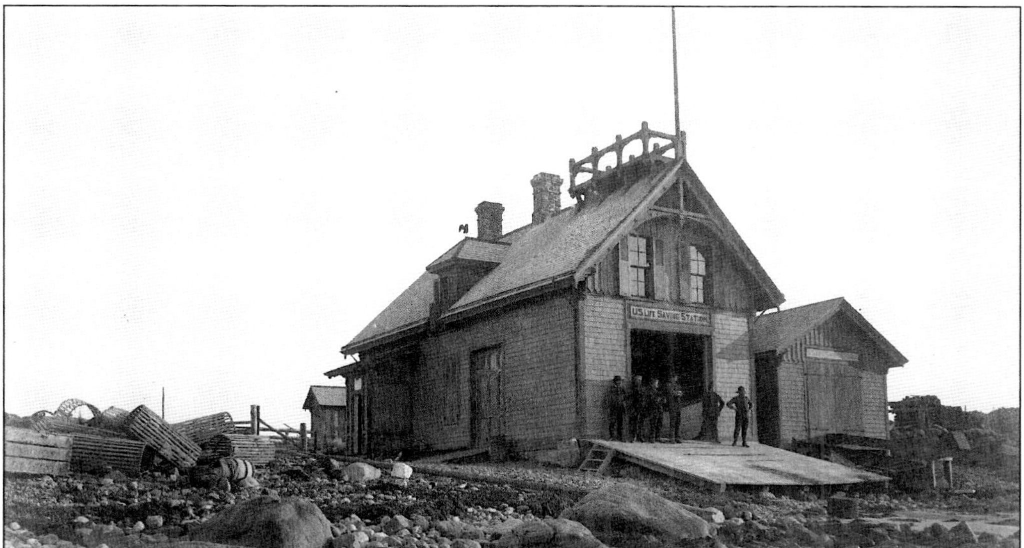

The Watch Hill Life Saving Station, built in 1879, stands dead center on Lighthouse Point. Life saving was an age-old and dangerous occupation for Watch Hillers. Regarding the wreck of the *Metis* in 1872, "they tell strange stories about manning these boats. Many hesitated about going out to what they considered certain death. Some stoutly refused, and one said he wouldn't go for $2,000,000" (*Seaside Topics*, September 1915). (GHU.)

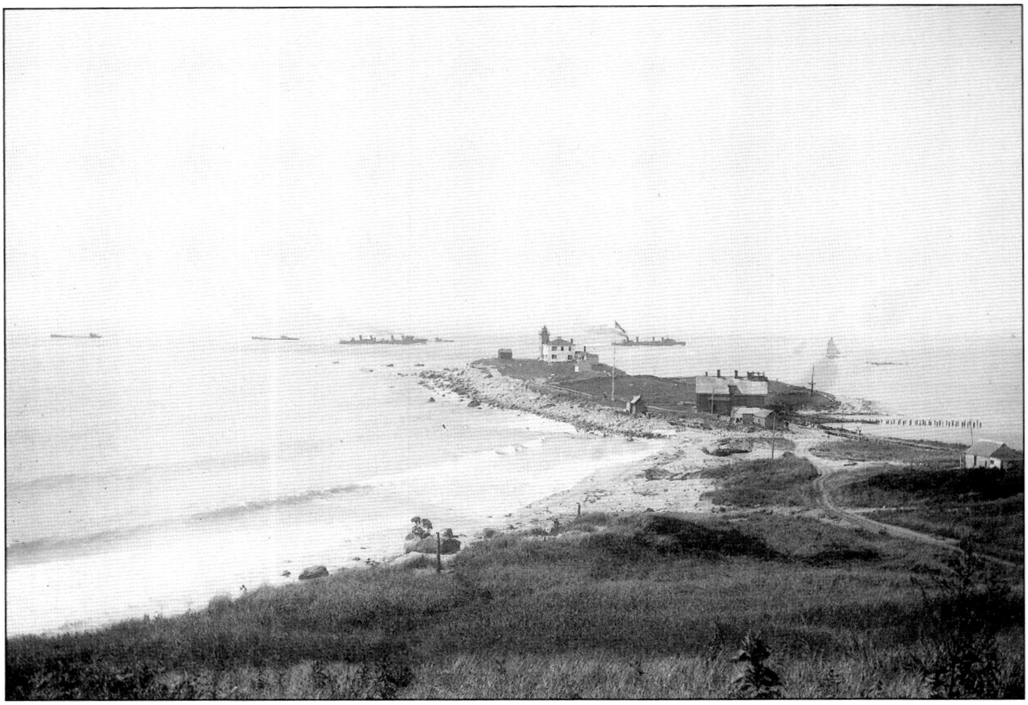

"So it can be seen that the light is not a lonesome place as many people think. Just to look out over the water and then up at the light watching the beams going out to sea and thinking of all the lives that have been saved, one can see that men here live up to their name 'keepers of the light' " (Mrs. F.C. Shreenan). (GHU-Burdick.)

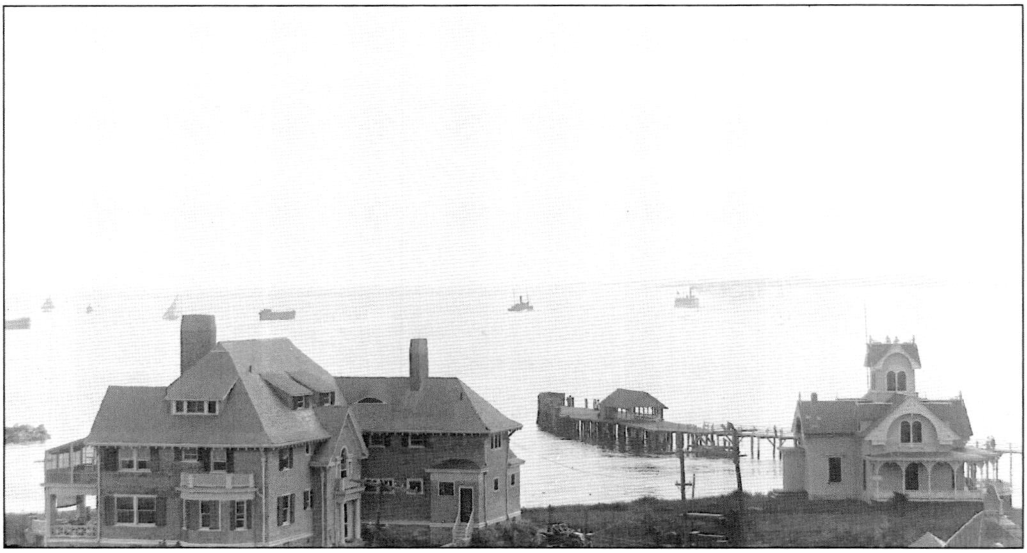

What is today a yellow Victorian house on Lighthouse Point overlooks the steamer dock and Fishers Island Sound in 1910. Note the *Block Island* on her way to New London to the upper right. (DB.)

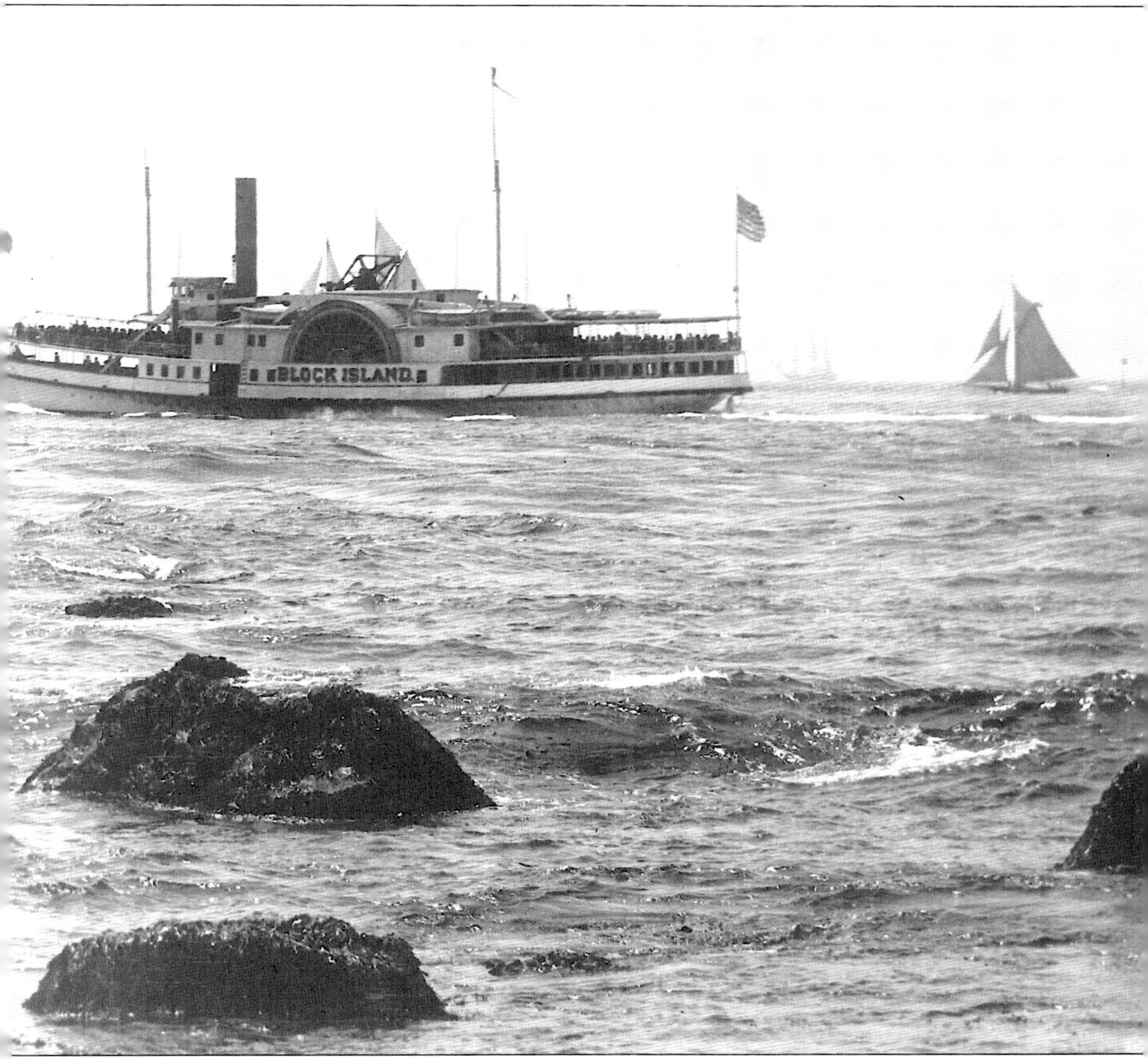

The steamer *Block Island* rounds Lighthouse Point en route to Block Island. During the 1890s and early 1900s, Walter Hiscox of Western Union would send a telegram to Watch Hill once the steamer disembarked from New London. This telegram, which was sent to the Watch Hill bathhouses and the Shore Dinner, alerted Watch Hill as to how many passengers were aboard. Hiscox noted in an article in *The Westerly Daily Sun* that "when the boat landed, people would run for the bathing beach, later for the Shore Dinner and then they were back to the boat again on their way back to New London and Norwich late in the afternoon." Note the staysails that the smaller sloops have set in the southeast breeze and the square-rigged ship in the rear center. (GHU-Burdick.)

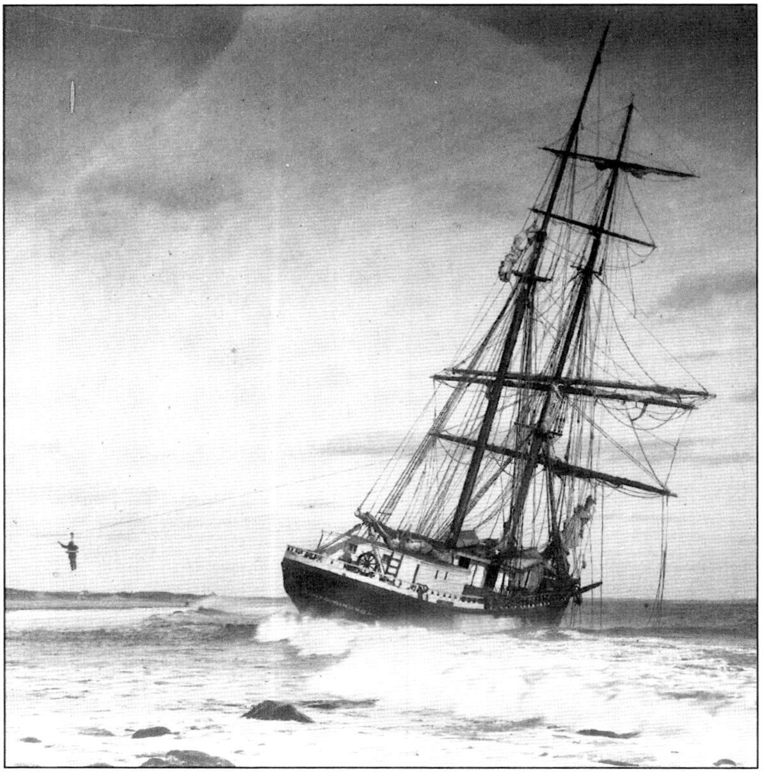

Her sails blown to tatters by a gale, the British brig *Toronto* of Windsor, Nova Scotia, was washed up on East Beach on the morning of November 25, 1886. Being unable to launch the lifeboats because of enormous surf, Captain Nash and the Watch Hill Life Saving Station were able to rescue eight men with the aid of a breeches buoy. Note the man swinging above the surf en route to safety. (WHS.)

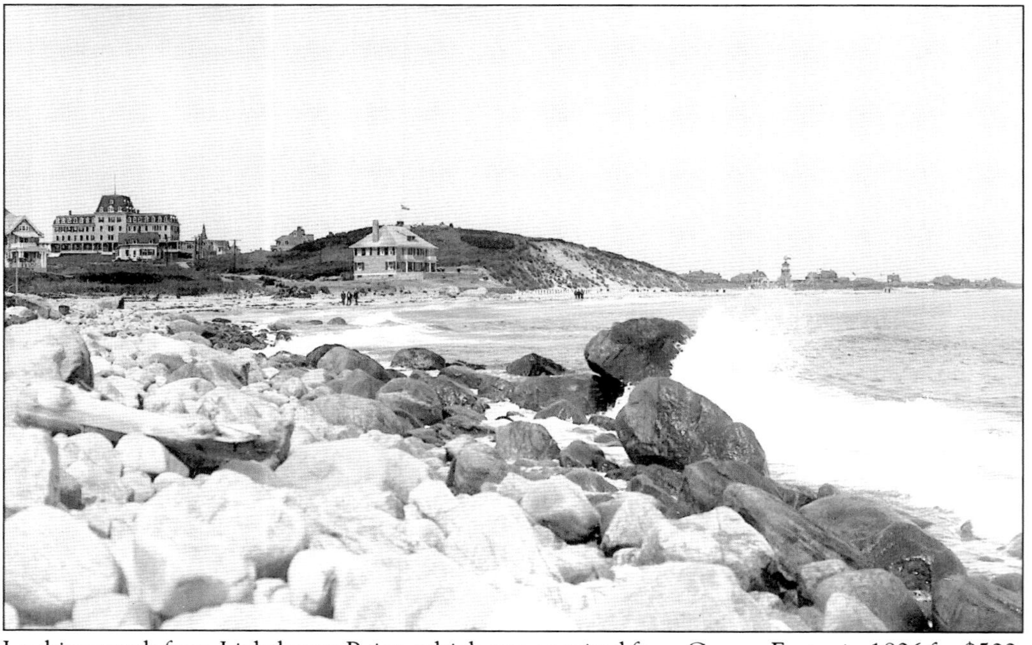

Looking north from Lighthouse Point, which was acquired from George Foster in 1806 for $500, a turn-of-the-century viewer would witness East Beach, its pounding surf, and the relatively undeveloped shoreline. (GHU-Burdick.)

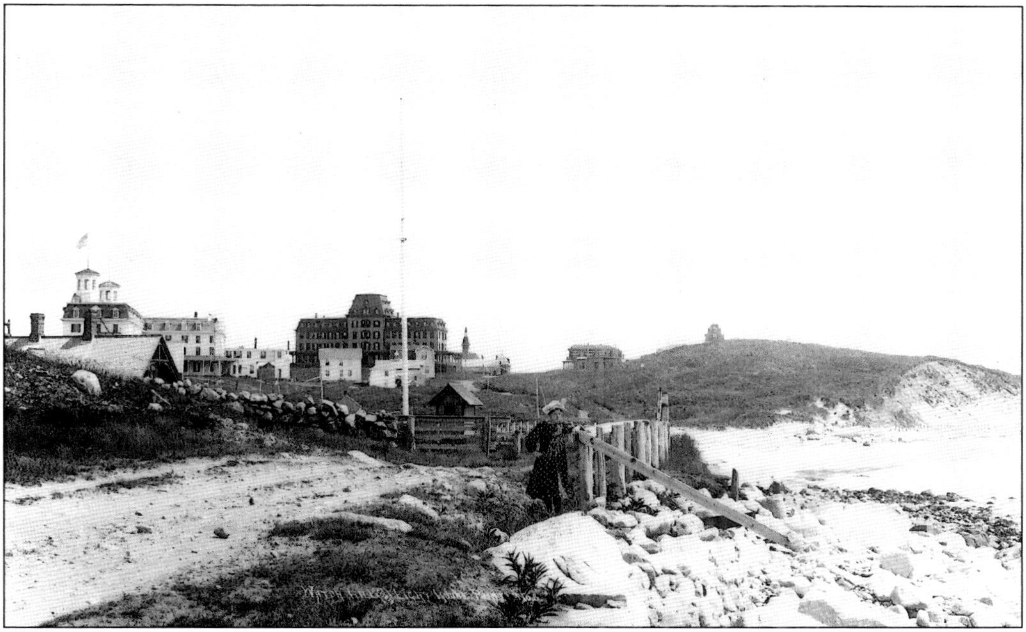

Strolling back from the lighthouse in the 1890s, one would note the undeveloped Lookout Hill to the right, the Watch Hill House behind the flagpole, and the twin cupolas of the Larkin House to the upper left. Also visible are the roofline and chimneys of the original life saving station above the stone wall to the left. A solitary woman peers into a light southeast wind. (GHU-Burdick.)

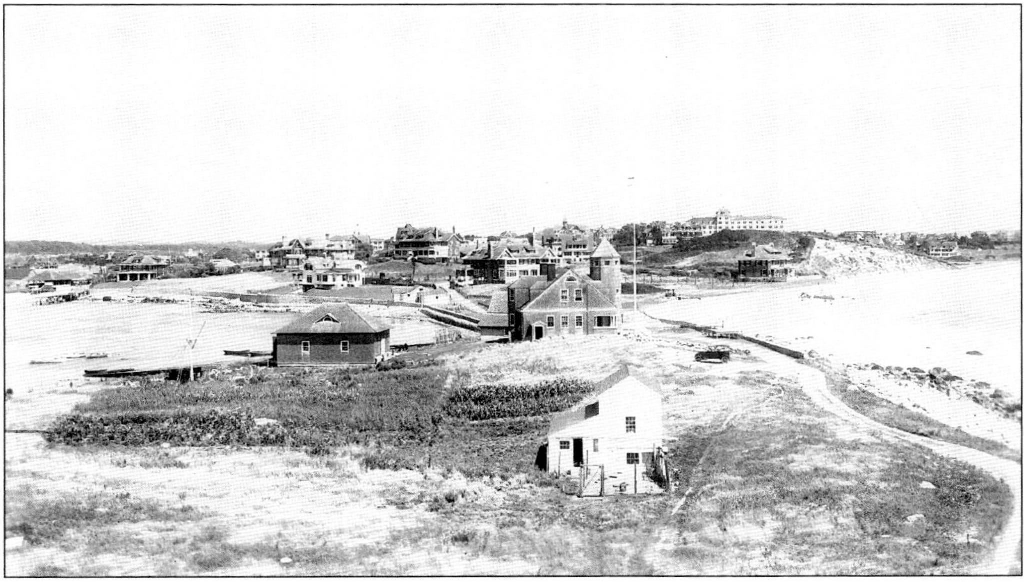

A panoramic view from the lighthouse looking northward is shown as the Ocean House looms above East Beach on the right, the steeple of Watch Hill Chapel is dead center, and the life saving station is to the left. In the early 1900s, an annual women's swimming race started on East Beach below the Ocean House and went out around the lighthouse to a private raft off Napatree beach, a distance of 1.5 miles. (DB.)

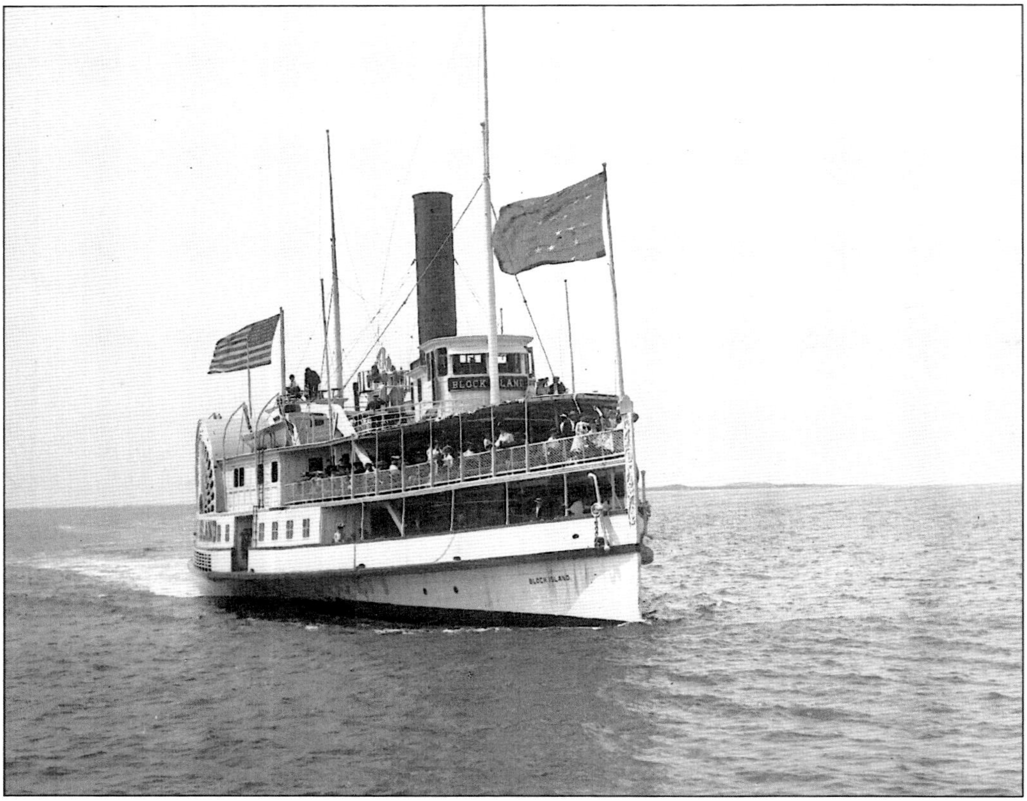

The *Block Island* had a busy schedule during 1899, calling outbound upon: Norwich, 8:15 a.m.; Montville, 8:45 a.m.; New London, 9:45 a.m.; Mystic Island, 10:15 a.m.; Watch Hill, 10:55 a.m.; and, Block Island, 12:30 p.m. By 6:15 in the evening, she was back in Norwich, awaiting the next day's journey. (GHU-Burdick.)

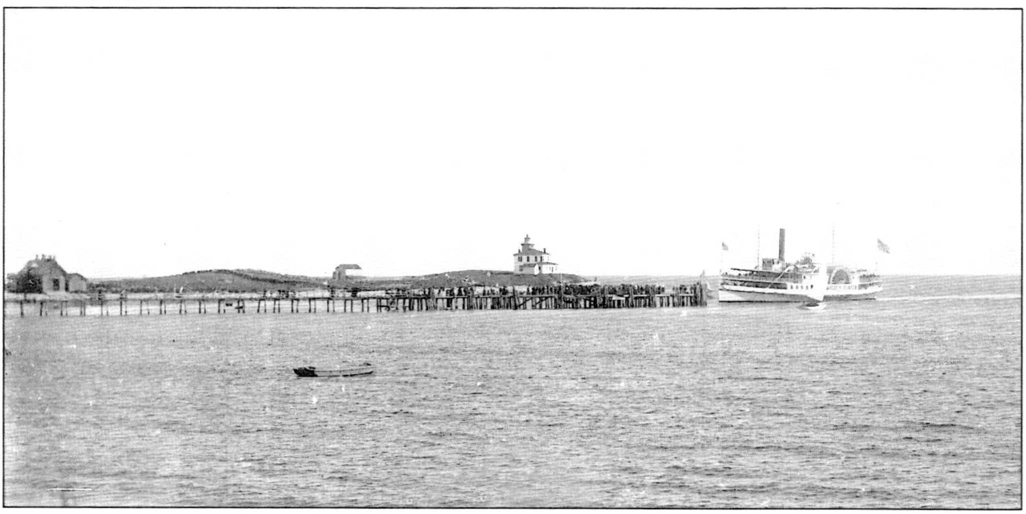

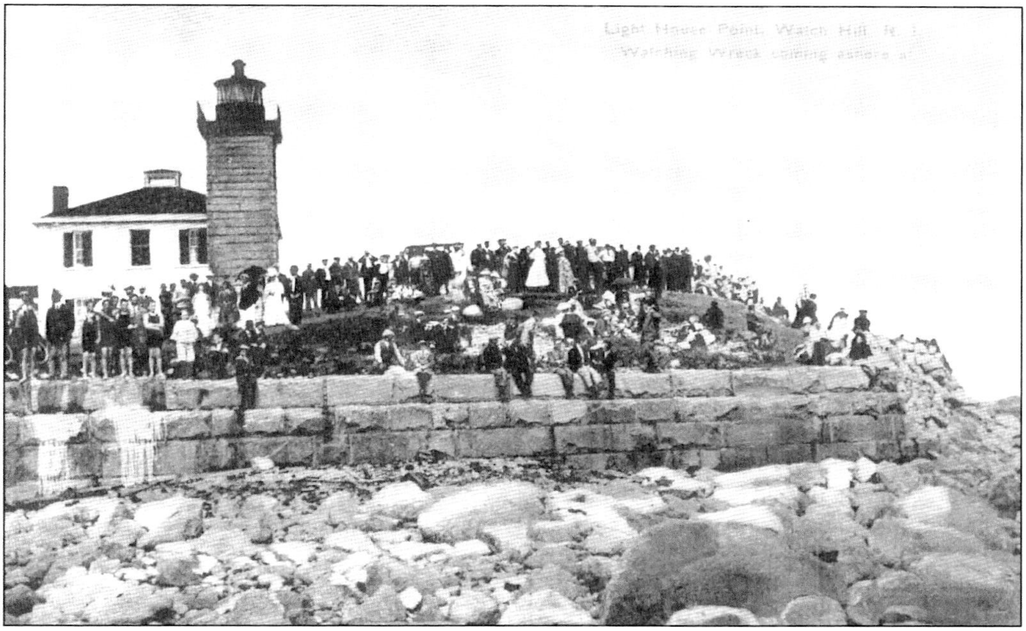

Folks gather upon the retaining wall that protects the lighthouse to watch a wreck that is being washed ashore. The massive blocks of granite that were used to construct this seawall were quarried at Millstone Point (the site of the current nuclear power plant) in Waterford and ferried to Watch Hill by Captain Jason P. West in his scow *Jason*. (BAFR.)

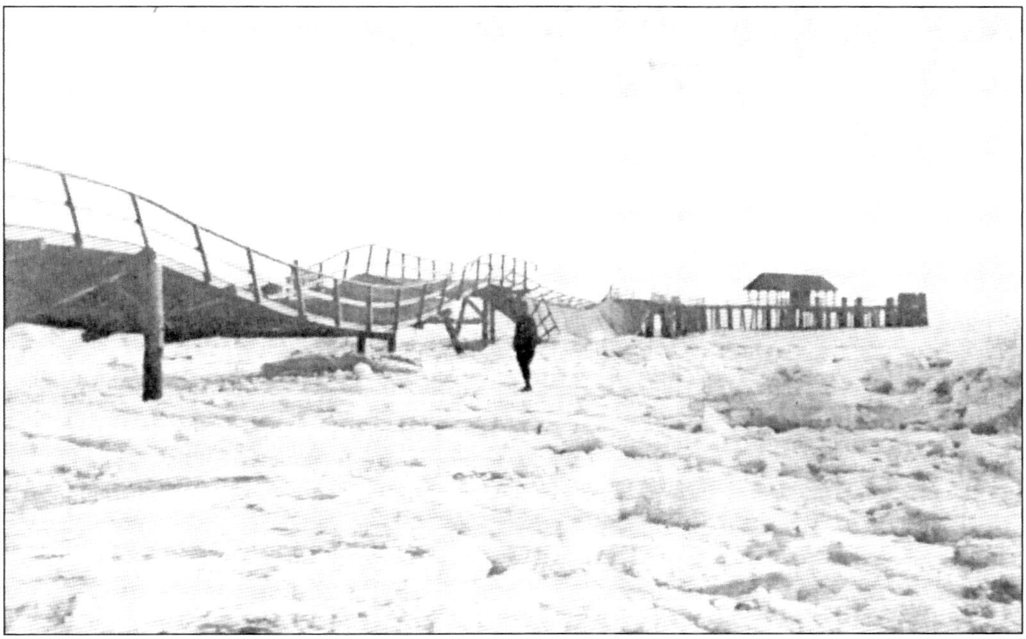

By all accounts, the winter of 1917–18 was one of the most severe on record along the Connecticut and Rhode Island coastlines. The Block Island steamer dock that jutted out into Fishers Island Sound was twisted, broken, and ultimately demolished, never to be rebuilt, by the winter ice that attended this harsh winter. (WPL.)

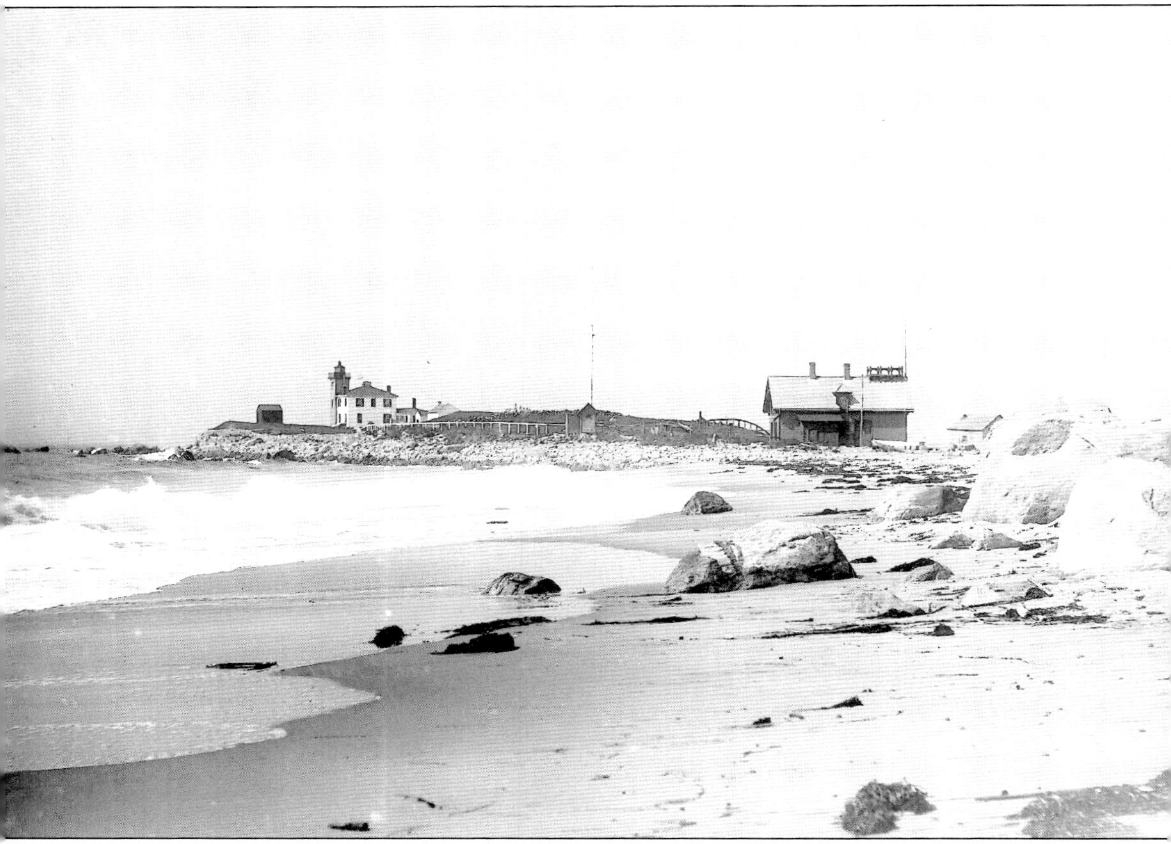

Looking south from East Beach in 1896, the second lighthouse and the first life saving station are visible on Lighthouse Point. The first lighthouse was constructed in 1808. The second lighthouse, which stands to this day, was constructed in 1855. The original life saving station was built in 1879 and supplanted by a new building in 1908. As regards the life saving station, "there have been four keepers—Captains Barber, Clark, John Nash and Walter H. Davis. Since the keeping of the present record books in 1883, there have been 54 disasters. Of these, only in two instances has there been a loss of life" (*Watch Hill Life*, 1895). (GHU-Burdick.)

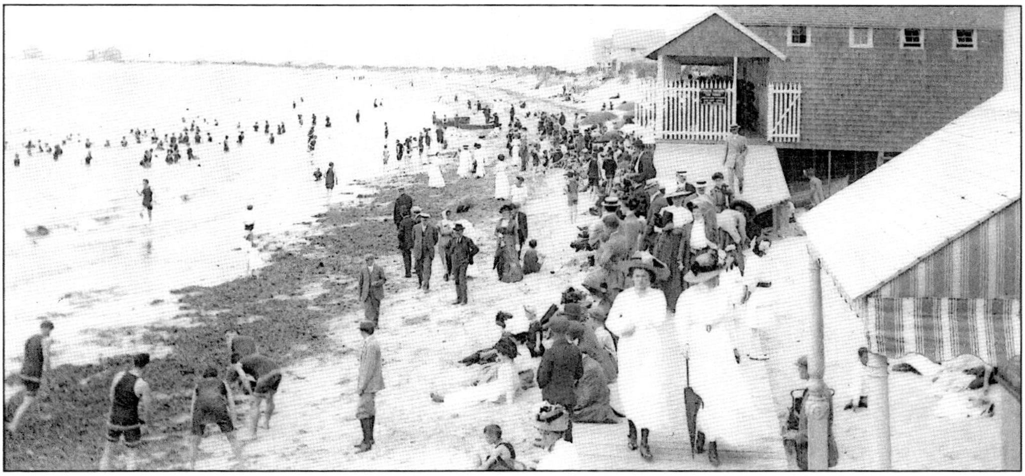

Looking west toward Napatree Point, note the restricted attire for the ladies. One longtime summer visitor remembered, "I wore a black, very full dress belted at the waist, very full shirred skirt that came down over my knees, and long black stockings with garters at the top and black sneakers . . . we were very, very discreetly clad . . . we didn't show any more of our skin than we did when we were on the street" (*Life's Little Pleasures*). (GHU-Burdick.)

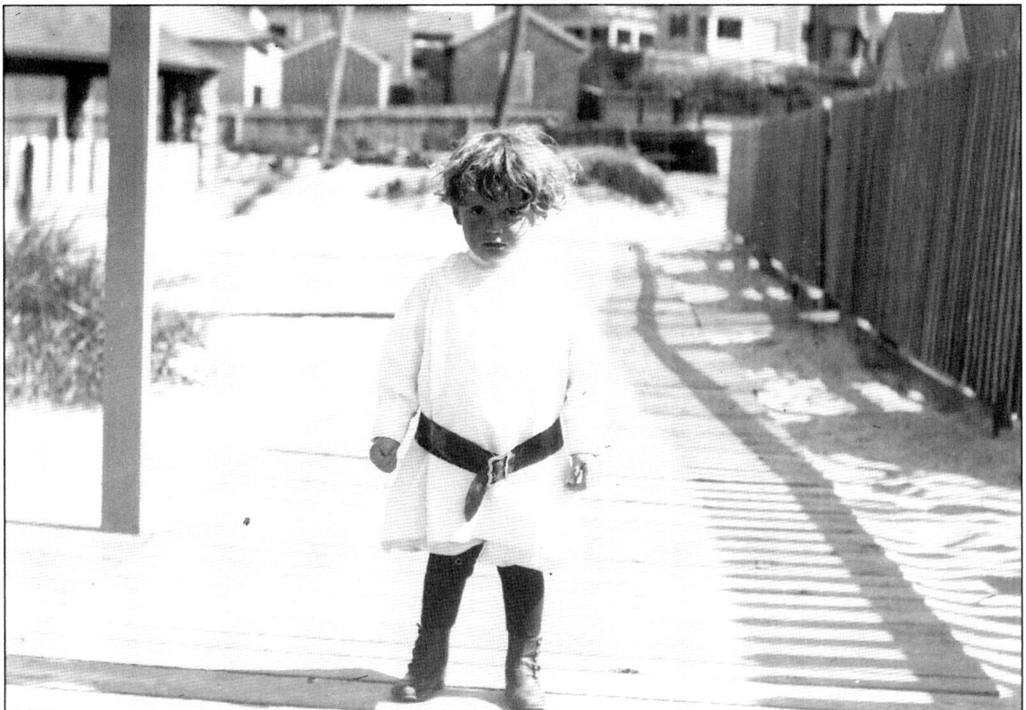

The wild hair suggests that this child just came off the carousel, which is pictured to the back left. Legend has it that the "live" horse that originally powered the carousel in the late 1800s would occasionally slip the confines of his warm stable in the wintertime and return to Watch Hill, where his master would "find 'old faithful' treading his circular path in winter solitude" (*Around and Around*). (DB.)

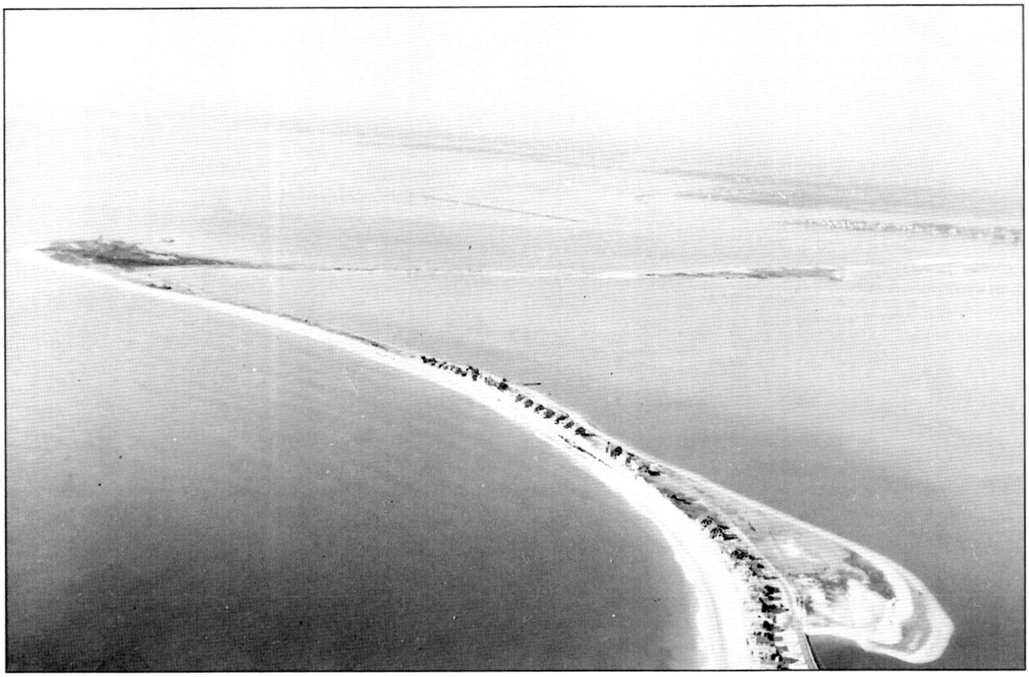

Prior to the infamous Hurricane of '38, Sandy Point was connected to and pivoted off Napatree from the "Naps" at a right angle—such was the way of things from the early 1800s. The hurricane amputated Sandy Point from Napatree in 1938 and Sandy Point has pursued a peripatetic journey north by northwest toward Stonington ever since. (DB.)

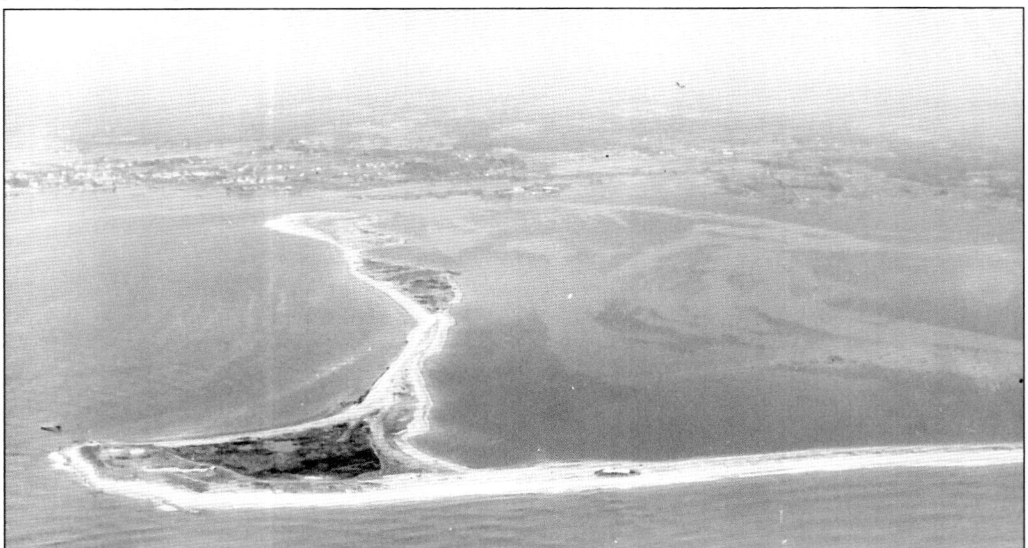

Napatree, so called because of the "Nap" of trees that once forested its western terminus, is now a concave peninsula that abuts Fishers Island Sound to the south and Little Narragansett Bay to the north. The Great Gale of 1815 permanently denuded the Nap and forever altered its topography. Lighthouse keeper Jonathan Nash claims that Napatree once ran in a straight line from Watch Hill to the Nap. (DB.)

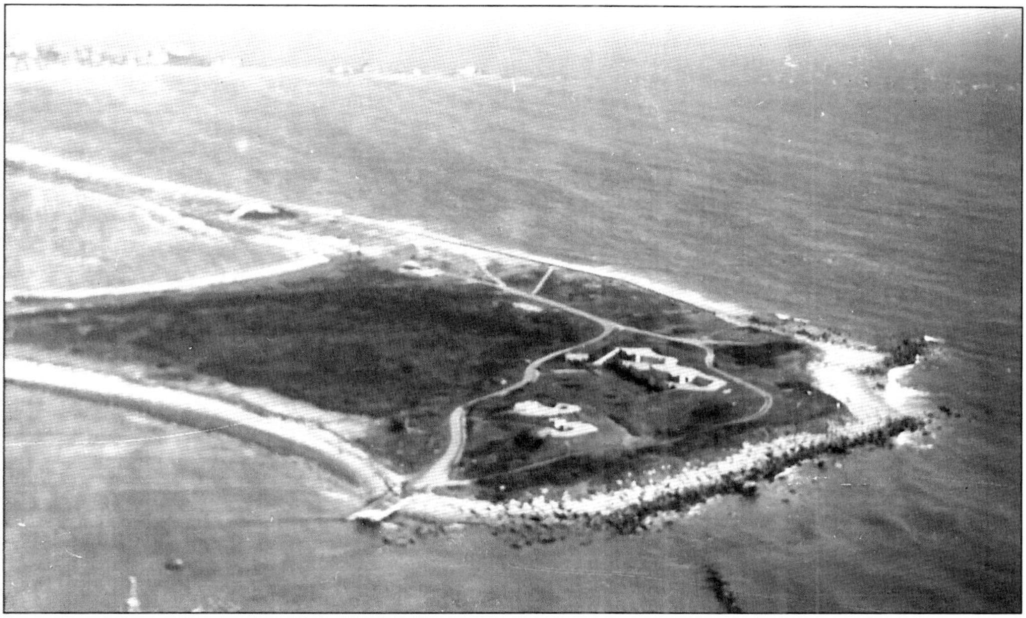

Fort Mansfield was built upon the Nap at Napatree in 1901. "It may be news to some Watch Hill people that the Hill is included in the government's plan of fortifying the eastern end of Long Island Sound. Some time ago a tract of sixty acres on Napatree Point, beginning a little beyond the Halcyon House, was bought by the United States" (*Watch Hill Life*, July 1898). (DB.)

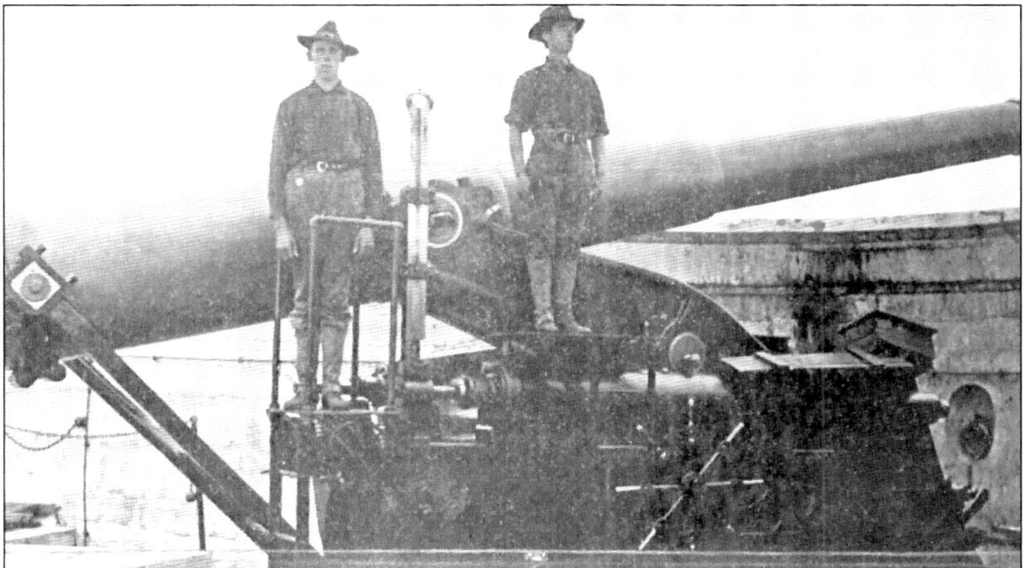

8 in. Gun, Fort Mansfield, R. I.

"Major Douglas MacArthur's visit at the fort yesterday showed that everything was in good condition . . . the most important [fortifications] are the two 8-inch disappearing Crozier guns, occupying the center emplacement and commanding the waters far out beyond the eastern end of Fishers Island Sound" (*The Westerly Sun*, August 1902). (BAFR.)

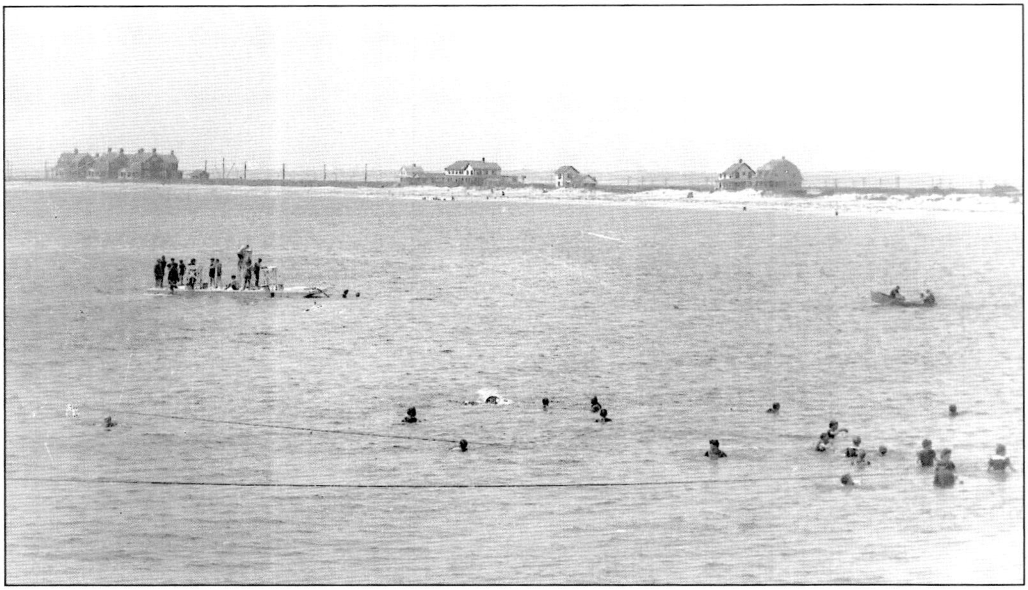

Looking from Lighthouse Point toward Napatree, summer revelers bathe and frolic before the site of the present-day beach club. The Halcyon House, which is the white structure with the gable facing the sea, was a boarding house that offered the following incomprehensible advertisement, "Finest Surf Bathing In America Free From The House." Note the swimming lines stretching out from the beach that timid swimmers could use as an aid for dunking themselves. (GHU-Burdick.)

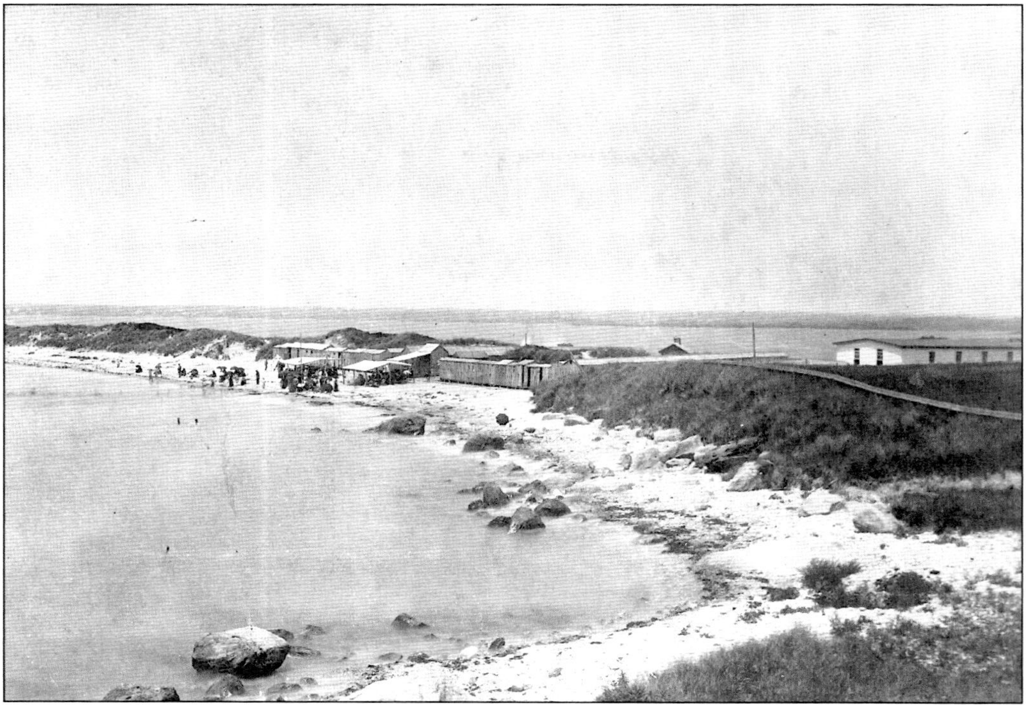

Way back when. (WPL.)

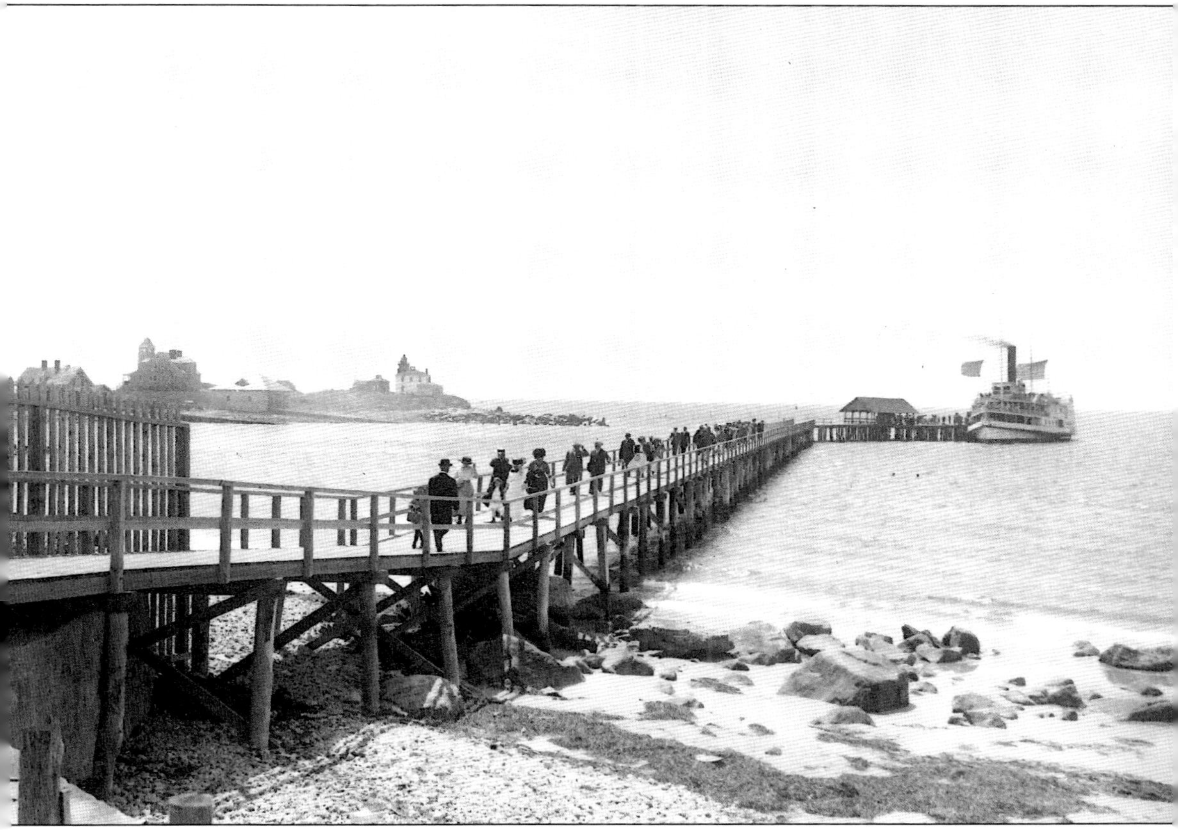

With its Union Jack and pennant cracking in the stiff southwest breeze and its bellowing smoke wafting toward Lighthouse Point, the steamer *Block Island* off-loads a parade of passengers on a summer's day. (GHU-Burdick.)

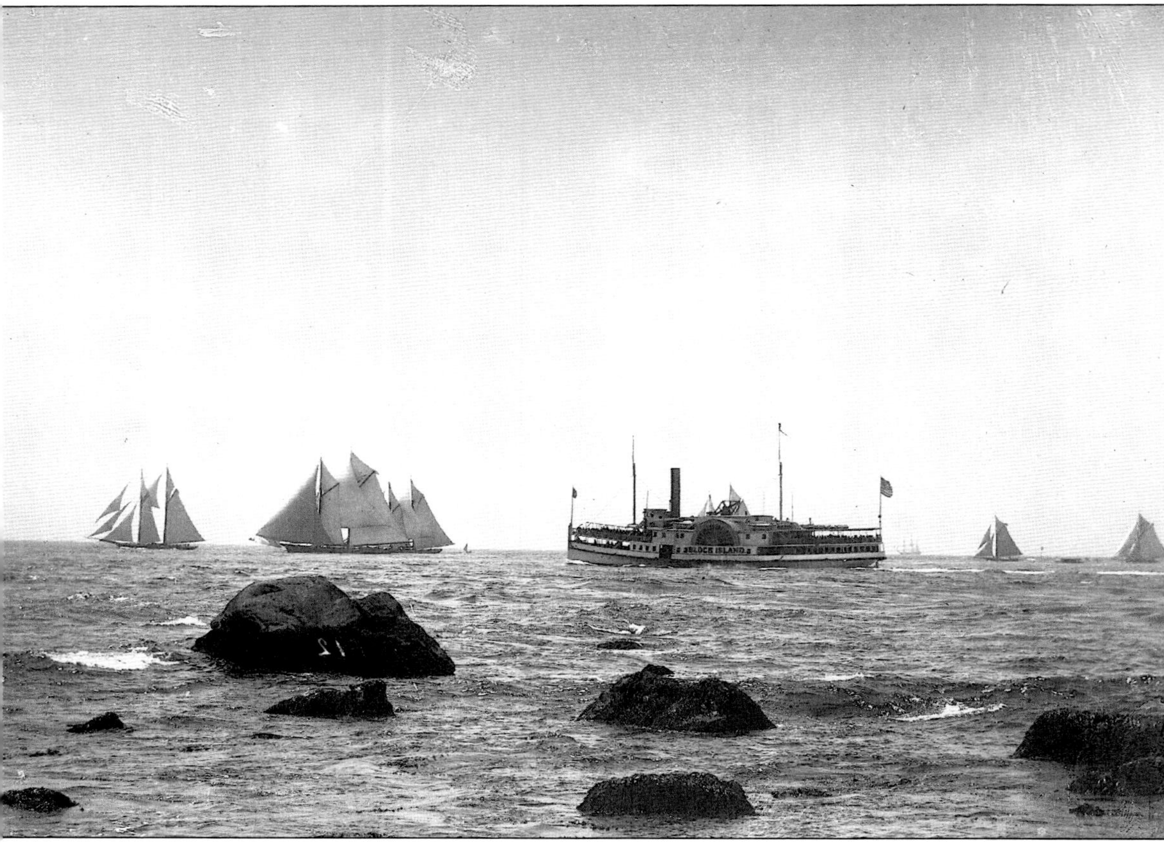

"A wet sheet, and a flowing sea,
A wind that follows fast;
And fills the white and rustling sail,
And bends the gallant mast."

—Allan Cunningham
Songs of Scotland, A Wet Sheet and a Flowing Sea
(GHU-Burdick.)

Six

DRIFTWOOD

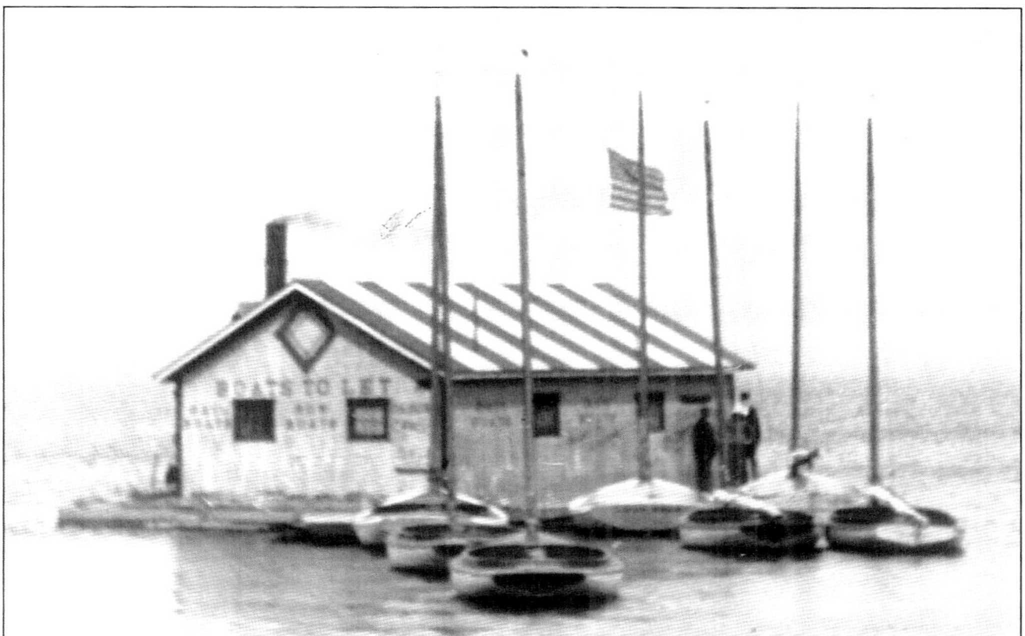

Each spring in the 1890s, George Barbour herded his fleet of "Boats To Let" down the Pawcatuck River from Lotteryville to Watch Hill Cove for the advent of the new summer season. His floating dock would be moored to the Plimpton Dock and his catboats, sails raised and luffing in the breeze, would patiently await their transient captains and crews. The northeast breeze that tugs at Old Glory and the smoke from the smokestack of the invisible tug give notice that summer has still not arrived. Note the lone passenger to starboard of the floating dock. (DB.)

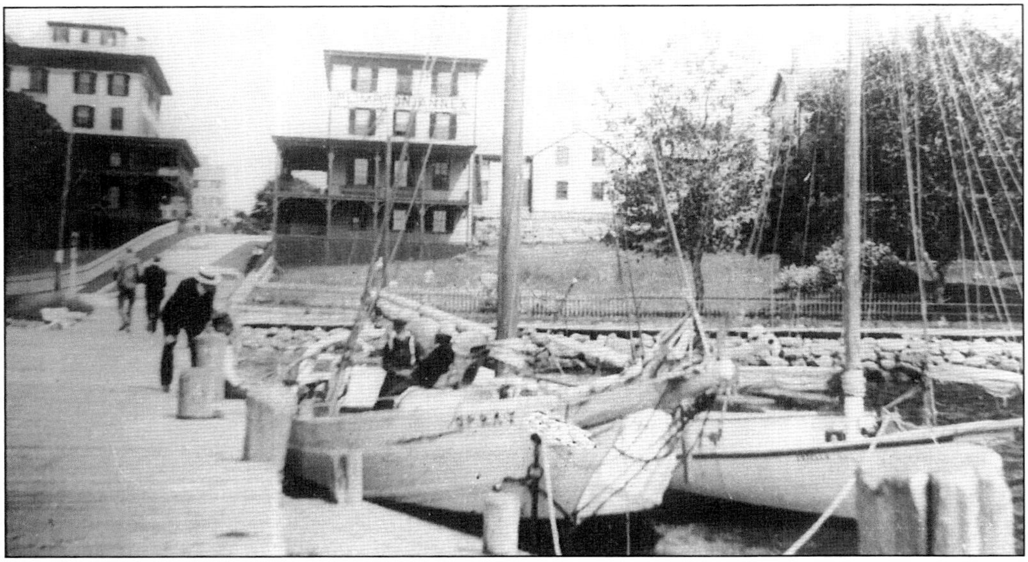

Captain Joshua Slocum, aboard his 36-foot-sloop *Spray*, was the first sailor to ever circumnavigate the globe under sail. His journey of nearly four years from 1895 until 1898 was an epic achievement. The *Spray*, moored quietly at Plimpton Dock in Watch Hill Cove, bore witness to murderous cannibals, desperate pirates, Cape Horners, and the goodwill of those who greeted Captain Slocum at his many ports of call. (DB.)

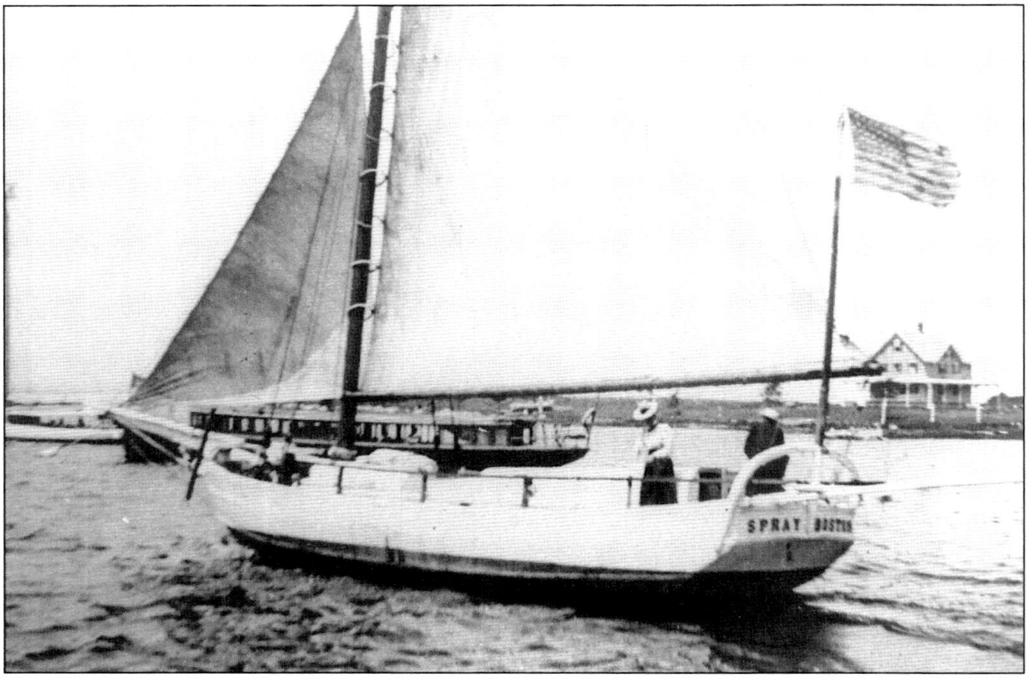

Captain Joshua Slocum and a lady friend sail the length of the cove. This inveterate voyager made additional solo journeys to the West Indies in the *Spray* during the winters of 1905, 1907, and 1908. However, during the winter of 1909, at the age of 65, Captain Slocum and the *Spray* commenced upon a journey from which they would never return. (DB.)

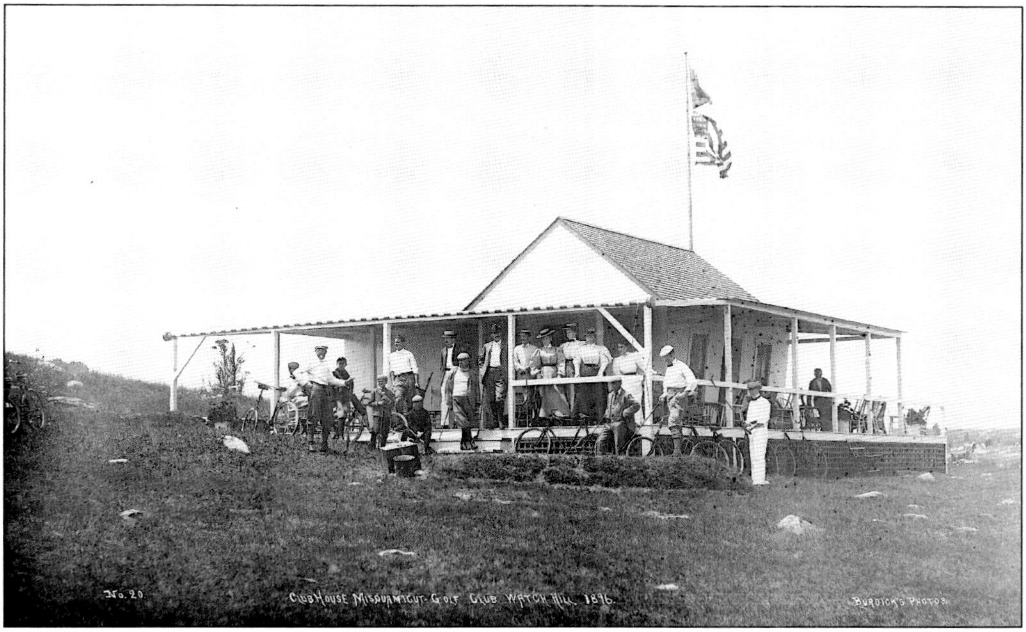

Combine a converted corn crib and a makeshift veranda, and you have the clubhouse of the Misquamicut Golf Club in 1896. Linksters of the day would ride their bicycles to the club while attired in "red coats with brass buttons and green collars, red and green being the Club colors" (*Seaside Topics*, 1942). Note the knickerbockers on the golfer on the first tee of this nine-hole golf course. (GHU-Burdick.)

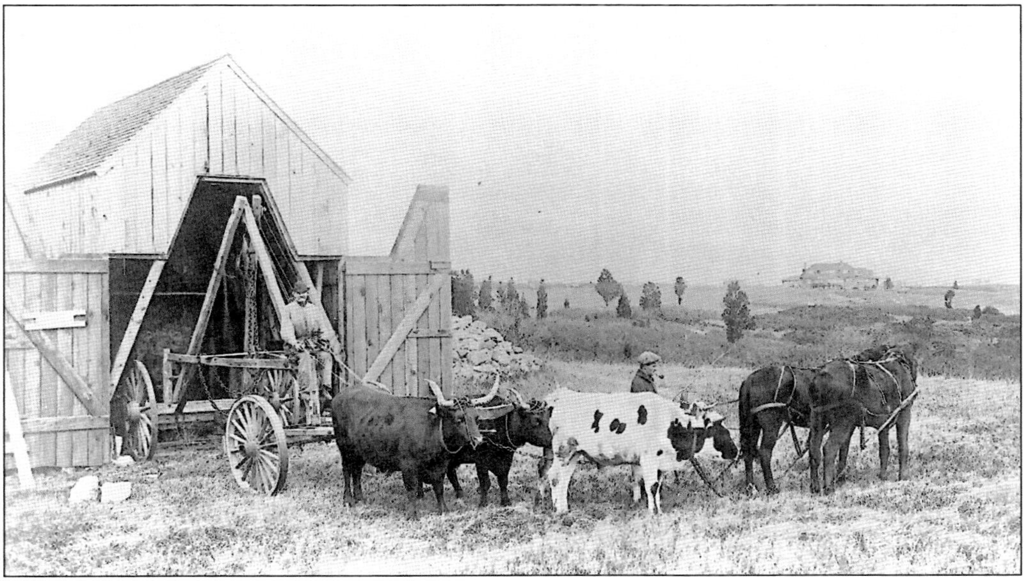

What is the hardest part about building a golf course on the rock-engorged fields of New England? Taking out the endless supply of stones and boulders! A team of oxen pull a "rock puller" out of a specially designed shed to begin assault on the grounds of the Misquamicut Golf Club golf course in 1902. Note the looming presence of the "new" clubhouse in the background that was built in 1901. (GHU.)

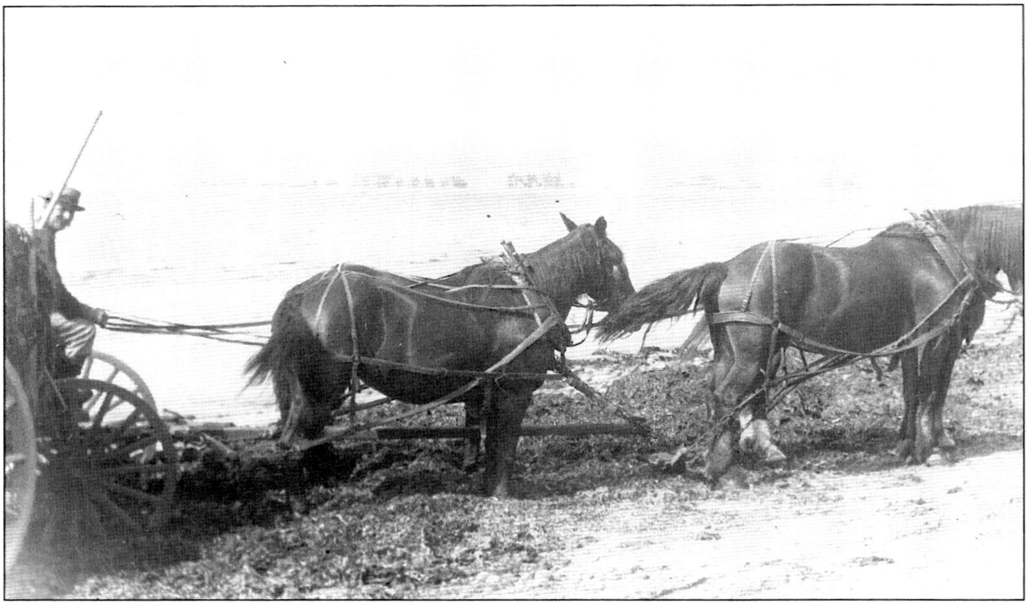

A team of horses, a wagon, and a strong back were the only ingredients necessary to harvest seaweed on the east shore of Sandy Point before it was detached from Napatree by the Hurricane of '38. The seaweed was used as fertilizer by the local farmers who tilled the land on the fields of Westerly. (DB)

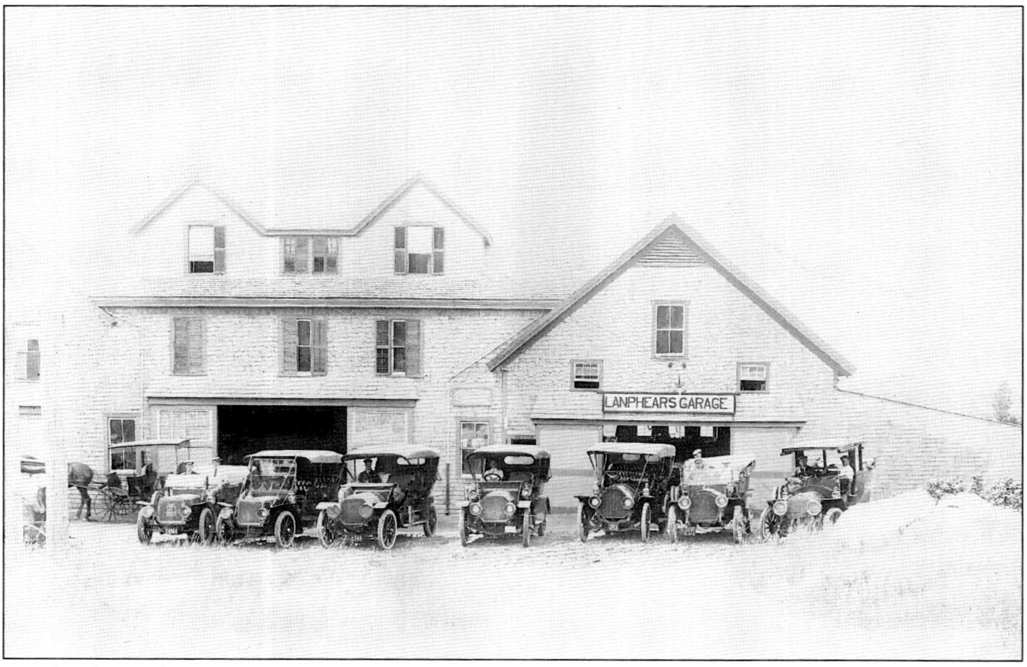

At the foot of Wauwinnet Avenue at the fork of Sunset Avenue stood Lanphear's Garage. The Watch Hill garages provided a gathering place for the chauffeurs of the day as few of the local cottages had their own private garage. The horse and buggy to the left seem particularly antiquated next to the line of automobiles in front of Lanphear's. (GHU-Burdick.)

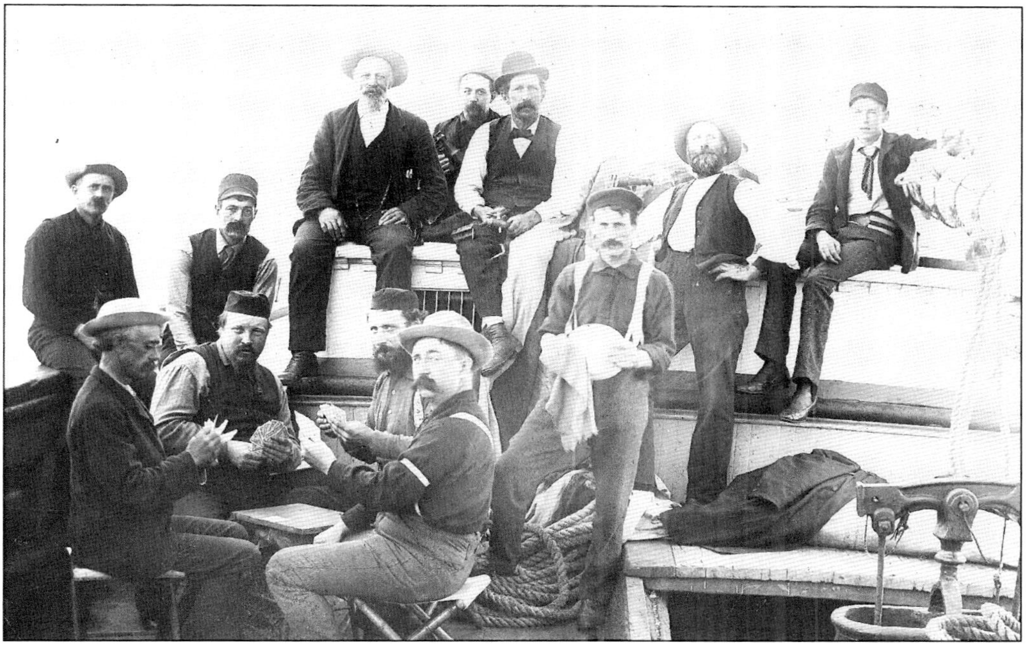

Four men play cards, one man is drying dishes, and two men are exhibiting their binoculars during down time aboard a local ship. A trip to Danbury, Connecticut, for some new hats would not have been a bad idea. (GHU-Burdick.)

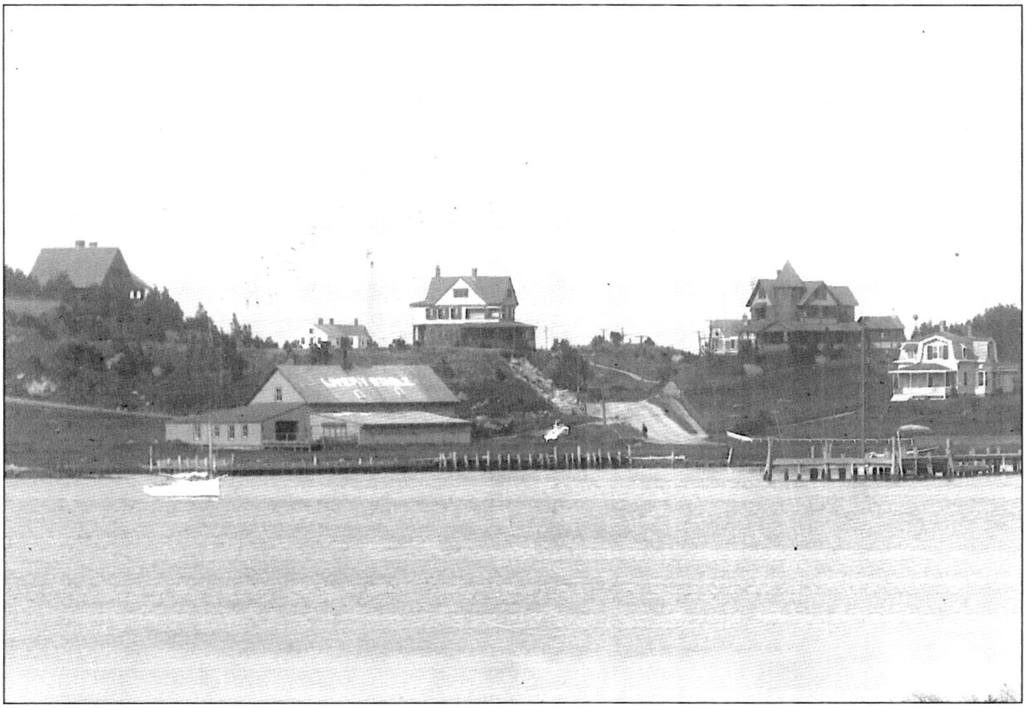

The northeast corner of Watch Hill Cove before the turn of the century provided ample "rooms with a view." (GHU-Burdick.)

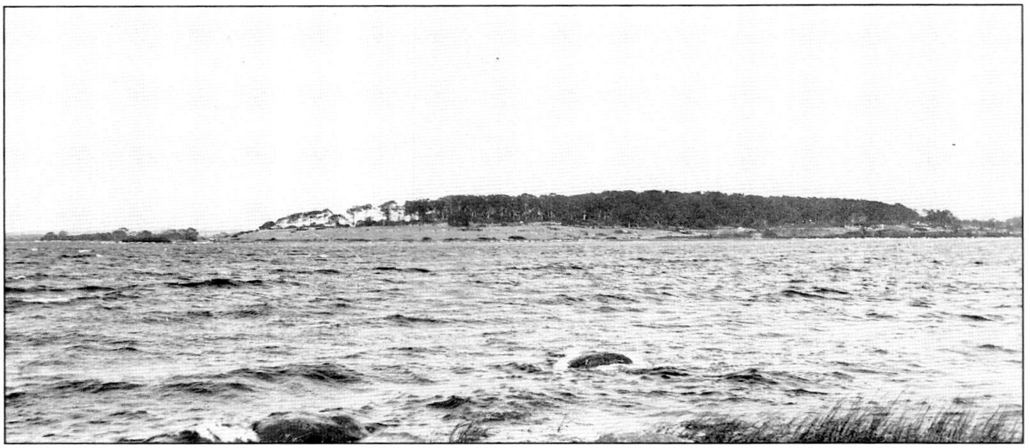

The contemporary boater who approaches Watch Hill Cove from the Stonington channel holds his breath ever so slightly as he passes the rocky outcroppings that guard Osbrook Point at the juncture of the Pawcatuck River and Little Narragansett Bay. A century ago, however, boats from Westerly and Watch Hill set sail for Osbrook Point on a regular basis for summer picnics and frolics. (GHU.)

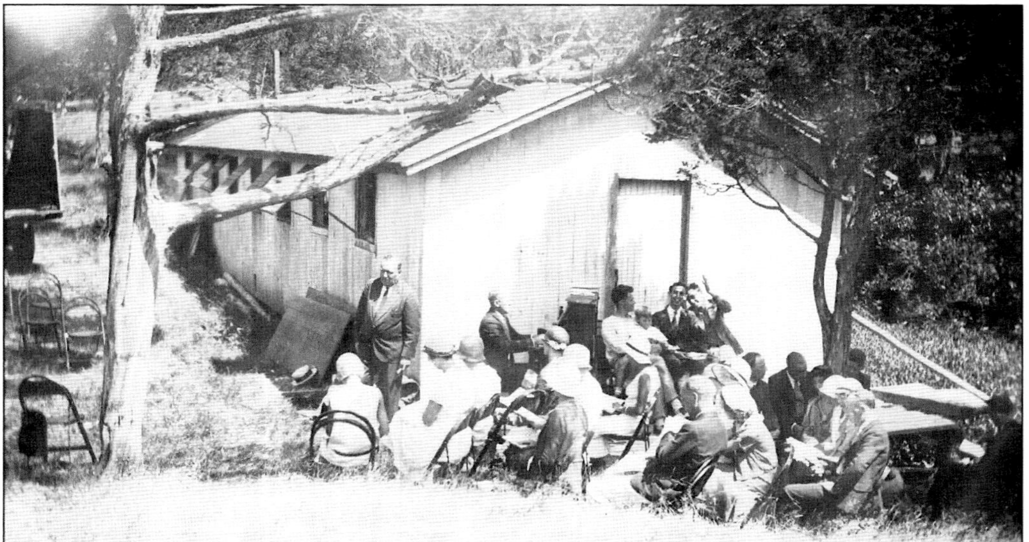

Picnickers revel at the old dance hall that was located on Osbrook Point during the mid-1880s. Their revelry was ended in 1877 when the dance hall was floated across the bay and plunked down at the mid-point of Napatree as a hotel. A "for sale" ad in 1880 noted that "there are two acres of land . . . thirteen lodging rooms . . . a barn . . . a cottage . . . a bowling alley . . . a dance hall . . . [and] a substantial wharf." (JM.)

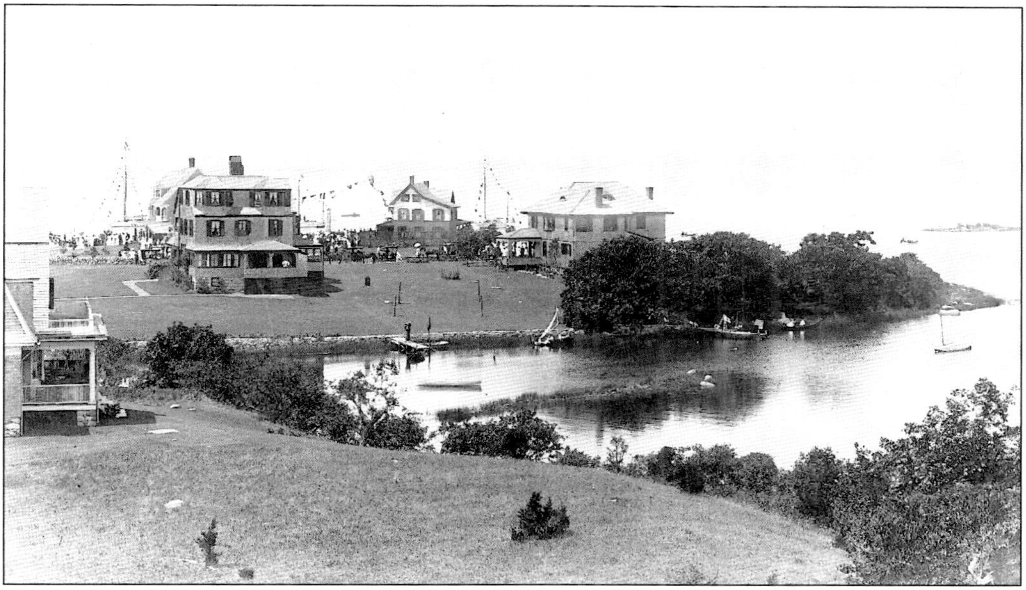

Breezy Lodge, the cottage on the right, and its three neighbors on Meadow Lane anchor the western shore of Foster Cove. The sailing craft on the far side of the cottages are flying their colors, suggesting a summer holiday. (GHU.)

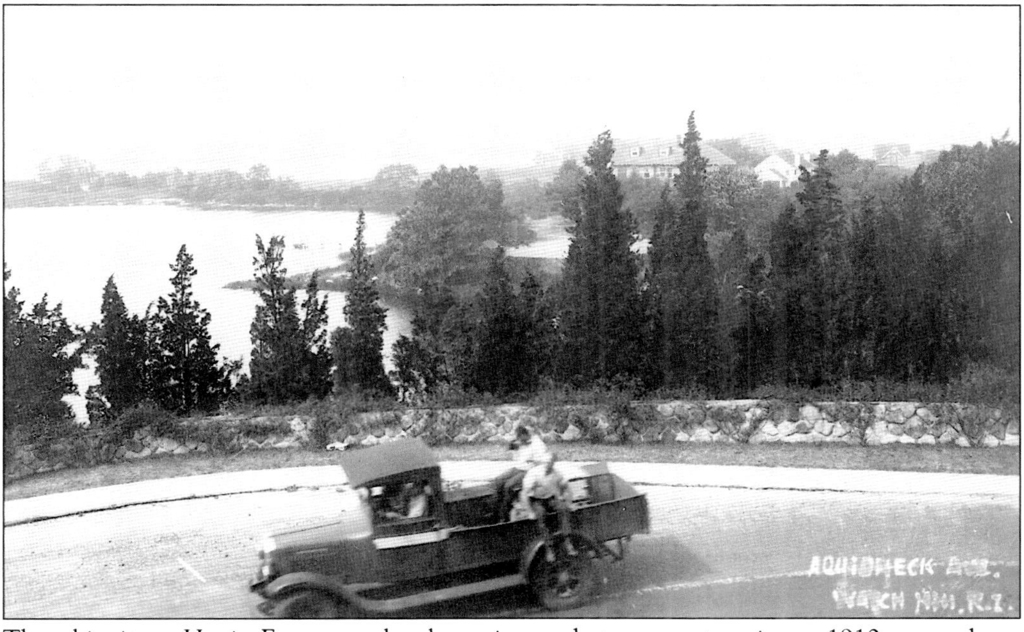

The ubiquitous Hoxie Express, a local moving and storage enterprise c. 1910, roars down Aquidneck Avenue toward Watch Hill. Foster Cove is visible in the upper left. (JM.)

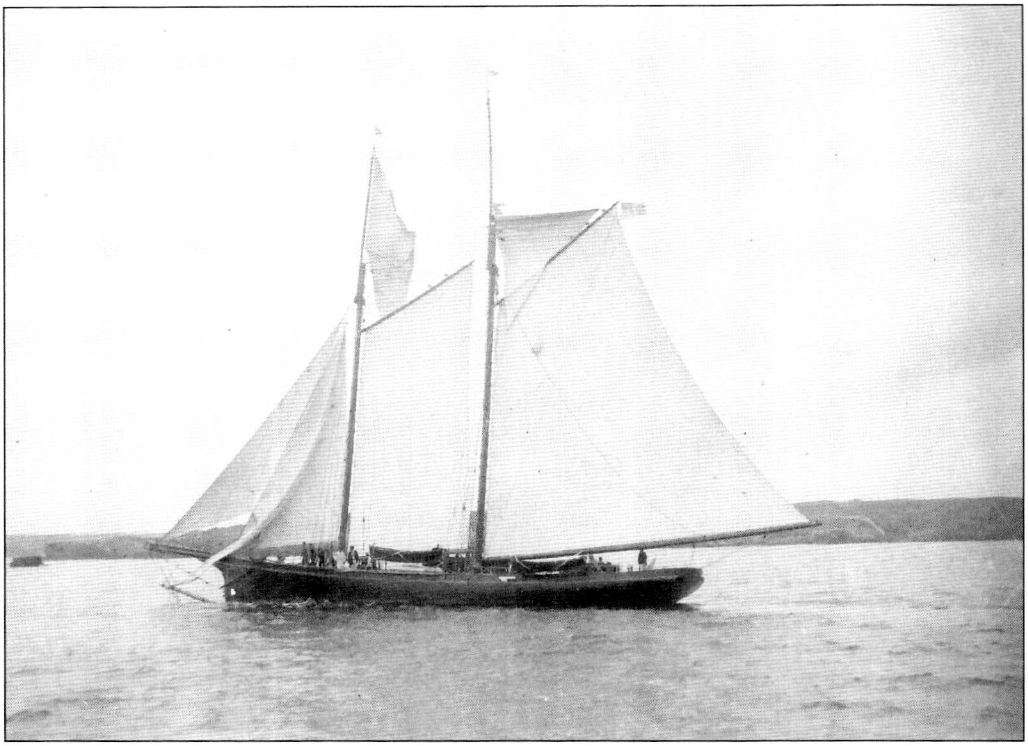

Plying the placid waters of Little Narragansett Bay, the schooner *Ruth* is depicted not long after a collision with the schooner *Grace P. Willard* on August 4, 1892. Commercial schooner traffic, more often at the end of a tugboat's hawser rather than under sail, was a common sight on the Pawcatuck River between Little Narragansett Bay and Westerly during the late 1800s. (WPL.)

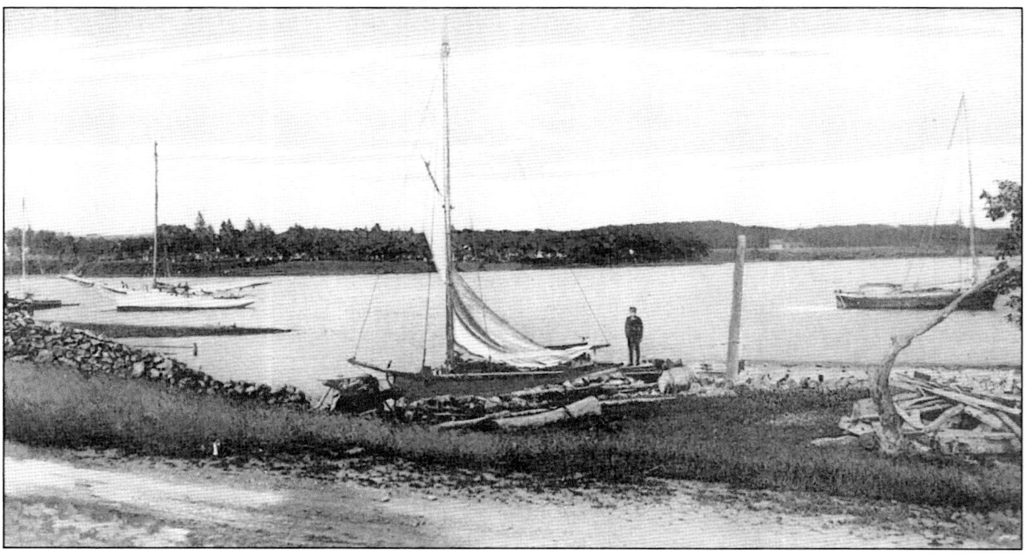

Partyboats rest at their moorings off Avondale before the turn of the century. The white-hulled Friendship Sloop to the left, the *Lucy E. Smith*, would depart for Watch Hill in the early morning during the summer season to take on passengers for half and full-day fares. (BAFR.)

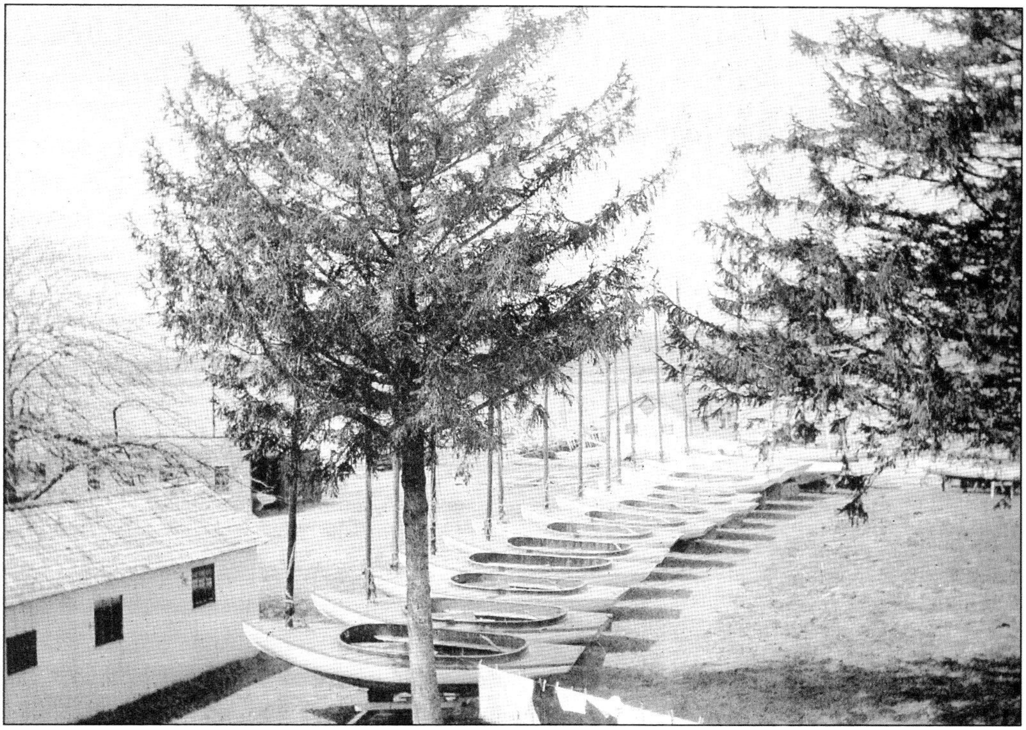

George F. Barbour's boathouse in Lotteryville at the turn of the century was the winter home to the Alden one-designs that raced in Watch Hill Cove during the summer season. The "Boats To Let" floating dock, which was moored to Plimpton's Dock in Watch Hill Cove during the summer months, is framed by the boughs of the pine trees that stand in the boat yard. (JH.)

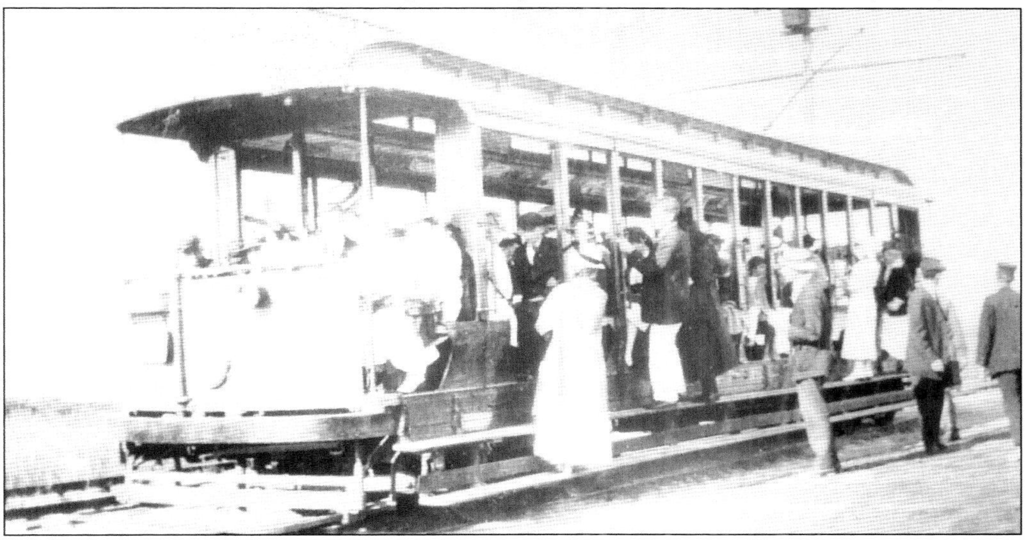

"The first [trolley] car this morning started for Watch Hill at 9:30 o'clock . . . the fare to Watch Hill is 10 cents each way, and to the cemetery it is 10 cents also. The cars have very brilliant headlights, and in the evening they may be seen at a great distance" (*The Westerly Sun*, July 1894). (BAFR.)

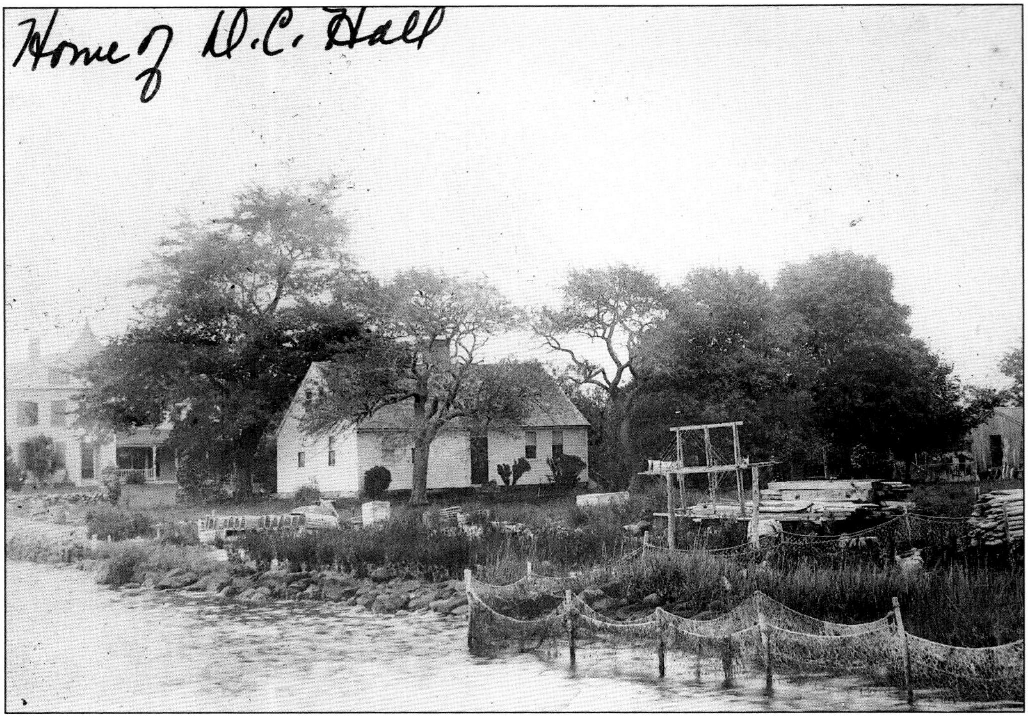

Daniel Coon Hall, the third of five generations of Halls to live in this riverside Colonial in Lotteryville, was the first Hall to own the home in the 1900s. Note the fish net drying racks to the right of the house and the fish weir in the Pawcatuck River. (JH.)

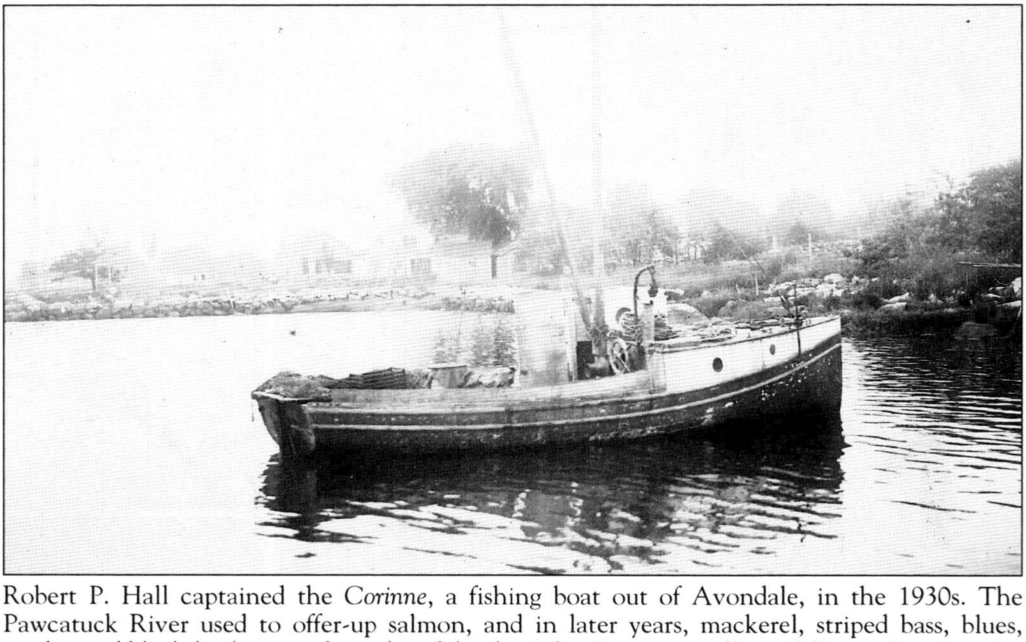

Robert P. Hall captained the *Corinne*, a fishing boat out of Avondale, in the 1930s. The Pawcatuck River used to offer-up salmon, and in later years, mackerel, striped bass, blues, smelts, and black-backs were the order of the day. The *Corinne* is still gainfully employed on the Pawcatuck River as a workboat at Frank Hall Boat Yard in Avondale. (JH.)

A local skater stays to the "safe" side of the number 8 nun that rides to this day off India Point in Avondale on the Pawcatuck River. (JH.)

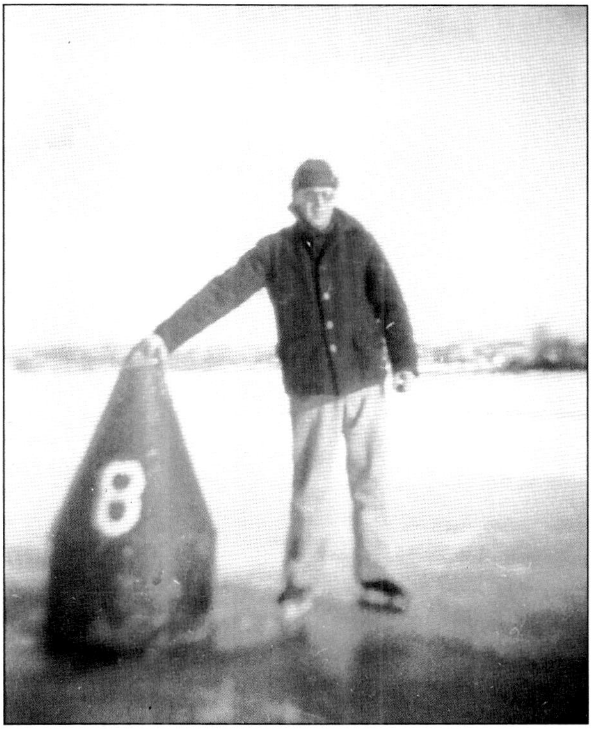

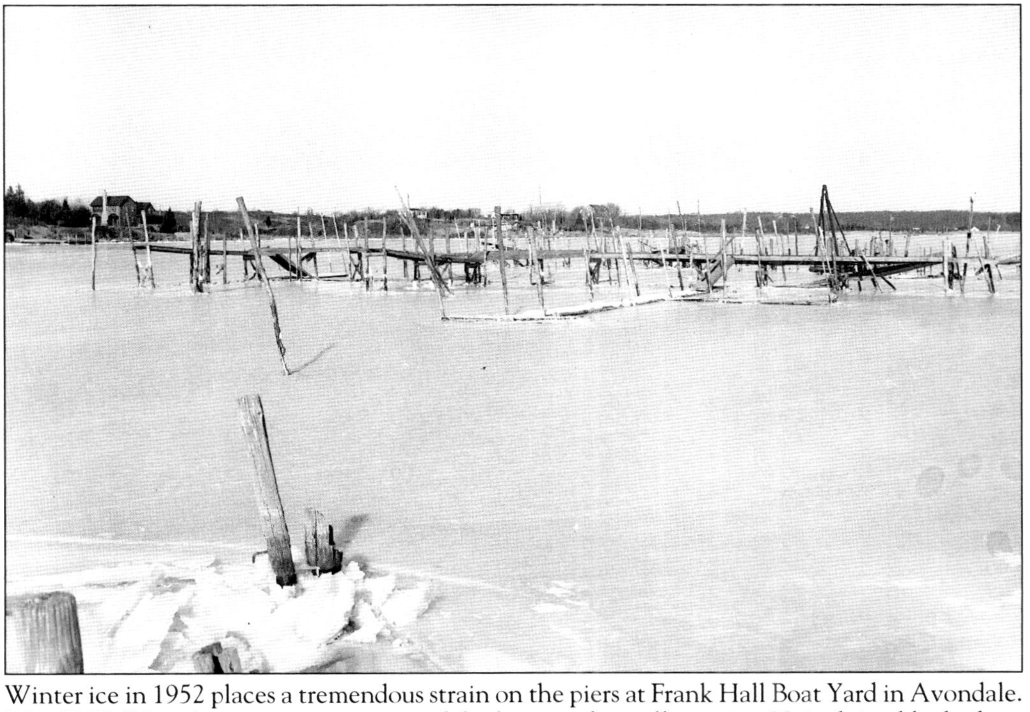

Winter ice in 1952 places a tremendous strain on the piers at Frank Hall Boat Yard in Avondale. John F. Hall Jr., the current proprietor of the boat yard, recalls cutting 22-inch ice blocks from around the pilings with a chain saw. (JH.)

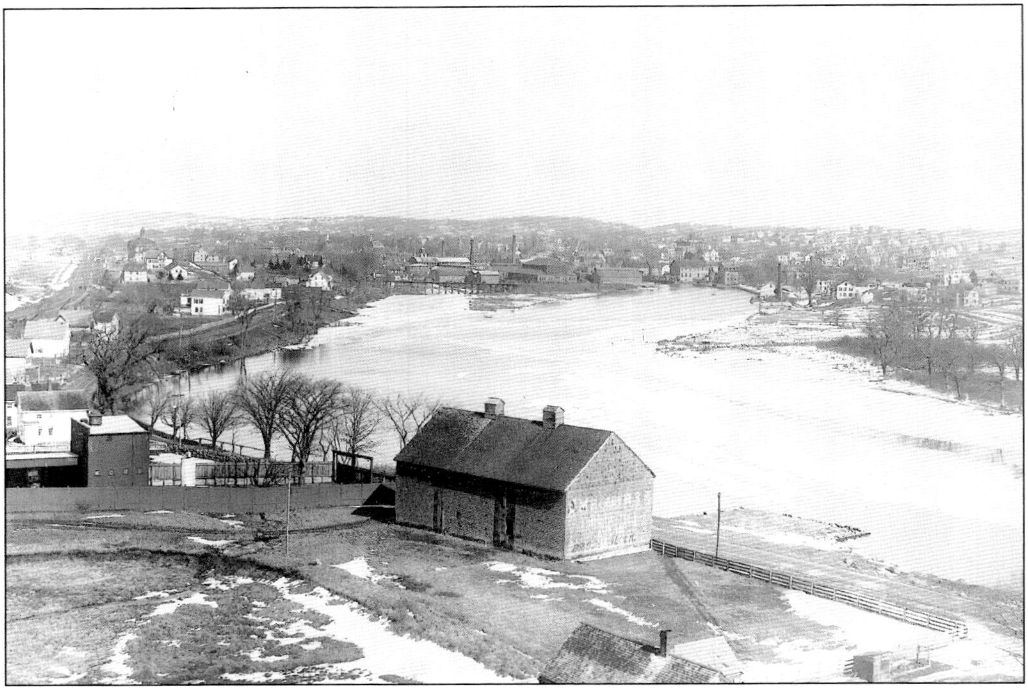

Standing atop the roof of the Clark Thread Mill and looking north up the icebound Pawcatuck River in February 1897, the smokestacks of both Pawcatuck and Westerly factories are clearly visible. The Clark Thread Mill factory is now the site of the ConnRi Paper and Supply Company in Pawcatuck. (GHU-Burdick.)

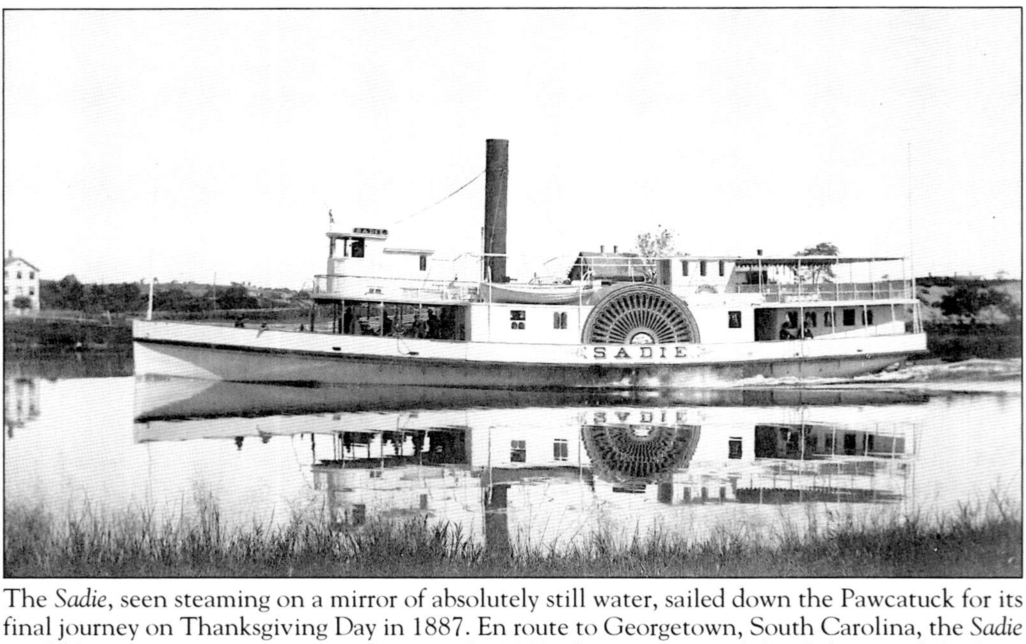

The *Sadie*, seen steaming on a mirror of absolutely still water, sailed down the Pawcatuck for its final journey on Thanksgiving Day in 1887. En route to Georgetown, South Carolina, the *Sadie* would begin a new career as a mail carrier. In 1898, she was renamed the *Caloosa* and she later called both Tampa, Florida, and then Mobile, Alabama, her home. (GHU.)

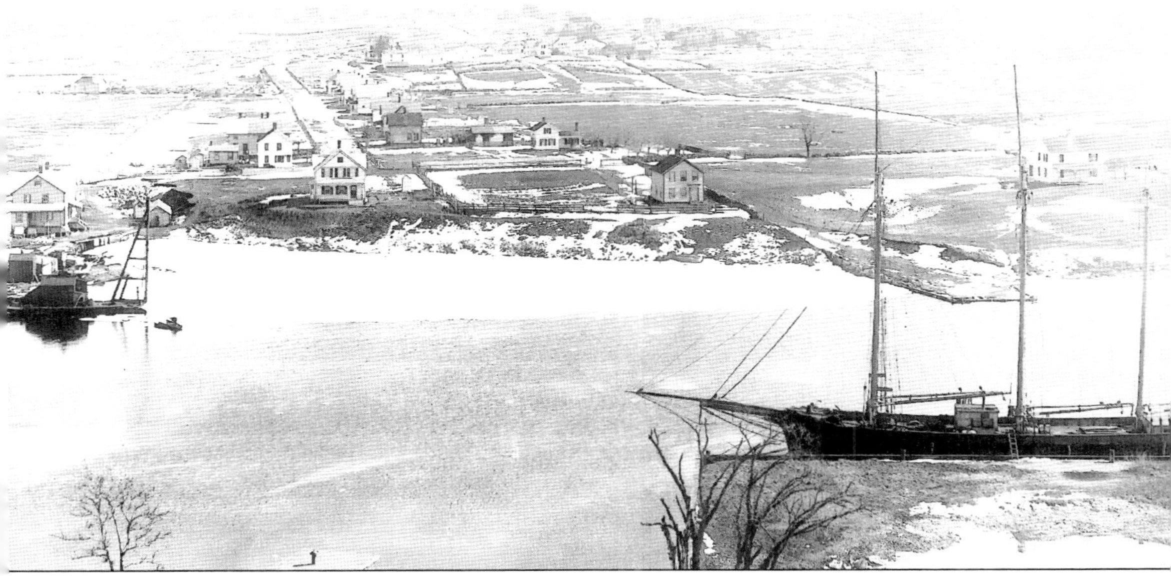

A three-masted schooner lies quietly off the Clark Thread Mill dock in Pawcatuck. This bulkhead is currently the home of Norwest Marine, a local marina. The house to the left, across the river, is located on Margin Street in Westerly, and is currently the site of Pier 65, another local marina. Elizabeth Fallon, a longtime resident of Pawcatuck, recalls that her grandfather, Joseph Ozanne, once owned and operated the ferry that ran from the old Pier 65 site to the Ozanne Corner on the Connecticut side of the river. The ferry carried passengers, cargo and, once, an entire home. (GHU-Burdick.)

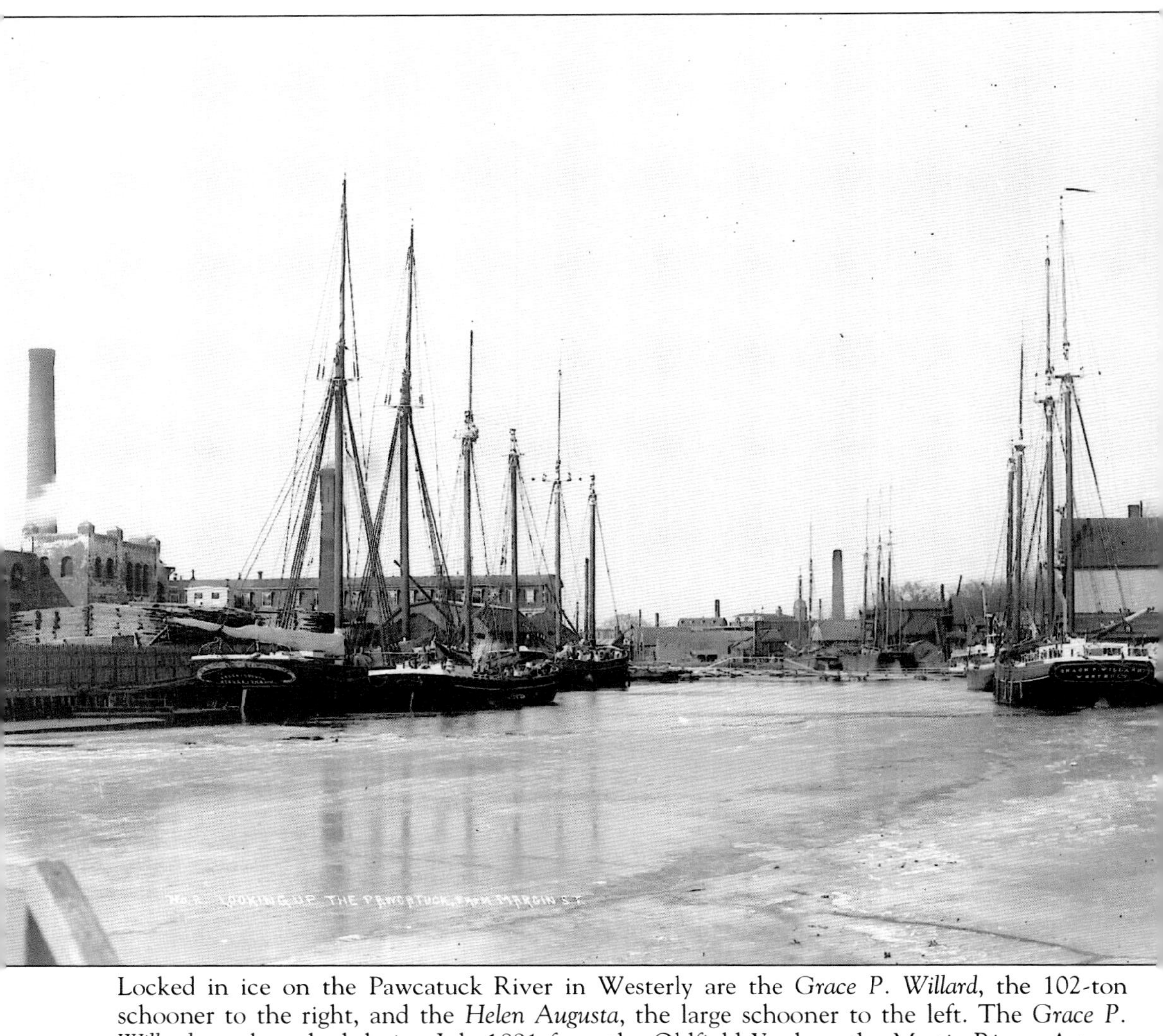

Locked in ice on the Pawcatuck River in Westerly are the *Grace P. Willard*, the 102-ton schooner to the right, and the *Helen Augusta*, the large schooner to the left. The *Grace P. Willard* was launched during July 1891 from the Oldfield Yard on the Mystic River. A two-masted centerboard schooner, she later foundered in the East River in New York in 1919. (GHU-Burdick.)

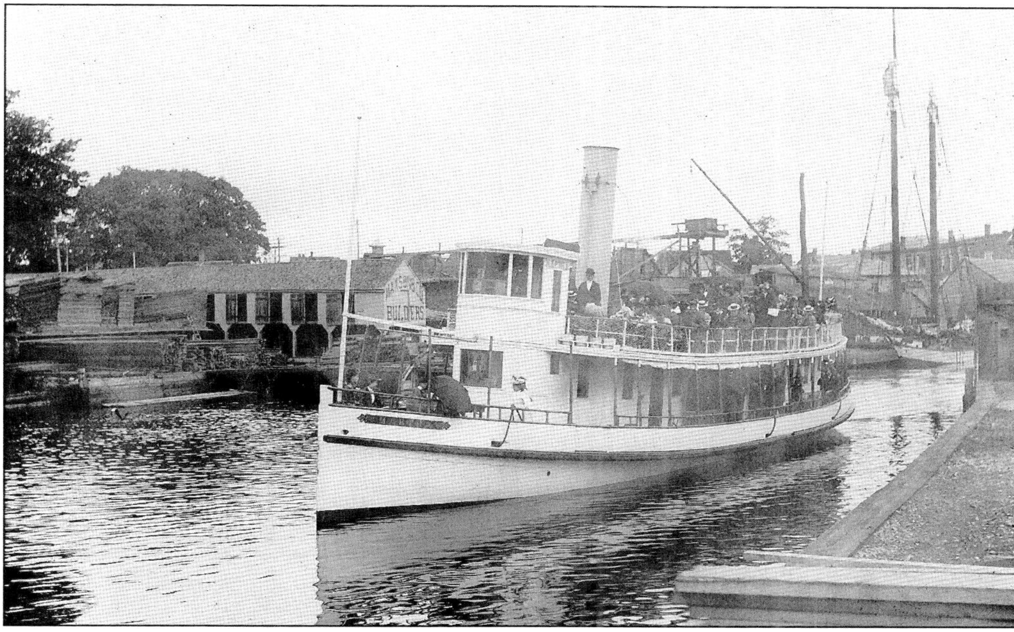

Named in honor of his youngest daughter, the steamer *Martha* was built by Orlando R. Smith in 1891. She began her career on the Providence River and later became a favorite among day-hoppers on the Pawcatuck during 1893 and 1894. The *Martha* was lengthened by 20 feet during 1894 to account for this new popularity. This 90-footer was sold in 1905 to new owners from New York. (GHU.)

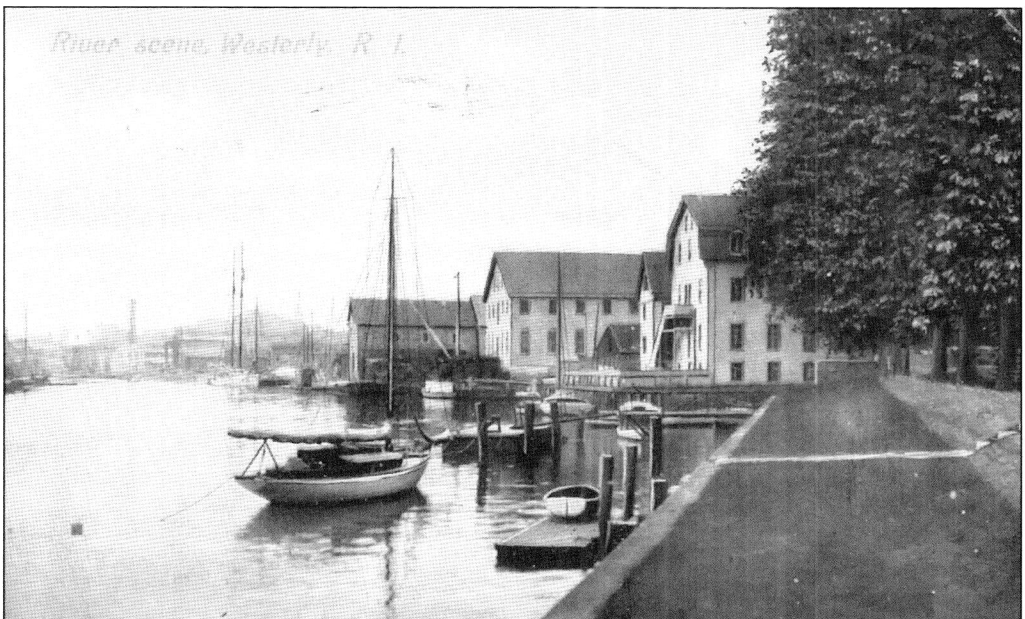

Pristine stairs and a walkway cut across the well-manicured lawn of a home on Margin Street in Westerly to a tidy dock in the Pawcatuck River. The warehouse, second from the right, stands to this day. (BAFR.)

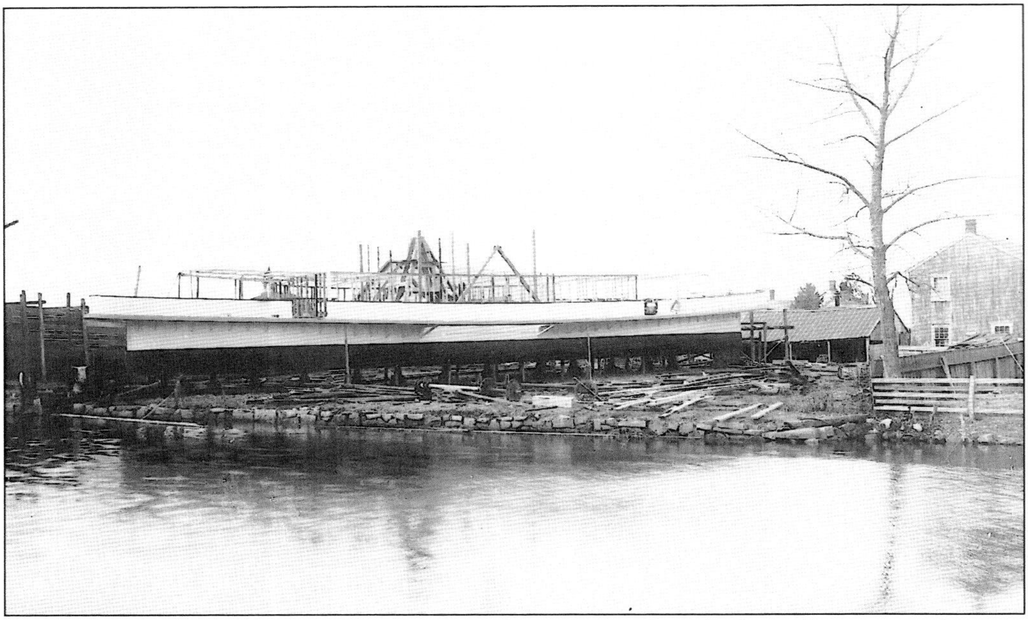

At 136 feet in length, the *Golden Star* was the longest steamboat built on the Pawcatuck River. She was constructed by George S. Greenman at the abandoned Hall and Dickinson lumberyard on the west side of the river during 1887. A "double ender," the *Golden Star* sported a rudder on both ends as well as two pilot houses because she was too long to turn around once she was upriver. (GHU-Burdick.)

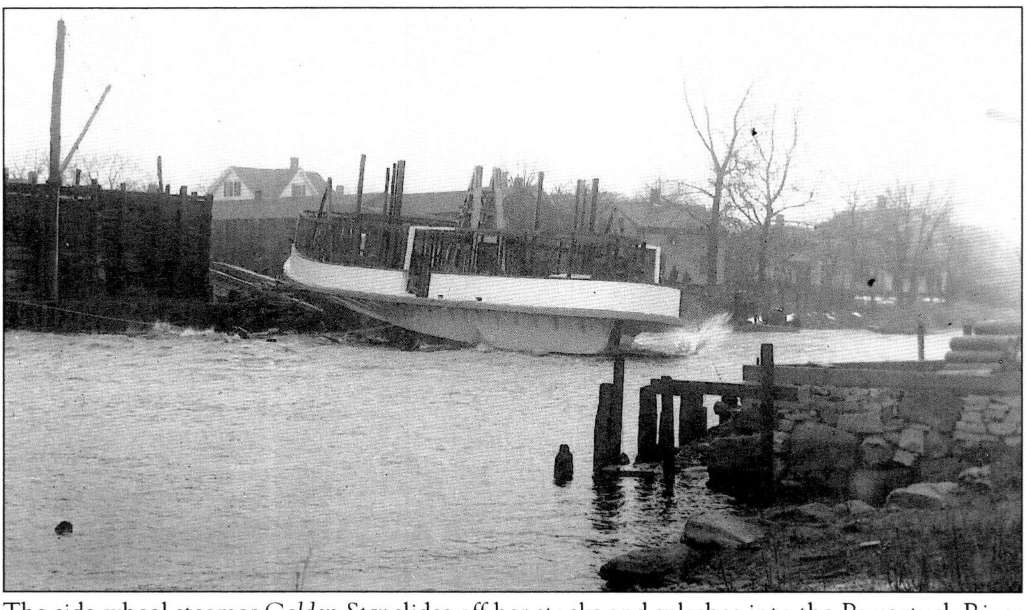

The side-wheel steamer *Golden Star* slides off her stocks and splashes into the Pawcatuck River on launch day. This massive 136-foot steamer made her first foray to Watch Hill on the Fourth of July in 1888. Her tenure on the Pawcatuck was cut short in 1890 when it became evident that she was too large for the river. She was shipped off to a railroad company in New York. (GHU-Burdick.)

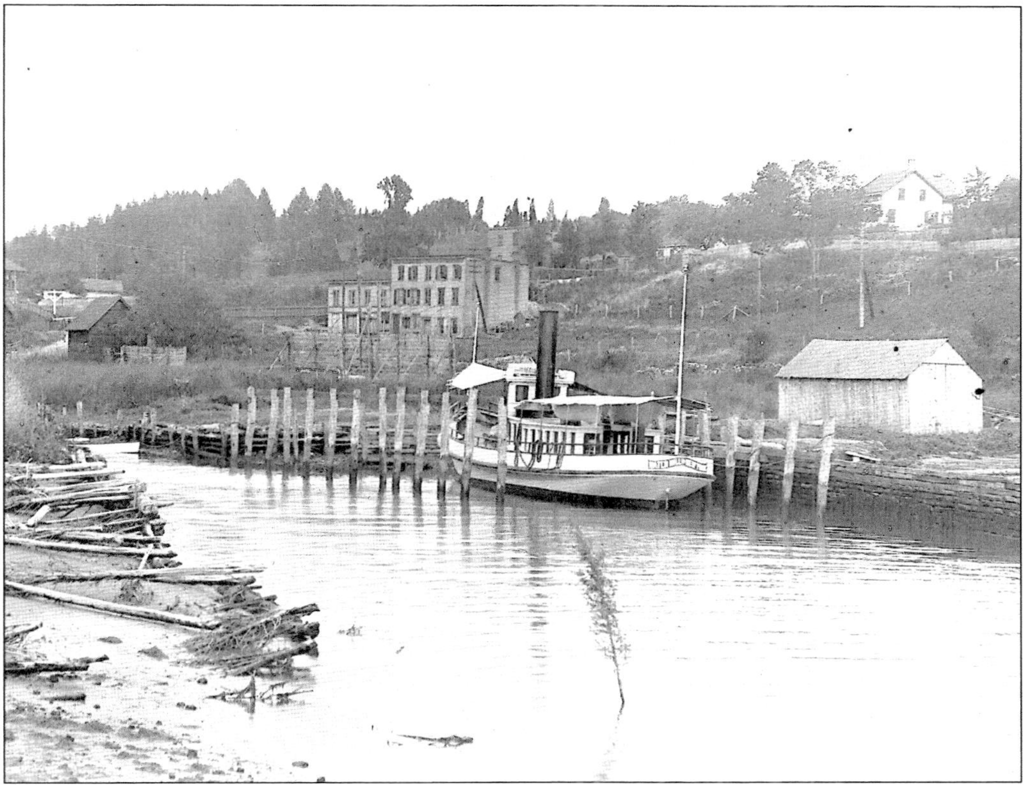

The *Watch Hill*, whereabouts unknown. (GHU.)

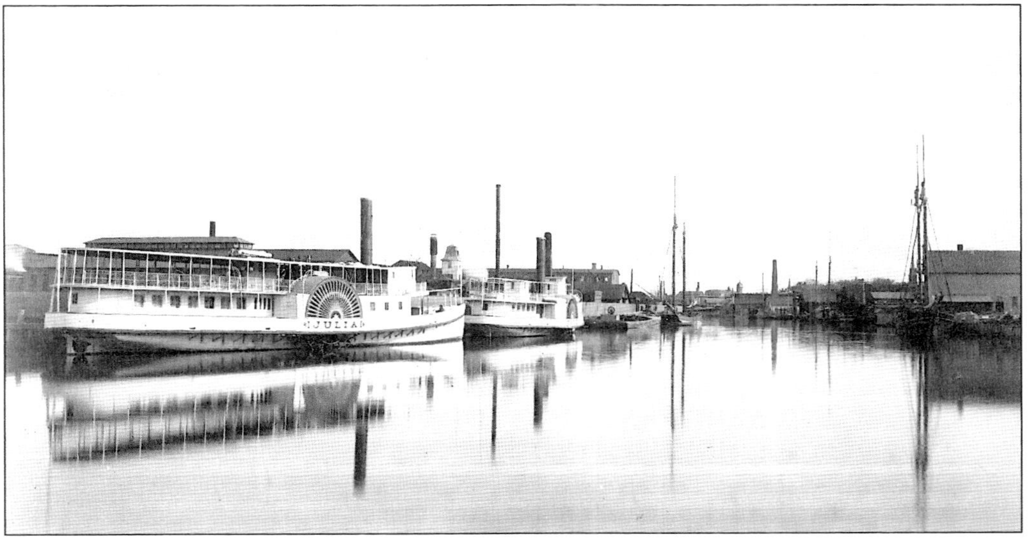

The 115-foot steamer *Julia* lies astern her sistership *Sadie* across from Margin Street in Westerly. The *Julia* may not be remarkable, but her engine plant is. Originally built for a vessel being constructed on the banks of a Peruvian lake, the engine was no longer needed when the lake became a dry valley as a result of an earthquake. Returned to the United States, it found a home in the *Julia*. (GHU-Burdick.)

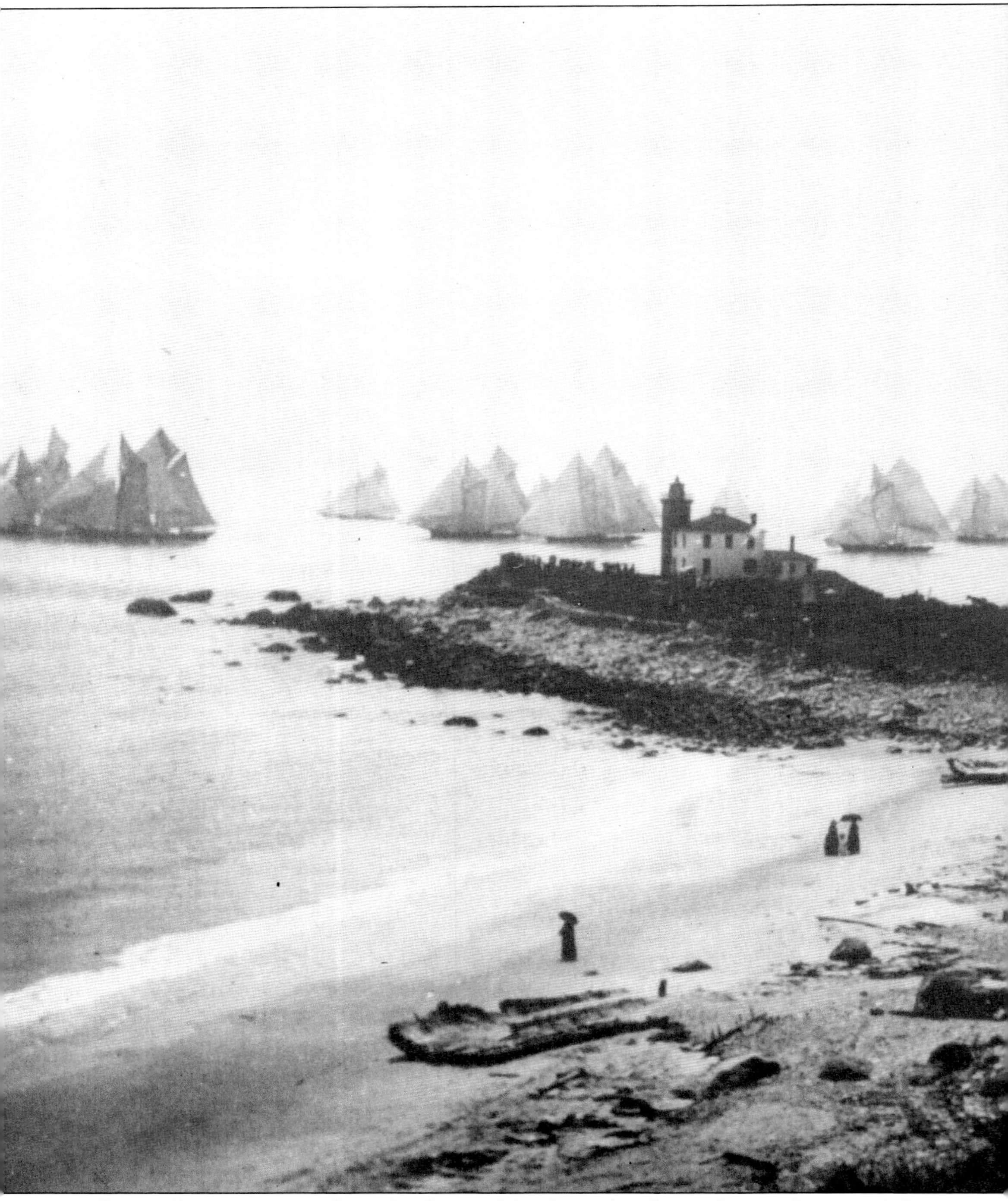

Responding to a query about the financial burdens of yachting, famous financier J. Pierpont Morgan said, "If you have to ask how much it costs, you can't afford it" (*Heritage Series*). Morgan served as the commodore of the New York Yacht Club from 1897 till 1899, and his yacht, the *Corsair*, may well have been part of the club's annual cruise that rounded Lighthouse Point

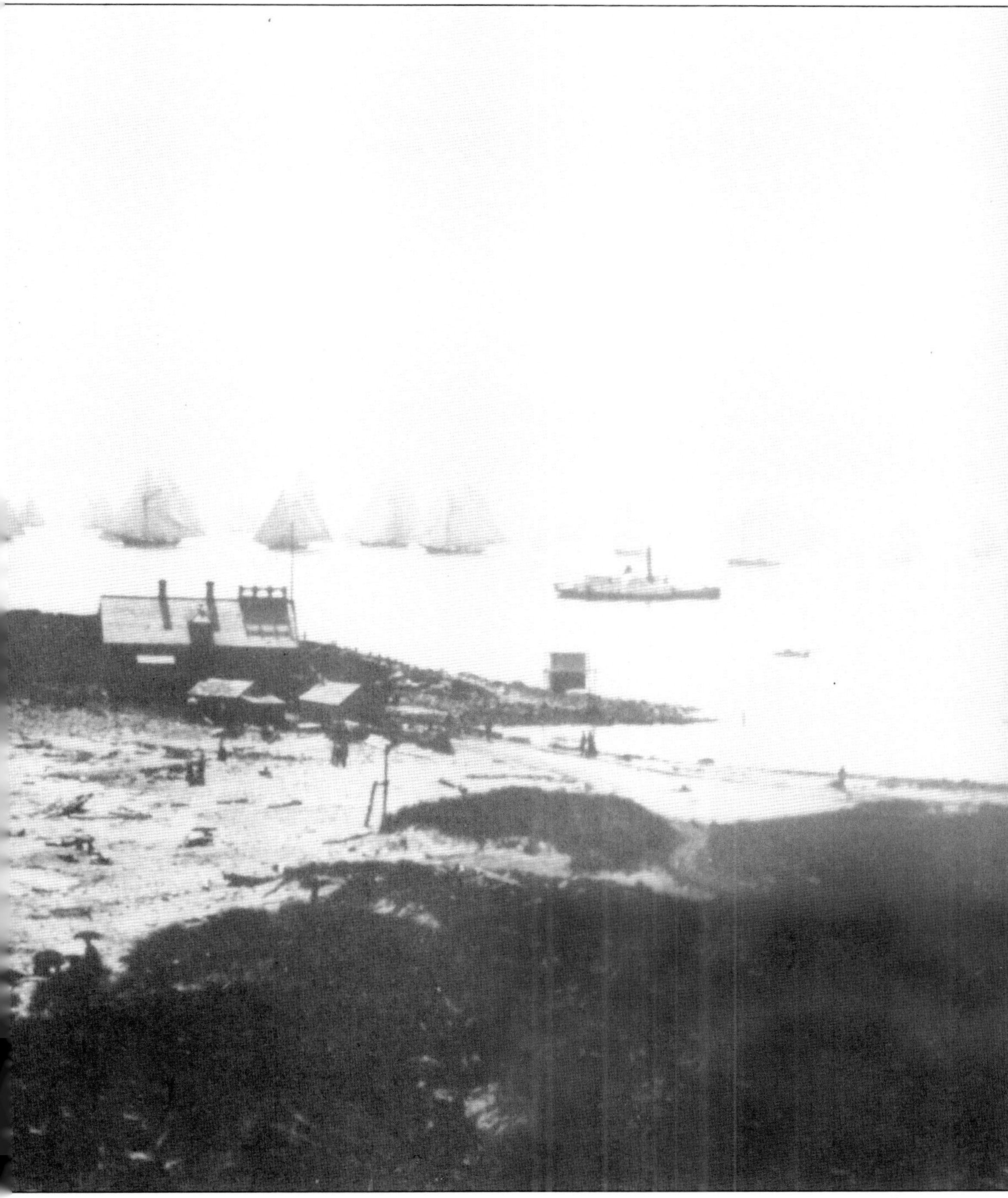

during 1892. Onlookers on East Beach stand under umbrellas to protect themselves from the rainy southeast breeze that is forcing the fleet to beat to windward on its journey to Newport, Rhode Island. (GHU.)

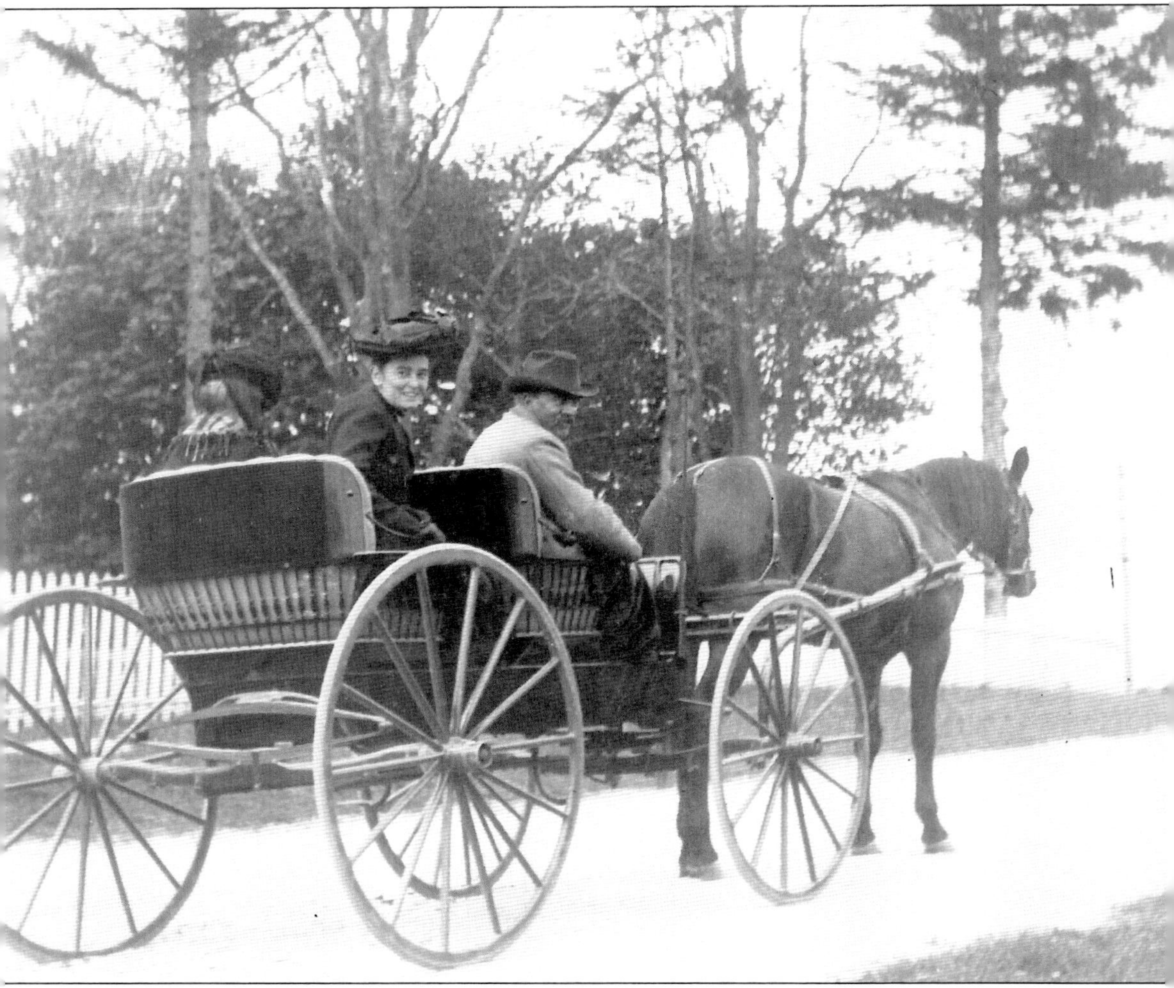

As we peek back at those who went before and wonder what they did, so too do they peek back at us and wonder what we are doing. Watch Hill is a jewel. Shine it, protect it, and administer to its setting. (DB.)

BIBLIOGRAPHY

Babcock, Louise Austin, Pendleton, Albert P., and Harvey C. Perry. *On the Banks of the Pawcatuck—Three Papers Selected From Earlier Publications of the Westerly Historical Society*. Westerly, Rhode Island: The Utter Company, 1963.

Barns, Everett. *History of Pawcatuck River Steamboats*. Westerly, Rhode Island: The Utter Company, 1932.

Burdick, Anne M. *Watch Hill Souvenir—The Stolen Bride or A Tale of Old Watch Hill*. Watch Hill, Rhode Island: The Book & Tackle Shop, 1977.

Burdick, Howard. *Along the Shore*. Westerly, Rhode Island: Westerly Historical Society, 1988.

Cooney, Ralph Bolton. *Westerly's Oldest Witness*. Westerly, Rhode Island: The Washington Trust Company, 1950.

Cunningham, Allan. *Songs of Scotland, A Wet Sheet and a Flowing Sea*, 1825.

Dayton, Fred Erving. *Steamboat Days*, Illustrated by John Wolcott Adams. New York: Frederick A. Stokes Company, 1925.

Foster, George H. and Peter C. Weiglin. *Splendor Sailed the Sound*. San Mateo, CA & Tucson, AZ: Potentials Group, Inc. & Midstate Associates, 1989.

Griscom, Clement A. *Fort Mansfield—Napatree Point, Watch Hill, Rhode Island*. Westerly, Rhode Island: The Utter Company, 1992.

Melville, Herman. *Moby Dick; Or, The Whale*, Illustrated by Rockwell Kent. New York: Modern Library, 1982.

Mochetti, Lido J. *Life's Little Pleasures—The Photographs of J. Henry Burk 1900–1919*. Westerly, Rhode Island: The Friends of the Westerly Public Library, 1979.

Moore, Harriet C. *Around and Around—The Story of the Watch Hill Carousel*. Westerly, Rhode Island: The Utter Company, 1980.

Moore, Paul Johnson. *The Search—An Account of the Fort Road Tragedy*. Westerly, Rhode Island: Sun Graphics, 1990.

Peck, Reginald, E. *Early Land Holders of Watch Hill*. Westerly, Rhode Island: The Utter Company, 1936.

Pendleton, Albert P. *The Watch Hill Road—Past and Present—Buildings and Tenants*. (Records & Papers 1913–22 Westerly Historical Society). Westerly, Rhode Island: The Utter Company, 1915.

Peterson, William N. *"Mystic Built"—Ships and Shipyards of the Mystic River, Connecticut, 1784–1919*. Mystic, Connecticut: Mystic Seaport Museum, 1989.

Pickering, Nelson W. *Notes on the Maritime History of the Pawcatuck Valley*. (Records & Papers 1940–54 Westerly Historical Society). Westerly, Rhode Island: The Utter Company, 1957.

Rousmanier, John. *The Heritage Series—Commodore J. Pierpont Morgan.*

Slocum, Joshua. *Sailing Alone Around the World*. Illustrated by James E. Mitchell. New York & London: Footnote Productions, Ltd., 1984.

Utter, George Herbert. *Old Pictures of Westerly, Rhode Island*. Westerly, Rhode Island: The Utter Company, 1991.

Historical Souvenir of Watch Hill, R.I.—Watch Hill, Rhode Island and Its Attractions as a Summer Resort. Watch Hill, Rhode Island: The Book & Tackle Shop, 1977.

Watch Hill, R.I.—A Description of Its Three Beaches, Its Climate, Scenery, Etc. Watch Hill, Rhode Island: The Book & Tackle Shop, 1994.

Various articles (identified by month and/or year in applicable captions):

The Day
The Providence Journal
Seaside Topics
Tidings
Watch Hill Life
The Westerly Sun

Index

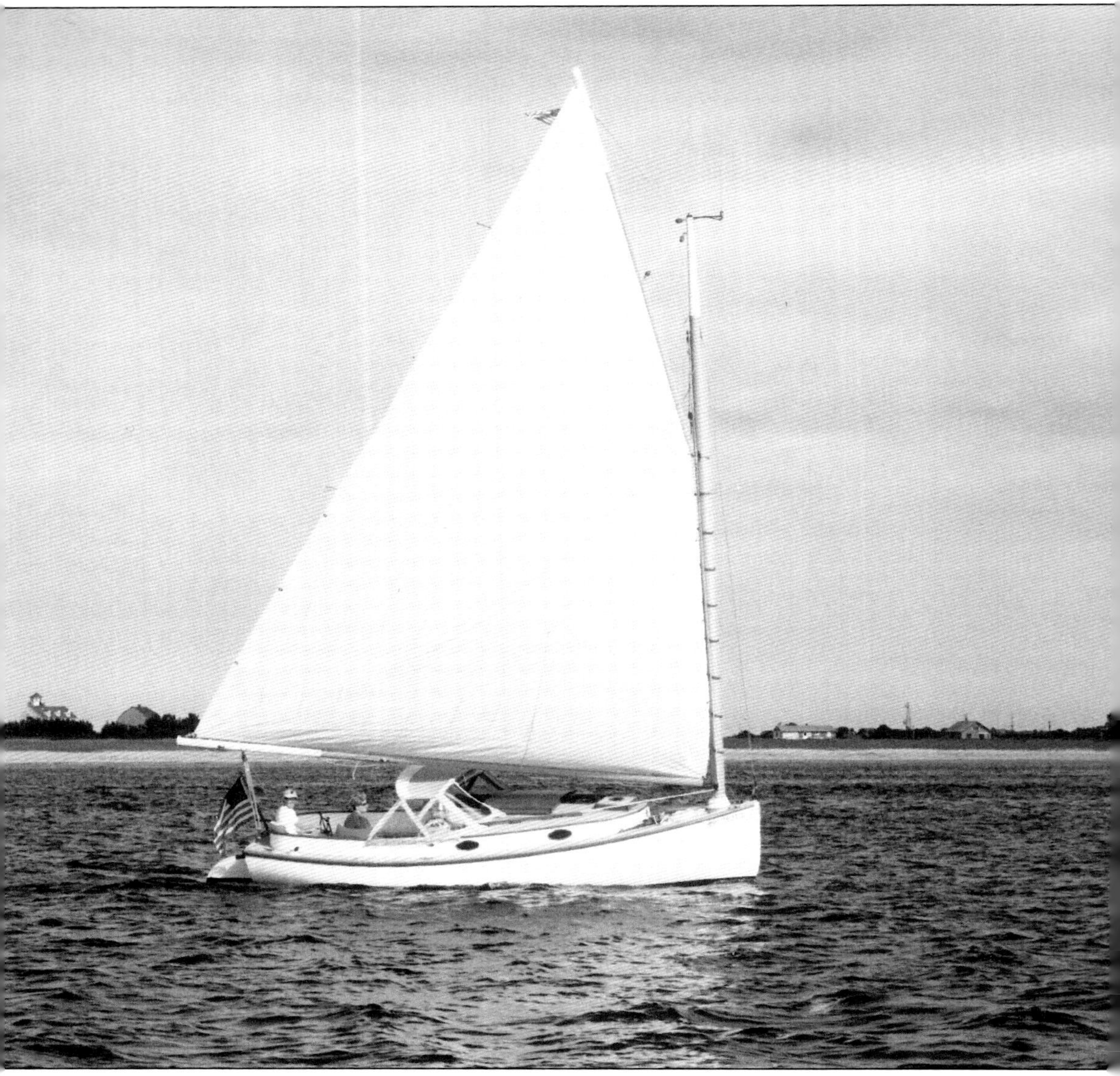

The *Nana* of Lotteryville, July 1998.

No wooden timbers has she, nor a duck cotton sail that can be hauled up to the heights of her white-tipped mast. There's neither hempen lines nor a fisherman's anchor nor even oil in her red and green lamps. She is a modern boat.

But the *Nana*, my *Nana*, is a catboat. She wears the short stubby bow and barn door rudder of a working craft. Her mains'l is gaff-rigged and nary a winch will be found by her lengthy sheets. The *Nana* is my transport to times long-forgotten, to skills no longer practiced, and to ports of call that beckon naught but shoal draft vessels.

Many thanks to my family for their love and support throughout this endeavor.